282
G37
a
Gilbert, Arthur.
　　　The Vatican Council
and the Jews.

THE VATICAN COUNCIL AND THE JEWS

THE
VATICAN
COUNCIL
AND
THE
JEWS

BY ARTHUR GILBERT

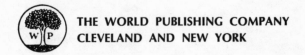

THE WORLD PUBLISHING COMPANY
CLEVELAND AND NEW YORK

Contents

Introduction

On October 28, 1965, Pope Paul VI promulgated an historic declaration on the Roman Catholic attitude toward non-Christian religions. It contained the revolutionary assertion that the Roman Catholic Church "rejects nothing that is true and holy in these religions. She regards with reverence those ways of action and of life, those precepts and teachings, which though differing in many aspects from the ones she holds and sets forth, nonetheless often reflect a ray of that truth which enlightens all men." This new openness to dialogue with men of other faiths coupled with a forthright repudiation of "any discrimination or harassment of them because of their race, color, condition in life, or religion" brought to climax a debate that had ranged over four years within the Church's Second Vatican Council.[1]

When this declaration is set alongside other Council decrees dealing with religious liberty, the Church's role in the world, and its attitude toward other Christians, it becomes evident that the Catholic Church in our time has given expression to a profound regard for the dignity and inviolability of the human conscience. It has articulated a sincere conviction that religion must bring hope to a world burdened with injustice, poverty, hatred, and war.

Stirring within all of these statements is a persistent awareness that the Church must reassess its role in the twentieth century. Although the Church continues to affirm that it possesses in fullness the saving truth to be spoken to all mankind in all times and places, the Council brought to the forefront not only a new sense of need for internal reform and renewal but a new openness to communication with the secular world and with other faiths. In the spirit of *aggiornamento* proclaimed by Pope John XXIII, the Council sessions and statements reflected a feeling that only by sharing in the world's problems and sufferings can the Church understand clearly the message of its Gospel for today. It recognized the disunity of Christians as an impoverishment of the Church, and it acknowledged that Christians would be "edified" by confronting the measure of God's truth to be found in other religions. In every corner of the globe men of all faiths, including Jews, hailed the Vatican Council as a remarkable event and achievement.

But there was also dissatisfaction. Some considered the Council's decrees inadequate. Among the Church's severest critics were leaders of the Jewish religious community. Jewish objections were raised despite the fact that the Council's action included a specific repudiation of anti-Semitism and clarification of Church teaching with regard to the Jewish role in the Crucifixion. It is important to understand the Jewish criticisms for they point the direction toward which the Church must now go, if it will be a force for reconciliation among men.

This book will examine the events of the Vatican Council at all of its four sessions, focusing particularly on issues that concern Jewish-Christian relations. These relations are a complex of many factors, which I shall try to describe as they appeared in the course of the Council deliberations. By placing them under scrutiny, we shall see how complicated they can be even under the best of circumstances. But I hope to demonstrate, also, how much we share together—a faith that calls us to a service of love to the one God and to humankind.

My primary concern will be to tell the story of the Council's treatment of the Jewish statement as the facts are known to me. Unfortunately, when attention is directed solely to the Council's action, the reaction of many Jews may be negative, for the emergent document, as Rabbi Abraham Heschel put it in a public address, "did not come up to the greatness of the moment."[2] On the other hand, the role played by many individual Catholics, and particularly the American bishops, was exemplary. And the final statement, when seen in the context of history, was a noteworthy advance. It set in motion a will for change that has already enabled the American Church, particularly, to develop a new relationship with the Jewish community.

The reader will recognize that there were implications for the theology of Jewish-Christian relations in every procedural and substantive question to confront the Council. Not only were there religious issues between Jews and Christians, but the conflicting theological views held among Jews and Catholics within their own communities also have to be considered. While some Jews, for example, favored some form of Jewish participation or attendance at the Council, others opposed it. Some Jews wished the Council to consider the Jewish question within the theological context of the Church's definition of ecumenism; others wished the Church to treat its relation to the Jews in a non-theological context, as merely another social problem. Some Catholics favored a statement on Judaism whereas others thought it never belonged on the Council agenda. Some Catholics wished to consider the Church's relation to the Jews in the context of its ecumenical concern; others wished to exclude Judaism from inclusion in a hope for Christian unity. Throughout this book I try to shed light on these theological issues as they emerged, rather than deal with them separately or independent of historical events. But the reader will appreciate that there is still much more to be said. Other books by other authors need to be written telling more of the history of the Council and deliberating on the theological issues at greater length.

This book is the first chronological history of the Council's effort to write a statement on the Jewish question as seen from within the Jewish community.

Catholic commentators were quick to confess that, as the English periodical *Catholic Herald* put it, "the dreadful memories of Belsen, Buchenwald, and the rest of the extermination camps and the apathy and indifference of so many Christians to them must surely have been nagging at the conscience of many of the Bishops since the Council began. . . . A declaration passed in 1965 can do nothing to wipe out the mistakes of the past, but it can help us to prevent the same mistakes being made in the future."[3]

Do Jews and Christians really agree on the mistakes of the past? How did anti-Semitism acquire such strong rootage in Western civilization? To what degree did Christianity nourish the seed of hatred of the Jews? Are some of the sources of anti-Semitism to be found in the New Testament or in the teachings of the Church? Or has it derived historically from no more than the perverse behavior of some churchmen? Is contemporary anti-Semitism a secularized version of an ages-old religious teaching, or is it a completely different breed?

Part One of this book considers such questions as these by reviewing the record of history from New Testament times to the modern day. This section could be no more than a swift survey of essential background to an understanding of the deliberations at Vatican II. Throughout history there have been powerful forces, including many Church spokesmen, that have found justification in Christian sources for condemning Judaism and for considering the Jews a reprobate people. There have also been some Christians who found in the Gospel the incentive to respect Jews and to treat them with justice and even love. Material describing the reconciling efforts of Christian leaders between the period of World War II and the calling of the Council forms the final section of Part One. That chapter reveals how widespread was the willingness of sensitive church leaders, Protestant and Catholic, to confront honestly the past in Jewish-Christian relations. Revision of textbooks, changes in liturgy, the initiation of theological conversation—these and other efforts commenced long before the Vatican Council was called. The Council built upon these foundations.

But, by lifting the issue of anti-Semitism up for world-wide public scrutiny, the Council went beyond any efforts of the past. By so doing, it compelled clergy and laity in Rome and around the world to take a stand. Many covert enemies of the Jews and Judaism showed their colors. Many quiet friends became outspoken. If there is dissatisfaction that the process should have taken so long, there ought to be gratification, nevertheless, that anti-Semitism was at last confronted openly and vigorously.

This book will describe what happened to the statement on the Jews in its various convolutions. At the end of the Council, the *Catholic Herald* stated that "Good as it is, the final declaration is not as strong as a previous one. . . ."[4] I shall analyze the various drafts prepared by the Secretariat for the Promotion of Christian Unity, in order to understand in what way one statement was "stronger" or "weaker" than another. Who were the parties to the various compromises and what was the Jewish role in all this?

Part Two is concerned with the procedural questions that confronted the Council administrators. These can be grouped under several headings: Should the Council adopt any statement on the Jews? If so, in what context and in relation to what other Conciliar statements? What Council commission should prepare the statement, and what relationship should that commission have to Jewish consultants? Who in the Jewish community ought to be consulted?

Parts Two and Three also discuss substantive questions that occupied the Council Fathers. Most of their energy seemed devoted to a clarification of the following questions: Were only *some* Jews implicated in the Crucifixion, or were *all Jews then living* to be held responsible? What were the consequences of Jewish complicity in the Crucifixion? Are the Jews of past and present to be considered a reprobate people? Are they to be considered collectively guilty of "deicide," even today? How shall the Church interpret the harsh passages about the Jews in Scripture? Should the Church express a hope for ultimate Jewish conversion to Christianity? Should it express an indebtedness to Jews or indicate in any way Catholicism's relation to Judaism? Who are the Jews of today, and after the revelation of the Gospel, what can be the Jewish mission in history? Can the Church say anything affirmative about Jews and yet avoid ill feeling among Arabs who look upon the State of Israel as evil? How strongly should the Church reprove hatred of the Jews? Can it "condemn" anti-Semitism as heresy?

The Council did not answer all of these questions. It is clear, after all, that four years is not long enough. The schism that took place centuries ago in the Household of Israel over the nature of the Messianic expectation is not a matter that theologians can neatly resolve.

Part Four, dealing with the fourth and last Council session, includes a critical analysis of the final text of the statement on the Jews. But the Council should not be judged by what it said in that document alone. The Church is in a period of decisive change. In the concluding chapters (13 and 14) I evaluate the Council's work from the perspective of hope for the future. It is my conviction that the Council has opened the door for Jews and Christians to enter into a new era of sincere and honest conversation about matters of faith.

The Appendices (p. 262) include the four versions of a statement on the Jews that were presented at the various sessions of the Council, and a translation of excerpts from the explanation Cardinal Bea prepared for the Church Fathers to justify changes in the text of the statement.

Much of the material in this book is reportorial in nature and I alone am responsible for what is included or omitted. No organization with which I have been associated during the past several years—the National Conference of Christians and Jews, the Anti-Defamation League of B'nai B'rith, the Jewish Reconstructionist Foundation—is to be held accountable in any way for the viewpoints expressed here. None of these organizations sought to censor what I felt I had to say, nor did they make available to me any "confidential material" that did not otherwise come my way by virtue of personal relationships and interest. But I am indebted to these organizations for being allowed to pursue this interest. Before the opening of the Council and throughout its deliberations I was independently invited by individual members of the Secretariat for the Promotion of Christian Unity to consider proposals and offer counsel. While at the NCCJ I was permitted the opportunity to visit Rome and confer with Vatican officials.

Needless to say, no one person knows all that took place in the development of the statement on the Jews. Nor can any one Jew speak for all others. Much was happening at many levels. Frequently, in both Jewish and Catholic communities, one hand did not know what the other was doing. In the Catholic community, important events were occurring, often simultaneously, within many concerned groups—the Vatican itself, the Curia, the Secretariat for the Promotion of Christian Unity, the Council's Coordinating Commission, as well as among the bishops and their experts, and among Catholic writers, editors, and laity. In the Jewish community, activity was going on within several religious and communal organizations—the leaders of which often disagreed with one another in their attitudes toward the Council. And, of course, the Protestant World Council of Churches, Protestant and Orthodox delegate-observers, Eastern Orthodox prelates, and Arab national leaders all were involved in expressing opinion and often exerting pressures to influence Council action.

In preparation for this book, I accumulated material obtained through channels of information developed over a dozen years of work in interreligious relations. "Leaks" of secret Council documents were not uncommon and were often intended to serve political purposes. I include such confidential material, obviously under the necessity of respecting the anonymity of friends and informants, where it is relevant. For the most part, however, the account is documented by reference to readily available sources.

I make an effort to be "objective" in the presentation of the historical data, but I confess that I am a partisan on issues of Jewish-Christian relations. I care deeply about the nature of the dialogue. Although the heart of my own viewpoint is contained in Chapters 13 and 14, I have permitted myself to respond to certain issues as they emerged in the course of Council debate. In some instances these "interruptions" are an attempt to interpret the general reaction of the Jewish community; at other points they are my own perspective. I have, however, tried to make the distinction clear.

I deeply hope that this book will make its own contribution to the honesty and depth of the ongoing conversations. I wrote it in deepest respect for the good will that most Catholics demonstrated toward Jews. The reader will discover that frequently there were in both communities wrangling, petty bickering, and smallness of spirit; but also there were moments of glory when both reached out to each other in forgiveness and fraternity.

I believe strongly that when Jews and Christians will speak to each other in a spirit of trust and mutual esteem. God may reveal Himself in new dimensions. I hope that this book, therefore, will not only provide background information but also continue the conversation that was started at the Council.

Finally, I am indebted to my wife and children, whose personal sacrifice made the writing possible.

Arthur Gilbert

PART ONE

BACKGROUND TO THE COUNCIL

1. Confronting the Past: The Consequences of Contempt

THE HORRORS OF THE NAZI PERIOD profoundly shocked all sensitive Christians. Out of the holocaust rose questions that haunted—and continue to haunt—the minds of historians and the conscience of mankind. Christians in particular were compelled to ask how it was possible for such a destructive form of pagan totalitarianism to emerge in "the Christian West." The brutal slaughter of millions of Jews posed even harder questions: How could such incredibly virulent hatred of Jews become established? What were its roots? Why did so many Christians by their silence or compliance permit such atrocity?

Historians and sociologists are still suggesting answers. Perhaps no adequate explanation will emerge in the foreseeable future. But in the post-war period, many Christians responded with a reappraisal of their past record and an acknowledgment of present responsibilities.

Protestant representatives of the World Council of Churches meeting in Amsterdam in 1948 unreservedly confessed, "We have failed to fight with all our strength the age-old disorder which anti-Semitism represents. The churches in the past have helped to foster an image of the Jews as the sole enemies of Christ which has contributed to anti-Semitism in the secular world. . . ."[1] In 1961 the same body, meeting this time in New Delhi, added a specific caution: "In Christian teaching the historic events which led to the crucifixion should not be so presented as to fasten upon the Jewish people of today responsibility which belongs to our corporate humanity and not to one race or community. . . ."[2]

Some individual Catholic leaders acknowledged that there might be a Christian component in the making of anti-Semitism. But indications of such concern were limited to occasional, unofficial statements by sensitive Catholic laymen and priests. The Church as a corporate body was not ready to act upon this question until Vatican Council II. One of the most constructive and important of the individual efforts was the evaluation of Catholic catechisms and parochial school textbooks. It was discovered that they contained many negative references. The concept of the Jews as a reprobate people guilty of deicide was not merely an outworn canard or the obsolete product of a medieval mentality. It was still being repeated. A study of French catechisms in 1952 disclosed the prevalence of teaching that fostered contempt for the Jew.[3] In a similar study of the intergroup content of American Catholic high school textbooks Sister M. Rose Albert Thering, O.P., recorded the following illustrative citations:

"When the mob saw this, the chief priest took up a cry that put a curse on themselves and the Jews for all time: 'His blood be upon us and our children.' "

"Since Pilate could not find anything wrong with Christ, he decided to disfigure his pure and beautiful body so that even the bloodthirsty Jews would back down and say that Christ had enough."

"The Jews are the invited guests who refused the invitation and were themselves finally rejected."[4]

Certainly it could be presumed that such a consistent and continual derogation of the Jews over the centuries would result in animosity.

If Christians since World War II had become aware of the consequences of Christian teachings of this kind, Jews, on their part, felt deep in their bones that the convictions behind them had helped to produce pogrom and pillage, the Inquisition and mass murder, the blood-libel accusations, and a painful Jewish alienation from the society of Christian Europe. Most Jews have been and are today still convinced that anti-Semitism is built into Christianity, even to a foundation in the New Testtment, and that Christian teachings are one of the most important sources of hatred of Jews. Christians are generally shocked at such a bitter and sweeping charge and some are angered by it. Those Christians who wish reconciliation with Jews often find that the Jewish proclivity for dwelling on the past becomes a stumbling block. It imposes a burden of claims and counterclaims, of guilt and shame, that is unpleasant and depressing.

Thus Father Michel Riquet, S.J., of Paris, in an article addressed to a Jewish-Christian audience, warns that friendship cannot grow in an atmosphere of mutual distrust and suspicion. He advises, "We should avoid any depressing and unpleasant talk about the Christian roots of anti-Semitism . . . [instead we should] build up true friendship by eliminating all the bad taints of the old and return to our common roots in the Bible, emulating each other in our knowledge, service and love of the one true God." [5] Like many other Catholics, Father Riquet is suggesting that it is enough in a new day of ecumenism for Jews and Christians to meet each other with their eyes directed toward the future.

This point of view, however, leaves many Jews dissatisfied. We do not believe that we ought to suppress or ignore the ghosts of the past. In order to create a tomorrow better for all mankind, we must build upon the wisdom derived from a knowledge of that past. The way in which the Church can be an agency of reconciliation, in fact, will depend on its ability to confront the realities of past Christian encounters with Jews. Knowledge of error provides wisdom with which to face future problems. It serves a corrective purpose and offers some assurance that contempt and hostility toward others cannot again emerge so readily. Does not the Church itself teach that confession is important in any effort at atonement?

It would be wrong, of course, to make of the Jew a "prosecutor of the Church." But it is equally foolish to think that history is of no account. There are important differences between Jews and Catholics that will test our patience and demand of all of us a genuine mutual comprehension. We cannot know each other unless we also know something of each other's history, for the past lives on in the present. Jews on their part can gain a more profound appreciation of their differences with Christianity. And when the distortions of the past are seen for what they are, the real confrontation with genuine issues of faith can take place. Finally Catholics will hardly comprehend the enormous emotion that Jews bring to any discussion of the Vatican Council unless they are aware of how Jews view the history that is background for the discussions completed in Rome. For the Jews, the prospect of a revision of Church teaching could only have aroused eager anticipation.

JEWS IN THE NEW TESTAMENT

Many Jewish scholars contend that the roots of Christian anti-Semitism are to be found in the New Testament. In light of this judgment, any hope for dialogue between Christians and Jews would require a forthright clarification of those passages in Scripture that seem to provide some Christians with justification for hatred of the Jews.

Jews are not merely being cantankerous when they claim that there are passages that feed the fires of prejudice; nor are they unaware of the many passages that speak of brotherly love. The fact is that in the past many Church Fathers defended their discrimination against Jews by citing biblical texts. And during the four years of the Vatican Council debate some Catholic and Eastern Orthodox prelates quoted the Gospels as justification for their belief that the Jews collectively bear a stain of shame upon their forehead. On the authority of such biblical lessons these conservatives fought any effort to alter traditional interpretations.

There have been Protestant scholars who have called for radical reformulations in order to offset the hateful implications of some of these biblical judgments. The very Reverend Charles H. Buck, Jr., Dean of the Episcopal Cathedral of St. Paul in Boston, unequivocally stated on January 17, 1960, "The basic doctrine of anti-Semitism in the Western World is the New Testament. Until the Church admits this and teaches its people to distinguish between the Gospel of Jesus and the anti-Semitism of some of the human authors of the New Testament books, this terrible problem will not begin to be solved. . . ."[6]

A. Roy Eckardt, editor of the *Journal of Bible and Religion*, expressed this attitude even more emphatically: "The Church must find that certain biblical lessons preserve and foster, in and of themselves, a derogatory image of the Jews. All the learned exegesis in the world cannot overcome the presence of a categorizing mental attitude within particular documents which are to all practical purposes tied to the Divine. . . . Until the Church admits concertedly, and goes out of its way to proclaim that there are roots of anti-Semitism in its own Scriptures, Christian anti-Semitism will not be overcome."[7]

During the Vatican Council debate on the declaration dealing with the Jews, the Holy Synod of the Coptic Orthodox Church communicated to Rome its forthright understanding that "the Holy Bible gives a clear testimony that Jews have crucified Lord Jesus Christ and bore the responsibility of His Crucifixion." The communication recalled that "the Jews repeatedly said to Pontius Pilate: 'Crucify him, crucify him (Luke 23:21).' 'His blood be on us and our children (Matthew 27:25).'" The Coptic Orthodox Church then provided documentation for the view that the Jews stand "condemned" according to the New Testament. "Said St. Peter the Apostle: 'but ye denied the Holy One and the Just and desired a murderer (Barabbas) to be granted unto you; and killed the Prince of Life (Acts 3:14–15).'" Furthermore, the condemnation rests upon all Jews in their collective existence whether in ancient days or in this time. "This condemnation does not include a specific group and not others; for St. Peter addressed the Jews 'of every nation under Heaven (Acts 2).' Jews will never be forgiven this sin of the Crucifixion," explains the document, "until they are led to repentance and belief in Jesus as the Christ. 'For I say unto you, ye shall not see me henceforth, till ye shall say, Blessed is he who cometh in the name of the Lord (Matthew 23:37–39).' This stands until they believe and get their sins removed."[8]

Certain Roman Catholic prelates also pressed for a similar statement based on New Testament accounts. They recalled the harsh censure imposed on Jews by Jesus as a consequence of their iniquity: the destruction of Jerusalem and the dispersion of the Jewish nation (Matthew 23:29–39, 27:25; Luke 19:42–44). They reviewed the Jews' loss of the Messianic blessing (John 1:11, 8:21–24; Acts 28:23–29; Galatians 4:25–26; Romans 9:30–31). Finally, in consequence of their hard-heartedness and blindness, Jews are no longer God's Israel; rather the Church has become "the true Israel, the new Israel, God's Israel, Israel according to the faith (Galatians 3:29, 6:16; Romans 9:6–8; I Corinthians 10:10)."[9]

As these citations indicate many New Testament passages suggest that the Jews are no longer "the people of God." Instead, the Gospels assert that God has established His covenant with a New Israel consisting of believers in Jesus as the Christ. Not only are the Jews displaced, but their covenant is made obsolete (Hebrews 8:13).

In the First Letter to the Thessalonians (2:16), evidently written some years after the destruction of Jerusalem, Paul justifies the suffering of the Jews as a proper retribution for their guilt. "For the wrath is come upon them to the uttermost" (KJV). Some Christians even considered their hostile behavior toward Jews as no more than fulfillment of divine wrath.

Despite the existence in the New Testament of such harsh judgments and notwithstanding their continual evocation by a number of Christian prelates, most Catholic Bible scholars repudiate outright any allegation of hatred of the Jews in Scripture. Thus, Father Gregory Baum in a book devoted to this very subject concludes, "There is no foundation for the accusation that a seed of contempt and hatred for the Jews can be found in the New Testament. The final redaction of the New Testament may bear the marks of conflict between the young Church and the Synagogue but no degradation of the Jewish people, no unjust accusation, no malevolent prophecy is ever suggested or implied."[10]

Similarly, Father John B. Sheerin is at pains to point out that the harsh passages were never intended to be a judgment for all times, upon all Jews. Nor is the Christian, on the basis of these passages, justified in committing any act of discrimination. Father Sheerin acknowledges that Church Fathers in times past misused and misread the New Testament, unfortunately bringing dire consequences for the Jewish people. For this reason, he concludes, the Vatican Council sought to clarify the exact Church teaching on these controversial points: "The reason why many people have the impression that the Gospel is anti-Semitic is due to the fact that these earlier apologists—the Church Fathers—often quoted Scripture to support their position. They realized that the religion of the Jews was still a formidable adversary to Christianity and they wanted to discredit it. . . . Unfortunately the preaching and writing of these early apologists seem to have had more influence on the mass of the faithful than did the Gospels. To read the story of anti-Semitism in the Middle Ages in Christian Europe is a bitter experience. Christianity crucified the Jews, inflicting on them incredible punishments and exile." [11]

What, then, does the New Testament teach about the role of the Jews in the Crucifixion and their consequent experience in history? Without anticipating all that this book recounts of the deliberations at the Vatican Council, I wish here to summarize what many Catholic scholars insist: (1) These harsh passages were meant to be read not as a judgment on the Jews but rather as a prophetic type of admonition and warning; (2) they are intended to refer only to the Jewish leaders of that time and not to all of the Jewish people; (3) certainly they are not intended to apply to the Jewish people of today; (4) Jesus himself, at the end of his ministry, in an act of reconciling love, asked forgiveness even for those who participated in the Crucifixion.

Such interpreters also point out that Apostle Paul underlined in his writings that sense of profound Christian kinship with the Jews that ought to preclude any form of anti-Semitism. Paul interpreted Jewish reluctance to accept Jesus as Messiah as God's divinely ordained occasion to provide a message of salvation to the Gentiles: "I ask, then, has God rejected his people? By no means! . . . God has not rejected his people whom he foreknew. . . . So I ask, have they stumbled so as to fall? By no means! But through their trespass salvation has come to the Gentiles, so as to make Israel jealous" (Romans 11:1–2, 11). As regards the Gospel, Paul acknowledged that the Jews are "enemies," but "as regards election they are beloved for the sake of their forefathers. For the gifts and the call of God are irrevocable" (Romans 11:28–29).

Perhaps the most telling point is that throughout the New Testament it is made clear that the message is one of love and that the measure of a Christian is his ability to love—even an enemy. In the First Letter of John, where it is contended that every spirit which does not confess Jesus is not of God (4:3), the Christian teacher also exhorts his followers: "God is love, and he who abides in love abides in God, and God abides in him. . . . If any one says, 'I love God,' and hates his brother, he is a liar; for he who does not love his brother whom he has seen, cannot love God whom he has not seen. And this commandment we have from him, that he who loves God should love his brother also" (4:16, 20–21).

There is, then, evidence and argument on both sides in interpreting New Testament passages with respect to judgment on the Jews. Some verses in some books seem to consign the Jewish people to everlasting condemnation, and others reflect gratitude, respect, fraternity. The future of Jewish-Christian relations will be vitally affected by the biblical interpretation of specific texts and the larger context of Christian Scripture. Such questions cannot be treated in this place or by this author, but it may be pointed out that the New Testament seems at best ambiguous and has been used from the first century into our own day to bolster anti-Semitic sentiment and action.

Certain basic issues of faith do emerge from a consideration of these New Testament passages. No one can deny that there are very real tensions between Christian and Jewish belief. I as a Jew, for example, can sense the problem of the Christian (and of the New Testament writers), who proclaims Jesus as Son of God, Mediator, and Messiah, when confronted not only by the refusal of the Jews to acknowledge him as Messiah but by the claim that the Jews, as "God's Israel," still have a divinely ordained role in history. Obviously I cannot pretend to resolve such a conflict for Christian theology; but I can outline some of the difficulties faced by Jews in the Christian affirmation.

Christian claims about Christ pose several theological prob-

lems for the Jew. The idea that Jesus is God Incarnate violates
the Jew's conception of the divine nature. The Jewish sense of
the indivisible unity of God, and His transcendence of human
limitations, is affronted by the claim that there is one God in
three divine Persons and that He appeared fully and once for
all in Jesus.

The affirmation that Jesus is the Messiah is perhaps the central
issue. Jews hold to a conviction that the coming of the Messiah
will be accompanied by an era of spiritual renewal and a rehabilitation of the People Israel. Only by a radical redefinition of
the Hebraic tradition about the meaning of the Messianic era could
Christian claims about Jesus' Messiahship be entertained. It
should not be surprising that Jews did not and do not acknowledge
those claims. And to the Jew, whose Messianic expectations
involve a transformation of life on earth, the evidence after
2,000 years of Christian "redemption" is not convincing. The
attitudes and behavior of Christians, and the spiritual condition
of the world, would not seem to justify their abandoning their
own faith and corporate existence for the Christian cause.

Indeed, Christian anti-Semitism may be related, in part, as
Father Dominick M. Crossan, O.S.M., suggests, to the very
fact that the Jews by their "stiff-necked" existence constantly
remind the Church that the promises of the redemption of man,
alleged to have been part of Jesus' legacy, have not yet been
realized even among the Church's faithful: "We have claimed
to be the fulfillment of the Old Testament's expectation of a
divine rule of love, mercy, forgiveness, compassion, patience and
peace: the Jew also knows these prophecies because he wrote
them and he looks for their fulfillment and does not find it.
Much of our Christian anti-Semitism is based on the fact that
the communal existence of the Jew is a divine accusation of
our failure to realize on earth the final vision of Jesus in
John 17:21–23."[12]

These are but a few of the many questions and issues divid-
ing Jews and Christians, and more will emerge in the pages to
follow. As a Jew I trust Christians to see that there is some
spiritual meaning and basis for Jewish beliefs, that to reject
Christian beliefs is not mere arbitrary, hardhearted stubbornness.

At least it should be apparent that there are more basic matters
than the Crucifixion and the charge of deicide to occupy our
attention. The account of the Crucifixion merely underscores
and heightens the evil already attributed to the Jewish people
as a result of their "blindness" toward Jesus. When it is suggested
that Jews abandoned God because of moral defect or perverse
motivations and were therefore replaced by the Church as God's
New Israel, then the seed of contempt is planted deep. The
charge of Jewish culpability for deicide merely nurtures a stock
taken root in controversy over other matters of faith.

This is not to deny that the New Testament dramatization
of Jewish leaders scheming and plotting to commit "murder,"
of the frenzied mob shouting "Crucify him, crucify him" and
"His blood be upon us and our children" does not itself contain the power to arouse enmity. Some Jews believe that as long
as the Passion is recounted, year after year, hatred of Jews is
inevitable. But antagonism does not have to remain the consequence of the Calvary account. In my opinion, the issue will
depend on how the Christian is taught to understand himself.
It is here that Christian theology becomes crucial.

Christians are taught to see themselves as members of a community that has received God's revelation and redemption through
Jesus as the Christ—particularly through the Passion. This basic
affirmation can be interpreted in more than one way, with
decisive results for interfaith relations. Sometimes emphasis is
placed on the exclusiveness and finality of the redemption: this
is the *only* way, and it has *completed* the redemption of the
faithful. In the past, such an attitude has not only precluded
meaningful dialogue, automatically consigning other faiths to
falsehoods and worthlessness, but stimulated contempt and even
hatred, particularly toward Jews. Jesus appeared among the Jews
and they rejected him; they had their chance and failed. And
they continue to insist on the validity of their own faith and
calling as the people of God. Jews provoke "exclusivist" Christians to angry rejection or to redoubled efforts at our conversion.

If, on the other hand, a Christian is led to feel that he belongs
to a pilgrim people *on the way* to redemption, resembling other
men who seek God in their own ways, then he will recognize

his at-one-ness with a sinning, struggling, striving humanity. He will see himself among the crowd at the Crucifixion. It is no longer Jews who are the enemy, but rather man's pride and sinfulness. He crucifies Christ today who hates his brother. Seen in this perspective the sacrifice of Jesus stands as a judgment upon all men who fall short in sensitivity and service to their brothers, of whatever race or creed. Contemporary theology can enable the Christian to find in the Passion, not a stimulant to hatred of the Jews, but on the contrary a reason to extend himself in sacrificial love so that all men may achieve their full humanity.

THE CHURCH FATHERS AND ANTI-SEMITISM

Whatever the significance attributed to the New Testament as a source of anti-Semitism, Christians stand ready to acknowledge that most Christian leaders from the fourth century on stimulated a "denigration of Jews" that assumed "something of a dogmatic character." In these words Father Edward Flannery, whose history of anti-Semitism is the first to be written by an American Catholic priest, confirms the Christian contribution to anti-Semitism in Western civilization. Father Flannery describes the situation: "At the end of the fourth [century] the Jew was a semi-Satanic figure, cursed by God and marked off by the State."[13]

In Flannery's account, Christians and Jews are seen as being in competition with each other in the Gentile world. Jews had a recognized status as a distinct group in the Roman world, a more privileged position than that attained by the struggling Christian communities. Some churchmen were ready to use any and all means to curb Jewish power. This became an even more pressing matter when "Judaizing" influences were found within the Church in opposition to newly formulated dogmas and teachings that appeared to some to be alien to the Church's original Judaic heritage.

Whatever may be the reasons for the development of a theology hostile to Judaism—and the antagonism of some Jews to the spread of Christian teaching may have been a factor—the fact remains that the Church, through many of its most sainted leaders and in cooperation with the state, nurtured the seed of hatred of the Jews in the western world. Churchmen violated the ethical spirit of Christianity by providing the religious justification that enabled Christians to consider themselves not only vindicated but even pious when they maltreated Jews. The following illustrations adequately demonstrate this thesis:

St. Justin, a second-century defender of Christian faith against non-Christians, explained in his *Dialogue with Trypho* that the exclusion of Jews from Jerusalem, the desolation of their lands, and the burning of their cities were "justly imposed on you for you have murdered the Just One."[14] In the very first of the Christian dialogues to be written in Latin, Minucius Felix Octavius explained the enslavement of the Jews by Titus in A.D. 70 in these words: "It was their own wickedness which brought about their doom. . . ."[15] In the third century Origen asserted: "We say in confidence that they will never be restored to their former condition, for they committed a crime of the most unhallowed kind in conspiring against the Saviour of the human race. Hence the city where Jesus suffered was necessarily destroyed. The Jewish nation was driven from its country, and another people called by God to the blessed election."[16] St. Jerome, who had studied biblical Hebrew under Rabbi Bar Chanina and had been reproached by his enemies on account of such Jewish studies, felt constrained to defend his orthodoxy: "If it is requisite to despise the individuals, and the nation, so do I abhor the Jews with an inexpressible hate."[17]

By the fourth century, anti-Semitic religious teaching was flourishing. St. John Chrysostom, the great Eastern preacher, provided it with a rare resonance and persuasive passion. For the Jews' act of deicide, he declared, there is "no expiation possible, no indulgence, no pardon. . . . Vengeance is without end." Jews, moreover, will always remain without temple or nation. Their rejection and dispersion was the work of God. Jews will live under the yoke of servitude without end, since "God hates the Jews and always hated the Jews."[18]

State power, soon allied with Church interests, was used to assign Jews to a servile position in the economy of Europe. The

first measures adopted by Church Councils and enforced by civil
legislation had been intended to remove the Jews from any
ability to impede the progress of Christian evangelization. The
goal was a Christianized Europe. Jews were already established
in colonies throughout Europe and were generally welcomed by
the local populace. In Spain, for example, Jews were asked by
Christians to bless their fields before setting in a new crop;
early Church Councils forbade such respect for Jewish prayer.
In time such Church decrees also became instruments of economic and social oppression.

An Ecumenical Council, called into being by the Emperor
Constantine in Nicaea in A.D. 325, snapped one of the many
threads that had connected Christianity to its parent stock. The
day fixed for Easter was made independent of the day fixed
by the Sanhedrin in Judea for the observance of Passover. The
prevailing mood was expressed by the Emperor: "It is unbecom-
ing beyond measure that on the holiest of festivals we should
follow the customs of the Jews. Henceforth let us have nothing
in common with this odious people; our Saviour has shown
us another path."[19]

Constantine forbade the Jews to make converts from among
their slaves. His son Constantius in A.D. 339 decreed a death
penalty to any Jew or Christian who entered a mixed marriage
or to any Jew who won "circumcision [conversion] from a Christian slave." The Third Ecumenical Council held at Ephesus in
431 was called by the Emperor Theodosius II, who also adopted
a code for the entire Roman empire prohibiting Jews from building new synagogues, or exercising the office of judge in suits
between Jews and Christians, or possessing Christian slaves. Eventually a slave was able to win his freedom from a Jew merely
by becoming a Christian. In an age when the possession of slaves
was the necessary requirement for engaging in productive labor,
such restrictions were designed to hasten Jewish servitude.

In Gaul, for example, a Church Council in Vannes in 465 prohibited clergy from taking part in Jewish banquets because when
Christians ate at the table of Jews, while the latter refused to
eat of (non-kosher) Christian dishes, "it made it appear as
though the clergy were inferior to the Jews." The Council of

Epaone, 517, forbade Christian laymen to eat at Jewish banquets. The Council of Orleans, 538 and 545, forbade Jews to
appear on the streets at Easter for "their appearance was an insult
to Christianity."

The great and revered Western Church Father, St. Augustine,
provided a theological perspective that undergirded this restrictive
legislation. While the hatred in St. Chrysostom's sermons seemed
unbounded and became a source of prejudice nearly unrestrained
in its consequences (explaining some of the animus still to be
found among Eastern Orthodox Christians and many Roman
Catholic prelates in the Middle East), St. Augustine tempered
his rejection with a Paulinian concern for the physical safety of
the Jews. His theology, nevertheless, justified placing the Jews
in a social position of humiliation and enforced poverty. St.
Augustine shared with the other Church Fathers a conviction
that the Jews bore a guilt for the death of the Saviour. "In your
ancestors you have killed Christ." The Jewish religion since
Christ was a corruption, yet Jewish survival in an impoverished
condition was to be seen as serving a providential purpose. The
Jews were to be a "witness people" (*Testes iniquitatis et veritatis
nostrae*—the Jews are, at once, to be witnesses to the dire consequences of their evil and to the Christian truth). Like Cain
they carry a sign, but they are not to be killed. As predicted
by Scripture, the Jews are the older brother who must serve
the younger (Galatians 4:22–31).[20]

Such teachings set in motion a policy toward Jews that was
to persist for generations and achieve its most emphatic statement during the papacy of the great Pope Innocent III.

In two letters—one of 1204 addressed to the king of the
Franks and the other directed to the count of Nevers in 1207—
Innocent stated the full theological justification for a church-
sanctioned civil effort to maintain Jews in a state of servitude.
Following the teachings of St. Augustine, he justified the Jews'
lowly status on the grounds of their corporate responsibility for
the Crucifixion, and he invoked again the Pauline analogy between
the children of Abraham by his wife Sarah and by the bonds-
woman Hagar. Pope Innocent also cited the fate of Cain, who

many were enslaved, their women were raped. Hundreds committed suicide rather than submit to such ravaging. Even those who chose to convert were hounded thereafter by the Spanish Inquisition, which suspected the sincerity of their conversion—not without good reason.

Among the sailors on Christopher Columbus' voyage of discovery in 1492 there were at least three Marranos—converts who practiced their Judaism in secret. The first settlement of Jews in the United States in 1654 consisted of twenty-three refugees from the Inquisition who had made their way north after being transported to Brazil. The history of the Jews in America has been from the beginning intimately intertwined with memories of persecution.

Jewish scholars have estimated that less than 20 per cent of the Jews were able to survive as Jews during the long torturous nightmare in Christian Europe from the fourth century to the twentieth. Many were murdered—such as those who were slaughtered by the Crusaders in the Rhine Valley. Others perished in transit, fleeing from one land to another; and many survived only by joining the Church. Six million Jews altogether were lost to the Jewish people during that sad period. Those who remained Jews, therefore, were a hardened remnant.

By Church Council action over the centuries Jews were compelled to give tithes to the Church on their houses and property, to wear a distinctive dress or badge, and to live in special Jewish quarters. They were denied admission to the universities and instructed to attend sermons on Christianity. They were constantly restricted in their right to publish, distribute, and study Talmudic literature or to build synagogues, and in at least one case, they were conscripted into forced labor groups to repair the walls of Rome.

By civic law, Jews were denied the right to own property, to join craft guilds, or to engage in gainful employment other than that which served the purposes of the prince. For the protection of their lives they paid exorbitant taxes and permitted themselves to be highjacked of their possessions.

During the Protestant Reformation Jews dared hope that a new Christian leadership was about to emerge in Europe and a new approach to Jewish-Christian relations would be instituted. Martin Luther had boldly proclaimed that "the perversions of the Christian Church" and not a supposed "hardening of Jewish minds" was the cause of the medieval Jewish tragedy. In his essay "That Jesus Was Born a Jew" (1523), he wrote: "Were I a Jew and saw what blockheads and windbags rule and guide Christendom, I would rather become a sow than a Christian for they have treated the Jews more like dogs than men."[25] Luther then suggested a revolutionary new approach to the social rehabilitation of the Jew: "My advice, therefore, is to deal decently with this people. So long as we resort to violence and slander—saying that they need Christian blood to keep from stinking and heaven knows what other idiotic rubbish—and so long as we forbid them to work and trade and mingle at our side thereby forcing them into usury, how can we expect to win them or better them? If we wish to help them, we must employ not papist law, but Christian love—we must give them a friendly hand, letting them work and thrive in our midst."

For whatever reasons—some suggest because the Jews refused to join Luther's Church—Martin Luther himself also turned upon the Jews. Twenty years later, using the sort of harsh language with which he had once attacked "papists," Luther called for the destruction of the Jews: "Let their synagogues be burnt for the Glory of our Lord and of Christendom, so that God might see that we will not tolerate right under our noses a meeting house in which God is blasphemed. Let their houses be razed so that they may know that they are not lords in our land. Let their prayer books and talmuds be confiscated. Let Rabbis be forbidden to teach. . . ."

To the reasons for rejecting the Jews that had already become a theological legacy of Christendom Luther added his own arguments. The Jews, he suggested, are a warning example for all men who think that they can achieve salvation by their own righteousness. Luther taught that, by rejecting Christ, the Jews had truly revealed their hatred for God. Since turning against Christ, they had lost their status as a chosen people; and to the degree in which they persisted in their Jewishness, they became demonic, "the mouthpiece of the devil." Thus he came to believe

that salvation for the Jews would be achieved, not by improving
their lot and status in life, but rather by requiring that they
supplement their Old Testament with the New. "They must be
forced through their misery . . . to profess that the Messiah has
come and he is our Jesus."

Lutheran scholars, on this account, suggest that Luther's
methods were "sharp kind-heartedness." They were meant to serve
the same missionary purposes which were expressed in his earlier
suggestions, namely, "to show love toward the Jew" and to save
some of them if possible "from the fire."[26]

Not all Protestant leaders were bitter against Jews. John
Calvin, for example, was far less hostile toward the Jews than
Martin Luther became; in fact, on this account he was severely
criticized. Both Catholics and radical Protestant opponents
accused him of being a "Judaizer" by virtue of his use of traditional Jewish commentaries on Scripture, his tendency to consider
Jews as though on an equal footing with Christians, and his zeal
for "the rigor of the Law." It must be recognized, nevertheless,
that Jews were never indigenous or welcomed in countries where
Calvinism flourished.

The Protestant Reformation had a constructive significance for
the Jew. It set in motion convictions regarding the rights of conscience, the importance of the biblical word—including the
Hebraic heritage in the Old Testament—and the necessity of
freedom for the exercise of one's religious responsibilities. Upon
such bases, some Christians rose later in history to defend the
right of Jews to citizenship and equal opportunity. Nor is it insignificant that Jews experienced a high degree of freedom in
America, a country whose roots are Protestant.

With the French Revolution and the emergence of a powerful
secular, humanistic, democratic ethos, Jews were able to move
toward the achievement of civil equality throughout Europe.
Many Christian leaders, and particularly Catholics, recognized
that there was an anti-religious, anti-clerical strain within such
liberalism. Frequently Jewish identification with the liberal cause
was enough to justify renewed antagonism. In Germany Jews
were attacked in the streets by armed mobs who cried out "HEP,
HEP (*Hierosolyma Est Perdita*—Jerusalem is lost)," the same

battle cry used by the Crusaders in the twelfth century when they slaughtered Jews in the Rhine Valley. Thus, disillusioned supporters of liberal reform in Germany were among those who, between 1815 and 1848, made up the second major migration of Jews to the United States; and a distrust of reactionary politics and church-state alliances accompanied these 200,000 Jews to the New Land.

In Italy Pius VII re-established a ghetto. In fact, Rome was the last major city in Europe to grant Jews their freedom and citizenship; Pius IX maintained a ghetto and enforced attendance at sermons until the Papal States were seized in 1870.

Even as late as 1898, during the Dreyfus trial in France, the semi-official Roman *Civiltà Cattolica* referred to Dreyfus—whose innocence was later to be fully established—as this "Jew by race" who bore on his forehead "the indelible sign of having betrayed his country. . . ." The author asserted that it had been the greatest error of the French Revolution to grant the Jews equal rights. They should never be admitted as fellow citizens; rather this "cursed and scattered people" ought only be allowed to reside in countries as "guests," segregated and enjoying an inferior social and political status.[27]

Between 1834 and 1914 the czars of Russia tried to solve their "Jewish problem" by enacting into governmental practice the proposals of the Procurator of the Holy Synod of the Greek Orthodox Church, Constantin Pobyedonostzev: to force one-third of the Jews to migrate, to baptize one-third, and to starve the remaining third to death.[28] Czar Nicholas initiated a policy that conscripted Jewish twelve-year-olds into the Russian Army for a thirty-seven-year period. Employing the most coercive measures, he succeeded, over thirty years, in winning a hundred thousand Russian Jews for the Orthodox Church. More than two million Jews fled the pogroms, the pales of settlement, the enforced conscription, for America. The third and largest Jewish migration to America was yet another flight from anti-Semitism.

Jews found here a greater measure of freedom than they had enjoyed anywhere else in the world. Christian leadership was supportive in hours of need. The problems of Abie in marrying

his Irish Rose were sympathetically treated in the theater instead
of prompting restrictive legislation. The democratic principles
on which America was founded prevented any efforts to promote
governmental support for religious bigotry. But movements characterized by anti-Semitic feeling and purpose still persisted. Examples of the animosity even in a free society range from the
extreme rantings of the Ku Klux Klan through the publication
of Henry Ford's allegations of an international Jewish conspiracy
to the existence of social discrimination, quotas in universities,
and obstacles to employment in certain professions. These inhibited
the Jew from experiencing a full measure of equality and security.[29]

In the contemporary world, anti-Semitism has taken on secularized features. It is now frequently accompanied by a hostility
to all religion. Pseudo-scientific theories of race can substitute
for religious teaching as justification. Nazism in its full fury
was a pagan revolt against God. Once hatred is given birth, from
whatever source, it no longer needs nourishment from any parent
but feeds on its own psychological aberrations and social distortions; and in turn it is manipulated and used. Anti-Semitic hatred
no longer needs Christian teaching as justification for itself.

The question remains, however: Why did Hitler feel that he
could count on anti-Semitism to gain him world-wide support?
What do Mosley in England, the Rockwell-type Nazis in America,
and the Tacura movement in Argentina have in common? Why
are anti-Jewish hatemongers at any moment of social crisis so
easily able to rally supporters? For most Jews there is only one
answer: Although anti-Semitism in the modern day takes on
secular form and justifies itself with non-religious explanations,
the likelihood is that it finds group support also because it touches
a deep, underground wellspring of animosity for the Jew that
was supplied for centuries by Christian teachers.

Father George Tavard provided a Catholic theologian's comprehension of this religious foundation for present-day anti-
Semitism: "To the mind of the anti-Semitic bigots, the idea that
the Jews are cursed because their ancestors crucified the Lord
explains a good deal of history. God would periodically visit the
murderers of Christ and incite them to penance through perse-

cution. All the anti-Semitic excesses of time past and present can thus be cheaply excused. They are freely granted the blessings of providence."[30]

And in Germany the brilliant Catholic professor Hans Küng was even more explicit: "The monstrous crimes of Nazi anti-Semitism would have been impossible without the hidden, often Christian,' anti-Semitism of more than 1,500 years. . . ."[31]

Obviously this review of history is far too sketchy. It ought to be sufficient, however, to explain why Jews are convinced that Christians must confront the legacy of contempt. It explains at least why many Jews viewed the Vatican Council deliberations both with uneasiness and with hope. Since much anti-Semitism seemed rooted in Christian Scripture, Jews hoped that the Council would clarify and more fully interpret the passages that have been so harmfully exploited. Since many Christians felt no conflict between their religious allegiance and contempt for the Jew, Jews hoped for a Council declaration that would condemn anti-Semitism as repugnant to the mind of Jesus and the Christian Scriptures. From an honest review of painful past history Jews sought healing action from Christian leaders that would promise a future based on a new foundation of respect and fraternity.

There were signs that these hopes were well founded. Happily, Christianity has always shown tendencies to view the Jew as a brother, sharing faith in the God of Abraham. Some Christians have always felt obliged to reach out to the Jew in love. Following the horrors of World War II many Christians took decisive action to change the tragic course of history. We turn to an account of some of their efforts.

2. Redeeming the Past: Efforts Toward Reconciliation

THE TRAUMA OF WORLD WAR II fostered a new ecumenical spirit between Protestants and Catholics. Both had suffered under Hitler's onslaught and both recognized that Christianity had failed to convert the bestial in the heart of man. Both experienced in a new way their shared heritage of faith. Theological conversations were initiated everywhere. A common conviction emerged that it was important for the Church to be in the world, concerned with man's social problems. And, in order to play a more prophetic role, the Church would have to free itself from dependence on governmental indulgence. Christians recognized too that religious pluralism was a fact, and that freedom of conscience had to be respected. A rediscovery of the biblical heritage provided another meeting ground for Catholic and Protestant theologians; at the same time it awakened them to a new awareness of Christianity's indebtedness to the Hebrew people. Both Protestants and Catholics found in the method of dialogue a constructive way of dealing with interreligious tensions.

Taken together these experiences paved the way for the Second Vatican Council. And they helped also to establish such a mood of openness as to make it likely that the Church would reconsider in depth its relations with the Jews.

RESOLUTIONS OF PROTESTANT CHURCHES

The first such response to the tragedy that had been inflicted upon Jews was a series of statements and resolutions formally adopted by Protestant Church bodies. In time both Catholics and Protestants initiated examination of textbooks and a review of materials that fostered contempt. Changes in the liturgy of the Catholic Church were considered. Eventually, theological conversations between Jewish and Christian scholars were organized. The desire to foster reconciliation led to the realization, at last, that Christians ought to engage in mutual study and dialogue with Jews. The survival of the Jewish people and their fidelity to their religious particularism challenged Christians to a new understanding of the role of the Jewish people in God's plan for history.

Protestants were first to initiate Church-wide reconsideration of traditional teachings. Since the Evangelische Kirche (Lutheran) had predominated in Germany, Protestants were led to reappraise the relation of Christian responsibility and anti-Semitism. Protestants had been more generally accessible to interfaith conversation; they were able to talk with Jews as a group about the ordeal they had suffered and to consider their common concern. Among Catholics, interfaith relations had been carried on by a few enlightened, courageous clergy and laity, while the Church itself remained officially aloof.

In the United States, as early as 1956, the National Council of Churches through its Department of Racial and Cultural Relations convened a workshop on Jewish-Christian relations. The workshop findings acknowledged that "The widespread misconceptions about the true meaning of the Crucifixion" were among the obstacles to the solution of anti-Semitism. The National Council of Churches called for "a more active effort on the part of the Christian Church to . . . correct the misconceptions about the meaning of the Crucifixion by reaffirming the Christian Church's historic belief: The Jews did not kill Christ; all men were responsible by their sins; Christ is still crucified today when men refuse to allow the will of God to rule their lives. To the Christians the true meaning of the Crucifixion is that Christ upon the Cross accomplished man's salvation. . . ."[1]

On June 5, 1964, the General Board of the National Council of Churches, "recognizing the ever present danger of anti-Semitism," renewed its call to the churches and community to be vigilant, declaring, "We confess that sometimes as Christians, we have given way to anti-Semitism. We have even used the events of the Crucifixion to condemn the Jewish people. . . ."[2]

Not only did Christian Churches issue such resolutions of contrition and reconciliation, but Christian educators began examining textbooks in order to remove any references that might be offensive to human dignity. The noted French historian Jules Isaac was the person most responsible for stimulating work in this direction. The author of textbooks studied in French schools, Isaac had served for many years as the distinguished director of French education. During the war, although his family suffered the same fate as most other Jews in occupied France, Isaac himself was rescued and hidden by friends. He turned his attention to the question that haunted his solitude: Why was it possible in Christianized Europe for such inhumanity toward Jews to be tolerated? Isaac became convinced that pagan, Nazi anti-Semitism flowered only because it had been engrafted on a stock of contempt for the Jews preserved by centuries of Christian teaching.[3]

Isaac helped promote the organization of a French society of Jews and Christians, *Amitiés Judeo-Chrétiennes*. He gathered around himself a notable group of individuals among whom were Father Paul Démann and Claire Huchet Bishop. Fr. Démann was later to undertake, on his own, an exhaustive survey of Catholic catechisms, and Claire Huchet Bishop, an author of many children's books, was later to stimulate the translation of Isaac's writings into English.

THE SEELISBERG CONFERENCE

Under the auspices of the newly organized International Conference of Christians and Jews, Jules Isaac, Father Paul Démann, and sixty-five other concerned religious leaders journeyed to Seelisberg, Switzerland, in August, 1947, to attend the first major international conference on the religious response to anti-Semitism.

The participants agreed on the following ten points "in order to promote fraternal love toward the sorely tried people of the Old Covenant."

1. To remember that it is the same living God who speaks to all, in the Old Testament as well as in the New.

2. To remember that Jesus was born of a Jewish Virgin of the race of David of the people of Israel, and that His eternal love embraces His own people and the entire world.

3. To remember that the first disciples of Jesus, the Apostles, and the first martyrs were Jewish.

4. To remember that the basic precept of Christianity, love of God and neighbor, promulgated in the Old Testament and confirmed afterward by Jesus, obliges Christians as well as Jews in all their human dealings, without exception.

5. To avoid debasing of Biblical or post-Biblical Judaism in order to elevate Christianity.

6. To avoid using the word "Jew" in the exclusive sense of "enemy of Jesus," or the expression "enemies of Jesus" to designate the Jewish people.

7. To avoid presenting the Passion in such a way that the odium of the condemnation of Jesus falls only on the Jews. They were not the only ones responsible, since "the Cross which saves all of us proves that the death of Christ was caused by the sins of all mankind," not by those of one part of it.

8. To avoid referring to the maledictions of Scripture and to the shout of the excited crowd, "May His Blood be upon us and upon our children," without recalling that this shout could not prevail against the infinitely more powerful prayer of Jesus, "Father, forgive them for they know not what they do" (Luke 23:34).

9. To withhold credence to the opinion that the Jewish people are reprobate, cursed, or destined to suffer.

10. To avoid speaking of the Jews as if they were not the first faithful of the Church.[4]

In order to make clear the need for introducing such concepts directly into the Christian curriculum, Father Paul Démann then undertook a thorough study of several thousand textbooks and catechisms used in French church schools. In a summary statement regarding his research, Démann asserted that he found certain grave instances "of fixed prejudice and hidebound opinion." He warned the Christian educator, "The Jews whom they will learn about in catechism, in sermons, in reading will be for many Christians, the first ones and sometimes the only ones whom they will ever meet. . . . There will be either a feeling of respect and sympathy toward the Chosen People of God . . . or it will be a feeling of aversion and scorn, of secret hostility toward a perfidious, condemned, fallen and cursed people, killers of God. Note the two reactions—Let us pray to God, that the second may not be the more frequent."[5]

STUDIES OF CHRISTIAN TEXTBOOKS

Father Démann's fruitful works and the enthusiasm with which they were accepted by Christian educators throughout Europe inspired similar effort in the United States. Early in 1960, the American Jewish Committee supported studies of Protestant texts undertaken by Yale Divinity School; of Catholic parochial school texts by St. Louis University; and of Jewish religious school texts by Dropsie College for Hebrew and Cognate Learning.

The Protestant and Catholic studies both revealed the Jews were more conspicuous in the church school material than was any other faith community. There was a tendency to mention Jews in a more favorable light when Old Testament content was discussed whereas harsh distortions and unfavorable images were frequently projected when New Testament material was examined.

The author of the Protestant study, Bernhard Olson, observed that the Crucifixion account, in itself, did not of necessity produce a negative image of the Jew. The quality of the image, he explained, depends "entirely upon the perspectives" brought to the New Testament themes. "The most favorable portraits of the Jew, as a whole, are made by those writers who show that they are most aware of the Jews as a continuing people, living among Christians, to whom Christians owe a spiritual debt, and are obliged to treat with consideration and fairness."[6]

Sister M. Rose Albert Thering, O.P., analyzed the intergroup content of 2,970 units (lessons or chapters) in the religion texts widely used in Catholic high schools. She observed that where the problem of prejudice or discrimination, as a social problem, was discussed, the image of the Jew was quite favorable. But this pattern was not well maintained when religious dogma was treated. "Often religious groups other than the Catholic were treated in the textbooks only when the representative group appeared chronologically on the scene of the Church's history as a schismatic or heretical group. Generalizations, over-simplifications, or negations in the textual content matter regarding another religious group may result, at least to some extent, in distorted knowledge for the students. . . ."⁷

Sister Thering also noted that materials published more recently were superior in their treatment of Jews than older textbooks—thus indicating a growing sensitivity. As Father Trafford P. Maher, Director of St. Louis University's Department of Education and supervisor of these Catholic studies, acknowledges, "Catholic textbooks published 35 to 40 years ago were incredibly awful. . . . People were taught that 'the Jews' crucified Christ."⁸

As a result of these and other studies many Protestant denominations and Catholic publishing houses, in America and abroad, undertook major revision of textbooks and curriculum materials. The content of Christian education not only came to treat key New Testament events with more sensitivity but also introduced presentations of contemporary Judaism.

CHANGES IN CATHOLIC LITURGY

Not only did Jules Isaac stimulate a significant process of textbook examination and revision, but his work was made known to Pope Pius XII and Pope John XXIII, both of whom invited him to private audience. By decisive action, both Popes demonstrated their own awareness of the problem created for Jews by the liturgy of the Church. They ordered changes specifically intended to remove any possibility of misunderstanding and to reveal their own benevolence toward the Jews.

In 1949 Pope Pius XII authorized that the Latin phrase *pro perfidis Judaeis*, which is in a prayer for Jews in the Good Friday liturgy, be translated in the vernacular as "for the 'unfaithful,' or 'unbelieving' Jews." The Latin phrase *perfidis* had frequently been mistranslated in such a manner as to apply to the Jews the derogatory connotation "perfidious." In full the prayer said,

"Let us pray also for the unbelieving [perfidious] Jews [*oremus et pro perfidis Judaeis*]: That our God and Lord will remove the veil from their hearts so that they, too, may acknowledge our Lord, Jesus Christ.

"Almighty, Eternal God, who does not withhold thy mercy, even from Jewish unbelief [perfidy], heed the prayer we offer for the blindness of that people that they may acknowledge the light of thy truth which is Christ, and be delivered from their darkness."

Although Jews are ready to acknowledge that they are "unbelieving" as regards Jesus, the prayer as corrected by Pope Pius XII was still objectionable because it seemed to imply that the Jews were also unbelieving in God, and that on account of their fidelity to Judaism they were in a state of "darkness." In March, 1959, Pope John XXIII did away with the phrase *pro perfidis Judaeis*, both in the Latin and in the vernacular. Jews hailed this act; but they hoped, still, that the day would come when the entire prayer would be revised. Pope Paul was to accomplish that change just before Easter, 1965, deleting all derogatory references.

In September, 1959, Pope John eliminated two other prejudicial sentences in Catholic liturgy: one in the Act of Consecration of the Human Race to the Sacred Heart recited every year on the last Sunday of October, and the other in the Ritual of Baptism of Converts. The portion eliminated from the Consecration to the Sacred Heart "out of respect" for the Jews read: "Turn Thine eyes of mercy toward the children of that race, once Thy chosen people; of old they called down upon themselves the Blood of the Savior; may it now descend upon them a laver of redemption and of life." The Ritual of the Baptism of Converts called upon the Jewish convert to Catholicism to "turn away from Jewish perfidy and to reject Hebrew superstition." The Latin *perfidia* is sometimes mistakenly translated "perfidy" when it really means "unbelief." Similarly the Latin *superstitionem* does not necessarily mean "superstition." Recognizing that these words, nevertheless, can be misunderstood, Pope John ordered their removal.

JEWISH-CHRISTIAN DIALOGUE

Throughout Europe, and then in the United States, Jews and Christians initiated conversation about the theology of Jewish-Christian relations and cooperative social action.

Several of the European Protestant denominations, for example, organized committees or conferences to deal with the Jewish question. In France the official Protestant Federation of France maintains a formal Committee on the Church and Israel. In Germany the Evangelical Church has a department called the Committee for Service to Israel. It holds annual study conferences on the Church and Judaism which are directed primarily to university students and are addressed by Jewish and Christian scholars. The General Synod of the Reformed Church in the Netherlands has organized a Council for the Relations Between the Church and Israel.

Every second year the Committee on the Church and the Jewish People of the World Council of Churches has conducted an international summer school on Jewish-Christian relations; and in the summer of 1965, for the first time, the committee convened a week-long conversation with a select group of Jewish and Christian scholars from across the world.

In the United States several Protestant denominations, notably those associated with the National Council of Churches, invited Jewish participation at summer youth conferences and at training institutes for church school educators. In several cases, Departments of Christian Social Concern published studies dealing specifically with contemporary forms of anti-Semitism. The National Conference of Christians and Jews and the Religious Education Association offered opportunities for Jewish and Christian leaders to engage in conversation. Throughout the country church Bible classes of children and adults visited synagogues and sought to gain a new understanding of their Jewish neighbors.

Catholic efforts in Europe and America were not official. Neither were they as formalized as the Protestant efforts. They were carried on chiefly by individuals. But some major movements are worthy of special mention.

Sisters of Notre Dame de Sion

Among Catholics concerned with the Jewish-Christian dialogue are the scholarly Sisters of the Congregation of Notre Dame de Sion, a religious institute for women founded in Paris in May, 1843. Recent changes within this Catholic Congregation are themselves illustrative of the new trends in Jewish-Christian relations.

The Congregation of Notre Dame de Sion was originally founded by two brothers, Marie-Théodore and Marie-Alphonse

Ratisbonne, who had converted from Judaism and had entered the priesthood. The purpose of the Order was "to work among Jews for their conversion." Growing quickly, the Congregation now claims sixty convents on four continents; most of these run schools and engage in educational work in the parish. Although its emphasis originally was on the conversion of Jews, the Sisterhood's major energies today are devoted to providing Catholics with information about Jews, in order to instill in them understanding and respect.

The Mother Superior describes the new attitude of some Catholics to non-Catholics: "Gradually too, what is valuable in other religions, is being acknowledged by Catholics. . . . They realize that all of us, as part of mankind, are called to form one Kingdom of God, one day . . . when God wills it, and in the manner He wills it. . . . The Catholic Church, too, will have to develop, correct Herself, and be transformed in view of the ultimate day. We are no longer insistent on unconditional surrender to a static and triumphant Church, since we admit that each man has a right and duty to follow the call of his own conscience and God alone can judge him. . . ."[9]

Mother Louis-Gabriel, a Sister of the Congregation in London, has further observed, "This new attitude is not just a new label for the old bitter medicine. Leaving aside all thoughts of conversion, the aim, today, is to establish Jewish-Christian relations on a new basis from which any suspicion, any trace of the former teaching of contempt, of enhancing one's religion at the expense of the other is completely banished. . . . Neither Catholic nor Jew is expected to minimize his religion or to compromise with his conscience but to correct the prejudiced views he may have inherited from the past."[10]

Dr. Gertrud Luckner

The work of Dr. Gertrud Luckner of Freiburg, Germany, has also been in sharp contrast to the traditional Catholic missionary approach. Dr. Luckner is a remarkable woman who risked her life many times during World War II in an effort to save Jews, until she was at last arrested by the Gestapo and sent to the notorious women's prison of Ravensbruck. Upon her liberation

she continued her works of charity. In 1950, she and three
other Catholics started a magazine called *Freiburger-Rundbrief*
aimed at improving Jewish-Christian understanding. As she
explained, "In the past Jews have been considered exclusively
either as objects of proselytizing or persecution and no attempt
had been made to enter into free and equal discussion with
them."[11] The *Rundbrief*, which now has a circulation of 16,000,
has tried to remedy this deficiency by carrying articles on Jewish
literature and the history of Zionism and the State of Israel.

Msgr. John Oesterreicher

The one Catholic scholar in America who has devoted his full
attention to Jewish-Christian relations is Msgr. John Oesterreicher,
founder of an Institute of Judeo-Christian Studies and editor
of a series of volumes entitled *The Bridge*.[12] Msgr. Oesterreicher
had so distinguished himself that he was selected to be one of
the consultants for the Secretariat charged by the Vatican Council
with responsibility for drawing up a statement on the Jews.

The choice of Oesterreicher raised some questions within the
Jewish community. It is natural that a convert from Judaism would
be subject to suspicion, particularly in view of a history of bitter
relations between converts and the Jewish people. The emphasis
on conversion of the Jews in his early writings only helped to
support fears about the probable results of his activity. To his
credit, he has frequently assumed a lonely role as a critic of both
Catholic and Jewish communities.

Other efforts toward dialogue were under way in the postwar
period. Under the auspices of B'nai B'rith's Anti-Defamation
League and with the cooperative leadership of Bishop John
Wright, a pioneer conference of Jewish and Catholic leaders was
held in Worcester, Massachusetts, in 1959. It paved the way
for a host of encounters, dialogues, and confrontations, chiefly
sponsored by Catholic universities and colleges.

THE SWASTIKA OUTBREAK

In the midst of the general movement toward Jewish-Christian
rapprochement two world events erupted that provided the occa-

sion for a new confrontation with the Nazi experience and the Christian attitude toward anti-Semitism. These events—the swastika epidemic and the Eichmann trial—also brought out the wide gulf still separating the Jewish community and some segments of the Christian Church.

On Christmas Eve, 1959, in Cologne, West Germany, two twenty-five-year-old men defaced a recently dedicated synagogue by daubing it with swastikas. When apprehended and brought to trial before a German court, the hoodlums delivered a violent anti-Semitic diatribe. Then, shockingly, as though by arranged signal, within a two-month period and despite vigorous government denunciation everywhere, more than two thousand similar outrages were perpetrated in almost forty countries. The largest number of incidents, approximately eight hundred, occurred in West Germany, but almost seven hundred such desecrations took place in the United States.

If there had been some growing sentiment that the Jewish problem was at last well in hand, these outbursts demonstrated that a virulent anti-Semitism lay not far below the surface. It awaited only the occasion to disclose itself.

The response of church bodies was a world-wide demonstration of sympathy for the Jews. Almost as with one voice, official statements were issued by Protestants and Catholics, all of whom recognized the need to fight anti-Semitism even more vigorously.

The World Council of Churches, representing 171 Protestant, Anglican, and Orthodox denominations, expressed the hope that "this dangerous recrudescence of anti-Semitism may be suppressed from the outset."[13] Archbishop Iakovos, Primate of the Greek Orthodox Church of North and South America, declared, "I think that this situation should alarm us Christians all over the world. Instead of talking sometimes, just to make headlines, we must work very conscientiously and responsively so that we may get back some order in our Christian thinking. . . ."[14]

The Catholic bishops of the United States, through the Administrative Board of the National Catholic Welfare Conference, called on "all citizens whether Christians or Jews" to protest privately and publicly against further manifestations of bigotry and deplored "any revival of the anti-Semitic prejudice which, in its earlier manifestations, culminated in such terrible disaster."[15]

Bishop Otto Dibelius of Berlin, Chairman of the Council of the Evangelical Church in Germany, sent a cable to Premier David Ben-Gurion of Israel expressing the "deep concern and disgust of German Protestants."[16] West Berlin church youth, Protestant and Catholic, turned out forty thousand strong in a torchlight parade to protest the anti-Semitic incidents.

Achille Cardinal Lienart used the swastika outbreak as the subject for a bristling, theologically oriented, Lenten pastoral letter. Specifically, he called upon his flock to

. . . defend ourselves against the ready-made, far too simple ideas that the Jewish people have become a people cursed by God because, through their responsible leaders, they rejected the promised Messiah in the person of Jesus; worse still, that they are a nation of deicides because they made the Son of God die upon the Cross. From premises like these, the conclusion may easily be drawn that they deserve the contempt and hostility of Christ's faithful disciples. And from there, it is only a short step to the assumption that anything is permitted to make them pay for their crime. The true doctrine of the Church is entirely different; the attitude she demands toward the Jewish people is exactly the opposite of this spirit of reprisals."[17]

But Vatican Radio, while expressing outrage at the swastika incidents, took pains to demonstrate that anti-Semitism was in no way furthered by religious factors and, in fact, stated that Jews by their own behavior fostered anti-Semitism: "Anti-Semitism, wherever it occurred in the past, was based mainly on social, national cultural, not religious grounds. These non-religious grounds have been the real basis of anti-Semitism ever since the Jews were driven out of the Palestine homeland." Reviewing the history of anti-Semitic persecution, Vatican Radio said, "The cultural isolation of the Jews was accentuated in Eastern and Central Europe by their different attire, language and customs and created an atmosphere which favored anti-Semitism." It added that, while Jews in Western countries "are careful to avoid emphasizing their differences," nevertheless, "with the increasing number of Jews in the West, the economic, social and cultural basis from which the whole Jewish problem stems, will be stressed more and more."[18]

THE EICHMANN TRIAL

If Christian response to the swastika outbreak was with the exception of Vatican Radio almost universal and unequivocal, such was not the case with the Eichmann trial. The Christian press in the United States, particularly, raised editorial questions about the means used to capture Eichmann and the role of Israel as the proper authority to bring him to justice. At the trial's conclusion, Christian statements disputed the use of the death penalty.

Jews felt that such matters were far removed from the central issue and that the church press could have used the occasion of the trial to probe deeper into the questions posed by the events of Nazi history. Whatever the points of proper legal procedure— Jewish and Christian jurists were to be found arguing both sides— for Jews in general they paled into insignificance before remembrance of the mass murder which Eichmann symbolized. Many believed that the Christian conscience of Western civilization had not seriously enough accepted the meaning and the significance of this trauma for the Jew, let alone the meaning of Christianity's contribution to an environment in which hatred of the Jews could have flourished.

In editorial response to such views, the editors of *America* pointed out that American Christians do not recognize a Christian component in anti-Semitism: "Christians in this country do not look upon anti-Semitism as anything essentially different from the discrimination practiced on the many other minority groups here. Christians will be shocked to discover that the United States Jewish community holds them responsible in part, at least, and remotely for Eichmann's deeds. Is this really a failure of Christian moral conscience? Or is it a sign of the vast gulf that still divides Christians and Jews, a division whose closing should be the continuing task of Christian and Jews alike?" Then, suggesting that "the recall of recent past tragedy has already begun to bring diminishing returns," the editorial asked, "Is it good psychology or good mental health to exhume in all their sordid criminal and tragic detail, the experiences of world Jewry at the hands of the Nazis? Can good understanding between Christian and Jew be built on such a foundation?"[19]

Robert Van Deusen, in his column in *The Lutheran*, a publication of the Lutheran Church in America, expressed a similar anxiety: "The Jewish people loses in the illness of mind and heart which results from the pouring of the old hatreds into the corporate blood-stream. . . ."[20]

With these typical reactions the difference for world Christendom between the swastika outbreak and the Eichmann trial became quite clear. In the one case, a new wave of anti-Semitic incidents by a "lunatic fringe" was decisively and properly repudiated. But with the Eichmann trial, it also became evident that there was deep resistance among many Christians to any suggestion of a link between the formerly Christian-inspired religious anti-Semitism and the pseudo-scientific pagan racism of Nazism. Furthermore, the raking up of the tragedies of this past period was considered morbid.

The claim that a relationship built on a foundation of accusation and penance is sure to be shaky has merit. There must also be a building for the future, based on mutual understanding. Most Jews, however, insist that without an honest facing up to the past no trusting relationship in the future is possible. Jews suspect that Father Flannery may be correct: "Historians can ask, moreover, whether the fact that the post-war world has not grasped the magnitude of Nazi anti-Semitism—as the quibbling over the Eichmann trial has amply shown—may not itself point toward an unrecognized anti-Semitism."[21]

But the American church press was not unanimous on this issue. James O'Gara, editor of the lay-published Catholic magazine *Commonweal*, asked, "Could the Nazi horror have sprung full blown out of nowhere without centuries of anti-Semitism to nourish it and give it strength in secret? And when the dark shadow of Nazism appeared over Germany, was the Christian response to this evil even remotely adequate? To my mind the painful answer to both questions has to be no."[22]

Similarly, the conservative Protestant journal *Christianity Today* had this to say: "While pagans inaugurated and implemented the

Nazi crimes against Jewry, Christians stood by and accepted them uncritically. Could the Nazi persecutions have been perpetrated without a long-standing atmosphere of anti-Jewish attitudes to which the Christian community had subscribed? Because the Jews had cut themselves off from Jesus of Nazareth, had the Christians, in turn, severed them from the bond of humanity?"[23]

In Germany the Eichmann trial became another occasion for Christians to assert a constructive responsibility in dealing with the brutal past in German history. "The trial taking place in Jerusalem concerns all of us," said the leaders of the 1961 Evangelische Kirche's Kirchentag celebration. "Evangelical Christians in Germany are realizing that by our guilt, we are involved in it."[24]

In similar spirit, the German bishops of the Catholic Church, meeting in June, 1961, under the chairmanship of Josef Cardinal Frings, Archbishop of Cologne, requested that the faithful in every church in Germany offer a prayer for the murdered Jews and their persecutors. A prayer was distributed which said, in part, "Lord, God of our Fathers! God of Abraham, of Isaac and Jacob. . . . We confess before Thee: Countless men were murdered in our midst because they belonged to the people from which came the Messiah according to the flesh. We pray Thee: Lead all those among us who became guilty through deed, omission, or silence, that they may see the wrong and turn from it. . . ."[25]

The response of Vatican Radio during the Eichmann trial was an apology for German Christians. It stressed that although "the existence of the concentration camps was no secret, skilled propaganda and the impossibility of direct contact with prisoners made the masses believe Propaganda Minister Joseph Goebbels' description of them as 'educational establishments.' " The Vatican Radio report conceded that many churchmen were influenced by the prevailing "national enthusiasms" and tolerated "excesses of party passions" and what they regarded as "mere temporary limitations on civil rights." It went on, "The want of foresight, resolution, and unity among these clergymen involves them to a certain degree in responsibility and should make them bow in humble confession under God's judgment. In spite of exceptions, however, the general attitude of Christians was so clear, outspoken and perceptible, that the Nazis recognized in believing Christians their most confessed adversaries."[26]

Despite the mixed reaction to the Eichmann trial, it focused world attention on the awesome consequences of unleashed anti-Semitism. It made even more imperative the need for a direct Christian encounter with the meaning of Jewish existence and the relations between the faiths. It contributed to the urgency felt by many for the Vatican Council to place the problem of anti-Semitism on its agenda.

An example of Christian opinion on the problem of anti-Semitism, as it finally emerged during the postwar period, was the hour-long program sponsored by the National Council of Catholic Men over the NBC network dealing with discrimination against Jews. An American priest opened the telecast on the eve of the Vatican Council by saying, "We should all be down on our knees in penance for the murder of six million Jews, but we don't know what to do about it so we forget about it." At the show's conclusion, however, the leading personality in the telecast summarized, "As Catholics we are told explicitly that anti-Semitism is immoral. As Catholics we have a duty to make reparation for any possible Catholic contributions to anti-Semitism in the past. Our special obligation is to wipe out any suggestion that a Catholic, who truly practices his religion, could at the same time practice even the smallest kind of discrimination against Jews."[27]

3. The Jewish Issue in the Context of the Council

The emergence of Pope John's pioneering personality was astonishing. Many in the Church had expected that this old man— he was nearly seventy-seven years old upon his elevation to the papacy in October, 1958—would do no more than put the administrative system of the Church in order. The Sacred College of Cardinals was then fifteen short of its full quota of seventy, and Church machinery needed overhauling. But Pope John was no tired watchman. Although aged in years, he was energetic and youthful in spirit. He knew what was going on in the world and he cared. To the delight of Catholics everywhere the Pope exercised his leadership with an enthusiasm, courage, and human warmth that was unparalleled.

The election of Angelo Cardinal Roncalli also awakened an unusual and profound interest among Jews. For this farsighted prelate, while Papal Nuncio at Istanbul, had made baptismal certificates available to Jews in order to save them from the Nazis. Chief Rabbi Herzog of Israel had said of him, "Cardinal Roncalli is a man who really loves the people of the Book and through him thousands of Jews were rescued."[1]

Before the first year of his papacy was ended, Pope John had revised objectionable references to Jews in Catholic liturgy "out of respect." He had informally acknowledged Israel's presence in the world by appointing a high-ranking Catholic prelate to serve as his Vicar General in Haifa. His first encyclical, *Ad Petri Cathedrum*, had demonstrated both his profound wish to improve the Catholic Church's relations with all men of good will, despite their religious differences, and his zeal for the Church's progressive involvement in the social and political problems of the world.

Pope John had also extended himself in genuine fraternal solicitude whenever Jewish delegations presented themselves to him. For example, when the B'nai B'rith officials visited him on January 18, 1960, with regard to the swastika outbreak, the Pope responded, "You are of the Old Testament and I of the New Testament but I hope and pray that we will come closer to the brotherhood of humanity. . . . It gives me great pain and sorrow to see these recent events which not only violate a natural right of human beings but destroy the understanding between brothers under God."[2]

No problem seemed to be beyond the range of Pope John's interest and concern: world economic reorganization and peace, the population explosion and the emergence of black nationalism, the scandal of Christian division and the heartfelt desire of all Christians to be in meaningful communication with one another, the age-old disorder of anti-Semitism and the disgrace of the denial of freedom of conscience in many parts of the globe, the authoritarianism of the Roman Curia and the hunger of Catholic religious and laity for a more vigorous involvement in the affairs of the Church.

Pope John recognized that the way the Church could grapple with all these problems in revolutionary fashion would be by the calling of an Ecumenical Council. It was on January 20, 1959, only three months after his elevation, that he first revealed his intentions to Cardinal Tardini, his Secretary of State. They were discussing the anguish of the world and the Pope's desire to provide men with an occasion for hope. Five days later the Pope broached the idea to seventeen cardinals who were among his closest associates. They were stunned. The suggestion met with immediate resistance.

There were reasons why a Council might be approached with caution. There had been only twenty such recognized Councils in the long history of the Church—the last in the Vatican in 1869; the one prior to that in 1562. Frequently the Councils had been the occasion for bitter harangue and conflict, extending even to physical encounter. At Vatican Council I, fifty-five bishops absented themselves rather than approve the dogma of infallibility, and in Germany, Switzerland, and France some fifty thousand Catholics defected from the Church, organizing their own Old Catholic or Christian Catholic Churches. Furthermore, the papacy by action of the First Vatican Council was recognized as infallible in matters of faith and dogma. There was no need for the Pope to call a Council. He could take whatever decisive action he himself felt necessary. Finally, the logistics and expense of administering such a Council must have seemed of staggering proportions.

Pope John understood what the administrators closest to him had failed to realize: To make the Church relevant to the problems of the world, to update it, required the involvement of all in the Church. Pope John revealed himself to be a wise pastor. He recognized that his far-flung hierarchy, in touch with the faithful in all corners of the globe, were better able to report on the condition of the Church in the world than even the wisest of the Curial officials from their Rome offices. He was confident that in collective assemblage the bishops would help to strengthen the Church.

Pope John was very much aware of the fact that in the course of years the Church had acquired ways of doing things, a pattern of responses, a language of administration which could stand revision and reformulation. He was aware too that in the opinion of many Christians the Catholic Church had for too long abandoned its prophetic heritage. Reacting to the past history of the Catholic Church, since the First Vatican Council, one of the most irenic and liberal of Protestant journals, *Christianity and Crisis,* had this to say: "We do not condemn Catholicism for failure to adjust to the spirit of the age. Fidelity to ancient truth in the face of modern temptation has often been its strength. But we lament lost opportunities to engage the contemporary world. In a time of perilous opportunity the First Vatican Council had made a

decision that cut off conversation with other Christians and
marked the Roman Catholic Church as outmoded in the eyes of
many perceptive and honest men." [3]

Pope John now clearly wished to make his Church a more
significant factor in the shaping of the present age. In addition to
this universal purpose, the Pope gave voice also to a revolutionary
intention. Once the Church had been "purified in truth and
charity," it could then turn "to those who bear the name of
Christian but are outside the fold" and say to them, "The way is
open. This is our Father's House. Take or retake your place in
it." [4]

ANTI-SEMITISM PROPOSED AS A COUNCIL TOPIC

Pope John appointed his Secretary of State Dominico Cardinal
Tardini, to serve as head of the Ante-preparatory Commission for
the Council and Msgr. Pericle Felici, Archbishop of Samosata,
as Secretary General for the Council. On June 18, 1959, Felici
set in circulation among the 2,800 members of the hierarchy in
134 countries a request for their suggestions regarding agenda
items. No restrictions were imposed on the subjects that might
be recommended or on suggestion for handling the subjects.
The response was overwhelming. Arranged in 2,000 files, the
suggestions ran to 9,424 pages of type covering fourteen volumes.

This unusual opportunity given clergy—and in some communities the laity—to speak their minds and to offer proposals for
consideration was itself a demonstration of vitality. It contributed
toward the realization of a measure of freedom within the
Church's authoritarian structure.

In the United States, it became evident immediately that proposals would be offered touching upon church-state relations and
freedom of conscience. Anti-Semitism and the problem of the
Church in relation to the Jew were also mentioned as a concern
of the American hierarchy. As Father Edward Duff, S.J., explained, "That the Second Vatican Council should formally discuss
the relations of Christians and Jews was inevitable. . . . The
systematic murder of six million Jews, occurring within our generation in what was thought of as a Christian civilization, called
imperiously for reflection on how this could have happened and

positive measures against the monstrous evil recurring in any guise."[5]

It has been revealed that at least one American bishop, John C. Dougherty, president of Seton Hall University in South Orange, New Jersey, officially petitioned the Council to consider revision of prayers "so that no undue offense be given and the true teachings of the Church be not misunderstood." The petition, signed by ten Catholic priests, urged also that the Church "denounce once more" hatred against the Jewish people.[6]

Requests that the Council deal with the relations between the Church and Jews were also made by the Pontifical Biblical Institute whose brief entitled, *De AntiSemitismo Vitando,* "On Avoiding Anti-Semitism," urged rejection of the notion of collective guilt and the myth of the Wandering Jew. And in August, 1960, Catholic clergy and laymen who had heretofore been involved as individuals in Jewish-Catholic dialogue met in Apeldoorn, Netherlands, and there formulated a detailed position paper later submitted to the appropriate Council authorities. Thus, from many quarters, Catholics insisted that the Jewish issue be dealt with affirmatively and courageously by the Council.

PREPARATORY COMMISSIONS APPOINTED

On June 5, 1960, the Pope appointed a series of Preparatory Commissions whose task it was to fashion the material that had been submitted by the bishops into a series of principles and proposals for discussion by the general meeting. These commissions were to be coordinated by a Central Commission, with Pope John as president and Archbishop Felici as secretary. The Theological Commission (or properly, the Commission on Faith and Morals), whose influence would be felt on all issues touching theology, was presided over by the powerful conservative Alfredo Cardinal Ottaviani. In addition to twelve commissions, the Pope appointed three Secretariats. The one of major concern to Jews was that over which Augustin Cardinal Bea, S.J., was to preside, the Secretariat for the Promotion of Christian Unity.

It was made known that Cardinal Bea would be responsible for finding ways to involve non-Catholics as observers or guests at the Council. The Secretariat would be charged also with drawing up the schema or decree that would spell out the Church's new approach to ecumenism. Jewish leaders were informed unofficially that Bea's Secretariat was responsible too for handling relations with the Jewish community and for writing any statements on the Jews that might become part of the Council deliberations.[7]

By selecting this outstanding Bible scholar to lead in the frontier area of Church unity, the Pope demonstrated that he supported an effort to speak in a language common to all Christians. Bea, schooled in Old Testament studies, was also equipped to comprehend many of the concerns of Jews. Jews were heartened but not fully reassured by Bea's appointment. They were uncertain as to the attitudes of powerful old-line conservatives in the Curia. Some degree of anti-Judaism bordering on anti-Semitism was suspected to exist within the Vatican. As I have already noted, the Vatican Radio response both to the swastika outbreak and to the Eichmann trial was hardly encouraging. The first appointments to the Preparatory Commissions seemed to include a very large number of conservative Catholic officials. Many in the Church who had achieved distinction as liberals were excluded, or invited too late to be of significant influence during the preparatory discussions. Among the men in this category who were known and appreciated in the Jewish community were the American Jesuits John Courtney Murray, whose work on church-state relations was much admired, John L. McKenzie, who seemed to understand Hebraic biblical insights better than many Bible scholars, and Jean Daniélou, who had been early involved in Jewish-Christian relations in France.

THE SECRETARIAT FOR THE PROMOTION OF CHRISTIAN UNITY

On October 24, 1960, the Secretariat for the Promotion of Christian Unity under Cardinal Bea opened its doors in Rome. In addition to Bea the staff included, as secretary, the Dutch churchman, Msgr. Jan G. M. Willebrands, who had served for nine years as European secretary to a Catholic Conference on Ecumenical Questions, and an outstanding American Paulist, Father Thomas Stransky, who was to be in charge of English language affairs.

The Secretariat made it known immediately that it had no intention of being merely the passive recipient of suggestions.

"It aims *to guide* the Council," explained Father Stransky, "in those theological and pastoral matters which directly or indirectly bear on the problem of Christian unity. It is a Secretariat for *Promoting* Christian Unity."[8]

From an early date, members of the Secretariat were appointed who were specially qualified to guide its relations with the Jewish community. Among those named as members or advisers who were known to have a background of interest in Jewish-Christian affairs were Father George Tavard, A.A., Father Gustave Weigel, S.J., and Msgr. John Oesterreicher from the United States; Father Gregory Baum, O.S.A. from Canada; and Abbot Leo Rudloff, O.S.B., from Israel and the United States. Abbot Rudloff was an expert on the Church's relations to the Jews and Arabs in the Holy Land. And as Archbishop John Heenan of Westminster, England, later explained, "The Secretariat for the Promotion of Christian Unity . . . had never taken a restrictive view of its terms of reference. Two of its members were Jewish by race, Father Baum and Msgr. Oesterreicher . . . because they would be able to guide it in its discussions on the larger unity which must include Jews."[9]

FEAR OF A UNITED CHRISTIANITY

Jews looked upon the quest for Christian unity with mixed feelings. For some, a united Christianity was threatening. Responding to a Catholic survey on the question, Rabbi Moshe Maggal in Los Angeles asserted, "We pray that the unity never comes into existence because Judaism will suffer tremendously from such a unity. . . . As soon as all Christian denominations unite, the first natural conclusion of this unity will be the exclusion of the Jews."

Others wondered how to distinguish between the old-fashioned missionary work of the Catholic Church and this new-fashioned ecumenism. Some Jews suspected that ecumenism might turn out to be just a more sophisticated way of manipulating others for the traditional proselytizing purposes of the Church. Furthermore, the use of Jewish converts as experts on Jewish affairs seemed an unfortunate omen.

Still other Jewish leaders, however, suggested that the changes

required of all Christian Churches in order to attain more effective
communication with one another might serve also to improve
their attitudes toward Jews. Rabbi Arthur Hertzberg offered the
following observation: ". . . the meaning of ecumenicity is in the
ultimate sense eschatological. It represents a largely unspoken
acceptance of the premise that the Church is likely to remain
divided on matters of faith and to live with this division; that
the historic denominations will, despite some normal traffic across
the various lines, not engage in an all-out attempt to destroy each
other; and that the question of which of the many churches is
Christ's true Church will be left for the judgment of God at the
end of time."[10]

In an article written for Reform rabbis I contributed my own
listing of Jewish expectations from the ecumenical movement:
"Jews of course cannot share the same excitement felt by Christians toward the Ecumenical Council, yet there is much here that
also stirs our hearts. As a result of this Council the Church, as
Church, has opened a door to conversation between Christian and
Jew. It has indicated an alertness to our conception of the
Church and our wishes for it and demands upon it. The power of
the Catholic Church has thus become available for cooperative
efforts in the struggle for peace, and in the good fight against
human disorder and anguish; hopefully it will specifically raise
its voice against anti-Semitism."[11]

The problem of defining ecumenism was critical in determining
whether there should be any Jewish participants or observers at
the Council and in deciding the rubric under which the question
of Jewish-Christian relations would be presented to the Council
Fathers.

THE MEANING OF ECUMENISM

The word "ecumenical" that characterized the Second Vatican
Council can have many meanings, and in the early days of the
Council's preparation it was often unclear just what usage was
intended. It was read in at least four different ways.

1. *The World-Wide Catholic Church.* As the bishops of
Holland explained in a pastoral letter, "The *oecumene* meant the

whole inhabited earth—it originally referred, therefore, to a geographical concept, that is, it meant in contrast to local and regional Church synods a gathering of the World Episcopate. After the east-west Schism, the word took on a dogmatic tone referring to the Council as an assembly of all Bishops who were in communion of faith with the Pope."[12] Insofar as Catholic traditionalists were concerned, an Ecumenical Council was the world-wide assemblage of the leaders of "Christ's Church," that is, the Roman Catholic Church.

2. *Christians in Relation to Each Other.* The word "ecumenism" could also be used, however, to include within its concern all those who had become "God's people" by their baptism into the Christian faith. It was perhaps in this sense that Pope John intended the word to be used. In his address on Pentecost Sunday, 1960, the Pope made it clear that Cardinal Bea's Secretariat was created in order "to enable those who bear the name Christians but are separated from this Apostolic see . . . to follow the work of the Council and to find more easily the path by which they may arrive at the unity which Christ wants." This was a revolutionary proposal. The Catholic Church was acknowledging that the exact nature of Christian unity was yet to be determined, according to the will of Christ. Furthermore, the Catholic Church now recognized that other Christian Churches, as Churches, were participants in the Christian communion, though it was still claimed that only the Catholic Church possessed *in fullness* all the elements required for salvation.

Cardinal Bea, when introducing a draft proposal on ecumenism to the seventh session of the Council's Central Preparatory Commission on June 12, 1962, contrasted this Catholic understanding with other interpretations: "The word ecumenical as it is used in most cases today by non-Catholics indicates a kind of federation of churches as equals. According to this theory no church can claim to be the unique, the true Church of Christ, but only one of its parts."[13]

Cardinal Bea was citing the customary Protestant usage of the term. In this perspective ecumenism demanded the following things: a sense of respect for the dignity of the other a willingness to hear what he had to say, a presumption of the possibility that the other by his difference might have remained faithful to an aspect of God's truth, and finally a belief that God's spirit would determine how and in what way all the participants in dialogue would have to change so as to achieve God's purpose. Such an approach to unity was the very antithesis of an attitude maintaining that the Catholic Church alone had the full light and that others could achieve salvation only by embracing the Catholic Faith as taught by the Church in its fixed, temporal, and institutional form.

3. *The Kinship of Jews and Christians.* The word "ecumenism," stretched a little further, could also designate a relation among all those who consider themselves in covenant with the God of Abraham. Thus Jews and Christians and the followers of Mohammed, all of whom boast of their monotheism and of their fidelity to the God worshiped by the Hebrew patriarchs, would be included. Certainly the kinship between Jews who call themselves "Israel" and Christians who identify themselves as "New Israel" would warrant a special consideration. This interpretation of the term would be the natural rationale for assigning the question of Jewish-Christian relations to a Secretariat for the Promotion of Christian Unity.

4. *The Fellowship of All Men.* Finally, in light of God's relation to all men through His covenant with Adam, the word "ecumenism" might apply to the involvement of the Catholic Church in the problems and needs of all humankind.

The Secretariat for the Promotion of Christian Unity was responsible for consulting Protestants and Orthodox churchmen to determine how their churches could take part in, or at least observe, the Council's work. Jewish participation in the Vatican Council depended, of course, on how Catholics intended to define and delimit their ecumenical concern. If they meant to refer to all men, or even to encompass all who shared the biblical heritage, then clearly Jews had a role to play.

But some Jews were wary of *any* involvement, in any way, with the Church, and particularly of any structure intended to "promote Christian unity." Although Judaism speaks of an eventual unity of all men in service to one God, this is usually interpreted to be an ethical harmony among men; it does not suggest the conversion of all men to the particular practices of Judaism. Christian expressions of man's unity in God, on the other hand, are usually accompanied by the additional assertion that it is in Christ that all men are called to eternal life and to the knowledge of God, and that the life of grace can be at least "more abundantly" achieved in the Christian faith.[14] Thus some Jews preferred not to be mentioned in the Church's theological formulations at all, no matter how liberal or benevolent the statement. They hoped merely that the Church would deal with anti-Semitism as a social problem, similar to other problems in the public order, without tortured attempts to define the nature of God's covenant with the Jews or the spinning out of an alleged spiritual relationship between Jews and Christians. What these Jews wanted from the Church, if anything, was a statement concerning past involvement in hatred of the Jews, a repudiation of distorted Christian concepts concerning the alleged curse on the Jews, and a clear, forthright condemnation of any form of anti-Semitism.

Not all Jews shared such a narrow view. It was the hope of many, for example, that the Church, in defining itself, might acknowledge and recognize its spiritual indebtedness to the Jews and the ongoing relatedness of Jewish and Christian thought. We have indeed differed on the meaning of the Messianic prophecies, but Christians and Jews share a rich heritage that compels us to define ourselves in such a way as to be of service to God and mankind. Instead of clashing with each other in order to prove one right and the other wrong, we ought to be teaching and learning from each other, for if God has been manifest in both of our faith communities and is still to be encountered in church and synagogue, then through dialogue we may each teach the other something of His truth.

THE NATURE OF JEWISH COMMUNAL ORGANIZATION

When Cardinal Bea's Secretariat turned to the task of considering the Jewish question, they did not know how to proceed. They were understandably bewildered by the maze of Jewish secular and religious organizational structures. They were not certain whom to consult and could not properly evaluate the various suggestions they received from Jewish sources.

There is no hierarchical structure in the Jewish community; we are not a Church. We are a *people*—a community. God's covenant was made with all Jews—the elders and chiefs, the men and women, the young and old. The synagogue is not regarded as a divine institution as is the Church. It merely provides a sanctuary where Jews in community express their love of God and hope for the experience of His presence. Rabbis have no closer relationship to God or spiritual status in His covenant than do the laity. They have no particular authority over the life of Jews, other than that earned by their piety and learning.

Particularly in the Western world, since the Napoleonic Emancipation, the Jews have created a vast network of lay-administered agencies and organizations, outside of the synagogal structure, that perform essential, even religious, functions for the Jewish community. In the United States, for example, the work of providing rabbis to serve the spiritual needs of Jewish college students is the project of the fraternal organization B'nai B'rith, and the duty of providing chaplains and religious services for Jewish servicemen is that of the Jewish Welfare Board, a coordinating agency of Jewish community centers.

World Jewry, therefore, boasts a multi-faceted structure of national and international organizations under countless auspices, which perform the varied services required by a dynamic, vital people. The work of community relations, including the battle against anti-Semitism, is carried on by such organizations as the American Jewish Committee, the Anti-Defamation League, and the American Jewish Congress, all of which have international affiliates and connections. The religious community also has its agencies and organizations. There are three denominations in Judaism: Orthodox, Conservative, and Reform. Each has its own national and international structures. There also exist coordinating agencies to provide the religious community with one voice on those issues on which they all can agree. Finally, a host of organizations are devoted to the welfare of the State of Israel.

(A brief description of each of these bodies appears in Appendix H.)

All of these organizations were properly concerned with the interreligious dimensions of the Vatican Council's work. Unfortunately, they did not always agree on the legitimate right of one another to engage in conversation with Vatican officials. Not only did this lack of agreement cause confusion and anguish for Vatican representatives, but it produced conflict within the Jewish community that remains a source of tension to this day.

Shortly after the Secretariat for the Promotion of Christian Unity had opened its doors, interviews were held by mutual agreement with representatives of the World Jewish Congress, International B'nai B'rith, and the American Jewish Committee. It was understood that each organization would prepare a memorandum indicating its concern. In light of later criticism inside the Jewish community concerning the manner in which Jewish "bureaucrats" approached Vatican officials, it is only fair at this point to emphasize that Cardinal Bea sincerely welcomed such representations. His Secretariat hardly knew where to begin in order to grasp the Jewish issue, and the members were truly dependent upon and grateful for all the documentation and suggestions they were to receive.

In February, 1961, a rabbi whose name was never disclosed revealed that he had been "informed by the Secretariat" that "Dr. Nahum Goldmann and other secular leaders had been rejected as possible participants in the Ecumenical Council. If Jewish observers were to take part in the deliberations, the Pope would want them to be experts on Jewish law and religion. The Vatican said that the Pope was certainly aware that it was not the Jews who crucified Christ and that no negative opinions about the Jews should be put before the public or students." Finally, "the whole matter was an internal Church matter. Should it be considered necessary to take advice from the Jewish representatives, the Vatican would take it only from experts in Jewish law and religion."[15]

As some Jewish leaders were later informed, the Secretariat had never rejected secular Jewish agency representation. In fact, the Secretariat remained indebted throughout for the availability of personnel, counsel, and information provided chiefly through the American Jewish Committee and the Anti-Defamation League. This report had probably been "leaked" by a Jewish religious official for internal Jewish political purposes: it was an effort both to dissuade Jewish organizations—and particularly the secular Jewish community relations organization—from maintaining contact with the Secretariat. Undoubtedly such sentiments, which were also voiced by Orthodox rabbis, carried some weight with Vatican officials, for like many Christian leaders, Protestant and Catholic, some members of the Secretariat were rather intimidated by or biased toward Orthodox rabbis, whom they thought to be the "authentic Jews" and the proper representatives of Jewry.

Not fully aware of the consequences of Western emancipation for the Jewish community, Christians have little acquaintance with the splintered pattern of Jewish communal affiliations. They do not comprehend the theological issues involved in the development of liberal varieties of Jewish religious expression. Some Christians wish that the Jews might maintain themselves as an ancient people who have carried on faithfully, to the present day, an unbroken chain of tradition and ceremonial life. Since Orthodox Jews are the closest to the Christian image of the Hebrews who lived in the days of Jesus, the more conservative Christian, particularly, sees in such a Jew the signs of authenticity.

Often Catholics suspect that Jews who are not scrupulously observant of ancient religious practices are to that degree less loyal to their own Jewish heritage. The Catholic thinks of loyalty in terms of his relationship to the Church and its observances, not realizing that many Jews conceive of themselves in terms of their heritage as a people. Catholics also respond to a kind of discipline that characterizes both Catholicism and Orthodox Judaism; the Catholic is disciplined by the Church and the Pope, the Orthodox Jew by the Halacha or the Talmudic law. To the Catholic, the liberal Jew appears frequently to resemble a type of heretical or radical Protestant.

Thus there was a germ of truth in the assertion of this unnamed rabbi. Some Catholics would have preferred to deal solely with Orthodox leadership and not with the officials of liberal Jewish religious secular organizations. But his statement, I surmise, reflected more his own predispositions and prejudices than those of the Secretariat, for there was no further evidence to support this claim.

A CASE FOR JEWISH REPRESENTATION AT THE COUNCIL

By internal decision the Church limited the category of official observers to those groups which comprised "the separated brethren," that is, Orthodox and Protestant Churches. This was a revolutionary enough step for the Catholic Church to take, and one that properly underscored its intention to prepare the way for Christian unity. On the other hand, many felt that it would have been a most inspired act had a category of observers representing the non-Christian religions been established also. The Church would have demonstrated thereby its readiness to cooperate with people of good will throughout the entire world—the majority of whom are not Christians.

The relation of the Church to the Jews is somehow unique, for it shares more with them than with other religions. The issue of anti-Semitism was to become a Council agenda item. For this reason alone, in my opinion, it would have been desirable if the Church had found some way to include Jewish representatives of the most important trends and tendencies in Jewish life.

The Secretariat had established a category of "guests," enabling Cardinal Bea to invite individual Christians, who by their attendance provided a presence for denominations that chose officially to refrain from representation of the Council. For example, Dr. Stanley Stuber, an noted Baptist churchman, was extended a personal invitation. At least one American Jewish scholar was approached to determine whether he would accept such an invitation. At that time, however, significant forces within Jewry opposed any involvement in the Council, so the invitation was never accepted. There were many rabbis and Jewish leaders, however, who would have welcomed the opportunity. In fact, by the time the Council concluded its several sessions, many Jews had visited Rome, consulted with bishops and cardinals, spoken to the Pope, and reported to their constituencies on the proceedings of the Council. But instead of being free to deal with the Council openly as did the official Christian delegate-observers, instead of freely being given documents and asked their opinions, the Jews involved in the Council always had to remain unofficial, behind closed doors and in the shadows.

MEMORANDA FROM JEWISH LEADERS

In November, 1961, a meeting of West European Orthodox rabbinical leaders resolved that, even if Jews were invited, they ought not to participate in any way in the Vatican Council. That very same month, however, officials of the World Jewish Congress and International B'nai B'rith made arrangements with Cardinal Bea to provide Church officials with a joint memorandum. Thus the division in the Jewish community on Jewish cooperation in Vatican discussions was apparent immediately. Catholic confusion in view of this dissension is readily understandable.

The leaders of the World Jewish Congress and the B'nai B'rith, conscious of their lay status and the opposition of the Orthodox rabbis to any theological connection between Synagogue and Church, took pains to cast their memorandum in such terms as to make of it clearly a document of social rather than theological significance. They dealt with anti-Semitism strictly as a human problem—"part of the struggle for the emancipation of all mankind." Although rabbis belong to both the World Jewish Congress and B'nai B'rith, and although the lay leadership of both organizations includes men who are religiously devout, the memorandum, as Dr. Nahum Goldmann pointed out, was signed only by Jewish laymen, "because it was felt that if rabbis had also done so, the document might be interpreted as involving theological problems."[16]

The World Jewish Congress represents Jewish community organizations in sixty-five countries, and B'nai B'rith, a respected and powerful fraternal organization, maintains affiliates in forty-four countries. This memorandum, therefore, was an expression of a sincere sentiment among a substantial sector of world Jewry. It received careful reading and serious consideration.

The joint memorandum spoke only in generalities, leaving it to "the authorities of the Church . . . to make specific or detailed proposals" and to "Catholic scholarship . . . to find the appropriate ways to deal with the problems." It was signed by Dr. Nahum Goldmann, President of the World Jewish Congress, and Label Katz, International President of B'nai B'rith, and submitted to Cardinal Bea on February 27, 1962. It asserted,

As Jews we regard the struggle against anti-Semitism as an integral element in humanity's aspirations for a better world. What is for us, as it must be for the Church, a source of deep distress, is that with rare exceptions, anti-Semitic agitation and incidents occur in European settlements in which Christianity is or has been a major formative influence. We venture to express the conviction that in the contemporary world wherever anti-Semitism is a threat to the Jewish community, it is equally at the same time, a challenge to the Church.

If we address ourselves to the Catholic Church on the Jewish question in particular, it is because there are [derogatory] references to the Jews and their place in history in its liturgical literature, in the catechisms in many of their forms, and in certain commemorative practices as well as in educational devotional manuals in wide use. It is unfortunately not to be denied that the ignorant or malicious may misunderstand or distort and exploit such references to foment hatred of others and to promote causes in patent conflict with the teachings of the Church on the brotherhood of men.[17]

The American Jewish Committee similarly had prepared a series of memoranda "at the invitation and with the encouragement of Catholic authorities with whom Committee representatives had consulted on several occasions."[18] Unlike the World Jewish Congress–B'nai B'rith memorandum, however, the proposals, prepared by the American Jewish Committee in cooperation with Jewish and Catholic scholars, were detailed and specific. It is pertinent to note here that this American secular Jewish community relations agency made use of religious authorities in the preparation of a document that spoke directly to religious issues.

The first memorandum, entitled "The Image of the Jews in Catholic Teachings," was submitted on June 27, 1961. It analyzed how the Jews were represented in the textbooks most widely used in parochial schools throughout the United States and was later supplemented by examples taken from educational materials used in Europe and South America. Specific derogatory aspects of these materials were presented:

1. The notion that the Jews are an accursed people, exclusively and collectively responsible for the death of the Son of God.

2. Partiality in the use of the term "the Jews." In many instances this term was applied to the enemies of Jesus but not to his friends and followers although they also were Jews. Often the term "the Jews" was used in describing situations that actually involved only a few Jewish individuals.

3. Unjust and inaccurate comparisons between Christianity and Judaism. For example, Christianity was often described as a religion of love, Judaism as a loveless religion of law.

4. Invidious use of language, including such phrases as "carnal Jews" and "bloodthirsty Jews."

5. Omission of facts that would serve to mitigate generalized judgments. For example, the Jews of the Middle Ages were described as "money lenders," without the corrective information that they had few other ways of supporting themselves, being barred from the craft guilds and forbidden to own land.

The memorandum pointed to the likelihood that such statements would produce prejudice in the impressionable minds of students. It recalled theological and doctrinal sources of Catholicism such as the Catechism of the Council of Trent, which could provide an effective antidote. The statement of the Council of Trent on the Crucifixion reads as follows:

It was the peculiar privilege of Christ the Lord to have died when He Himself decreed to die, and to have died not so much by external violence as by internal assent. . . . Should anyone inquire why the Son of God underwent his most bitter passion, he will find that besides the guilt inherited from our first parents, the principal causes were the vices and crimes which had been perpetrated from the beginning of the world to the present day, and those which will be committed to the end of time. . . . In this guilt are involved all those who fall frequently into sin. . . . This guilt seems more and more in us than in the Jews, since according to the testimony of the Apostle "if they had known it they would never have crucified the Lord of Glory" (I Corinthians 2:9); while we, on the contrary, professing to know Him, yet denying Him by our actions, seem in some sort to lay violent hands on Him. . . . [Article IV].

The second memorandum entitled "Anti-Jewish Elements in Catholic Liturgy" was submitted on November 17, 1961. It called attention to the fact that "Anti-Jewish passages remain within the Catholic liturgy," particularly in "homilies and officially-approved commentaries upon the public liturgy, which guide and inform a priest in the preparation of his sermon, and in texts belonging to the monastic ritual or to the Breviary . . . and in devotional materials prepared locally by sodalities, fraternities, etc." In a carefully documented, thickly footnoted text the American Jewish Committee quoted from patristic commentaries that point explicitly to Jewish collective guilt for the crucifixion. In the Gospel lesson for the Triduum, for example, the widely-read explanation from St. Augustine warns: "Let not the Jews say: We did not kill Jesus Christus. For exactly this was in their minds, when they handed Him over to Pilate, so that they might themselves appear innocent of His death . . ."

Although the American Jewish Committee acknowledged with appreciation the changes in the liturgy which Pope John had ordered, the memorandum quotes from commentaries published since World War II, several of which refer to the Jews as a "deicide people" and evoke the image of the Jews as "Cain-like fugitives" who are doomed to wander the Earth enduring "slavery, misery and contempt."

After an interview with Cardinal Bea in Rome late in November 1961, Rabbi Abraham Joshua Heschel of the Jewish Theological Seminary of America prepared a document that examined tensions between Catholics and Jews from a religious viewpoint and offered proposals for relieving these tensions. Rabbi Heschel urged the Council in order to strengthen their attack on anti-Semitism, specifically, "to reject and condemn those who assert that the Jews as a people are responsible for the crucifixion of Christ . . . and to declare that calling a Jew 'Christ-killer' is a grave sin." He expressed the hope that the Council would "acknowledge the integrity and permanent preciousness of Jews and Judaism . . . Genuine love implies that Jews be accepted as Jews." In this as-

sertion Rabbi Heschel pressed the Catholic Church to reconsider
its conversionist approach toward Jews. This was a revolutionary
proposal, but it directed attention immediately to the underlying
theological relationship between Jews and Christians. This was an
issue even more significant than the deicide charge and infinitely
more complex. Then pointing to the fact that "few Catholic priests
and laymen possess adequate information about Jewish life,"
Rabbi Heschel called for official programs "to eliminate abuses
and derogatory stereotypes." He recommended that permanent high
level commissions both at the Vatican and on the local diocesan
level be appointed to watch over Jewish-Christian relations and to
stimulate cooperative endeavors "to further the demands of justice
and love."

It was evident that Cardinal Bea appreciated the cooperation
he received from Jewish sources. He was particularly responsive
to the spirit in which the memoranda were submitted. He was
aware that, although the American Jewish Committee was a lay-
controlled organization, it had drawn upon the foremost religious
scholars available, several of whom were his personal friends or
were deeply respected by him, such as Rabbi Heschel in New
York and Professor Jules Isaac in France.

Leaders of the American Jewish Committee also had long
supported financially a unique international college and center
for social studies in Rome, Pro Deo. In January, 1962, Cardinal
Bea spoke at a "fraternal agape" at the University. The meeting
included representatives of eighteen non-Catholic religious groups,
including Protestants, Jews, Moslems, Hindus, Buddhists, and
Copts. Among the Jewish leaders present were the Chief Rabbi
of Rome, Elio Toaff, and the European Director of the American
Jewish Committee, Zachariah Shuster. As though responding to
the hope of all the world's religions for the Council, Bea asserted,
"The greatest challenge to our generation is the problem of group
antagonism. It is the primordial duty of all groups of mankind
to unite for the purpose of overcoming the hatreds of the world."[19]

According to some Catholics close to the Council, by May the
Secretariat had already agreed on the general text of a statement
on the Jews. Entitled *De Judaeis,* it was a short forty-two line
statement that made four major points: (1) the roots of the

Church are found in the Old Testament; (2) Christ has united both Jew and Gentile; (3) Jews are not *maledict* (accursed), they remain *carrisimi propter patres* (beloved for the sake of their fathers); (4) anti-Semitism is a special danger because it attacks Jesus of the House of David.

THE WARDI INCIDENT

Then an event occurred that led to misunderstanding and upset hopes for an early consideration of a statement on the Jews. On June 12, 1962, the World Jewish Congress announced the appointment of Dr. Chaim Wardi to serve as its "unofficial observer and representative" to the first session of the Vatican Council scheduled to open in October. Dr. Wardi is the distinguished counselor on Christian affairs for Israel's Ministry of Religion. Only a few months before he had served as an observer at the Third Assembly of the World Council of Churches in New Delhi, where he assisted in the development of a forthright statement against anti-Semitism. He had also attended the Pan-Orthodox Conference in Rhodes, and he was held in high regard by world Lutheran leaders. Without doubt, Wardi is one of the most eminent scholars on the history of Christianity in the Holy Land, and he has been a most sympathetic and understanding interpreter of Christian affairs to Israel's officialdom.

But Dr. Wardi is an Israeli.

There was no category of "unofficial observer" in the Council structure. No official invitation had been extended, and Cardinal Bea had not been informed that the World Jewish Congress intended to make such an appointment. Most damaging of all, the public announcement that Wardi's designation had been endorsed by Israel's Foreign Minister Golda Meir and the Israel Minister of Religious Affairs, Dr. Zerah Warhaftig, gave his appointment a political connotation. The Vatican was immediately besieged with protests from Arab countries and requests for similar representation at the Council. Jews protested too. Leaders of Jewish agencies and representatives of the rabbinic organizations charged that the World Jewish Congress had breached an (unpublicized) agreement by Jewish leaders to seek "no representation in any form at the Vatican Council . . . since the Council was a Christian theological parley."[20]

In explanation, Wardi underscored the fact that his mission was unofficial. He stressed that he would merely be "available to those Church circles which may be interested in contact and consultation." A spokesman for the World Jewish Congress denied that Dr. Wardi's stay in Rome was "directly related to the Vatican Council." He said that "Dr. Wardi would be in Rome for the designated period merely as a representative of the World Jewish Congress."

Msgr. John Oesterreicher later pointed out that the manner in which this announcement had been made "spoiled" the possibility of any representation by Jews at the Council. As he explained, "Not only was no one in Rome consulted—which, to put it mildly, was a breach of etiquette—the news item also gave the impression that although invitations had been extended to religious groups only, the Church was, in the case of the Jews, dealing with a political body and the State of Israel."[21] Cardinal Bea also confirmed that the announcement of Wardi's appointment in June, 1962, "produced some vociferous protests on the part of the Arabs. It was, therefore, considered prudent to allay anxiety by removing the schema on the Jews from the agenda of the Council. On December 13, 1962, Pope John associated himself with this decision of the Secretariat."[22]

Religious News Service correspondents in Rome reported that "nine Arab States have taken steps for authorization of a Moslem representative with the same status as Israel's." The Arab nations saw the designation of Dr. Wardi as benefitting Israel, a country which Arabs regard as a bitter enemy.[23]

Subsequently, Dr. Wardi's appointment as a World Jewish Congress representative in Rome was dropped. In a cable to the *New York Times* from Switzerland, Dr. Goldmann asserted, "World Jewish Congress never favored observers for the Ecumenical Council like most other Jewish organizations. Congress has always had representatives in Rome, as in many other communities, and will continue to have such representatives."[24]

It is worth noting, however, that with all this uproar over the naming of an Israeli Jew and a distinguished expert in Jewish-

Christian relations as an "unofficial" representative of the World Jewish Congress, the fact remained that Arab government officials were themselves officially present at the opening session of the Council in the role of "delegate-observers," representing non-Catholic Christian Churches. These included Father Youanna Girgis, an inspector for the Egyptian Ministry of Education, and Dr. Mikhail Tadros, an advisor to the Egyptian Court of Appeals, both of whom were Coptic Christians. Also present were official delegate-observers from Jordan, Lebanon, and Syria. Israel accepted the religious function of these observers and made no protest, even though these leaders were later to engage in active lobbying against a Jewish statement.

In addition to the Wardi incident, some tension also arose over a proposal that the issue of calendar reform be placed on the Council agenda. The possibility of moving toward a fixed world calendar constituted a threat to the preservation of the Jewish Sabbath. So disturbing was this possibility that a committee to combat the world calendar proposal was organized in Jerusalem under the auspices of the chief rabbinate, and Chief Rabbi Isser Unterman of Tel Aviv warned that in view of "Vatican intentions to touch the Jewish Sabbath . . . Jews should not be present at the Council in any capacity."[25] Orthodox Jewish interventions on this issue were undertaken with Vatican officials. By the end of the year the Vatican informed Dr. Shaul Colby, director of Israel's Department of Christian Communities, that the issue of calendar reform had been "postponed indefinitely."[26]

THE PROMISE OF A JEWISH STATEMENT

Cardinal Bea valiantly tried to offset the confusion and allay Jewish uncertainties. In an interview granted the foreign editor of the *London Jewish Chronicle* he disclosed how and in what ways he personally felt the Council should ultimately deal with the Jewish question. As editor Joel Cang reported,

The Cardinal, a biblical scholar of great eminence, is anxious to dispel, in whatever form the Council might deem right, the erroneous theory by which all Jews are often held responsible for the death of Jesus. This he considers a mistake.

"It was of course," he stated, "impossible now to change the wording used in the Gospel to describe that event, which very often was misunderstood. But it was possible, and even necessary, to give it the right interpretation so as to point out the true sense intended by the writers of the New Testament. This," he explained, "would remove much of the misunderstanding which had arisen and which has caused so much suffering in the past.[27]

So at last the issue had seemingly been clarified. Although there would be no Jewish observers at the Vatican Council, the issue of the Church's relation to the Jews, and particularly the problem caused by distorted conceptions of the Jewish role in the Crucifixion and the problem of anti-Semitism, would come within the Council's concern—if not at the first session, then at a later one.

PART TWO

ADVANCE AND RETREAT IN SESSIONS ONE AND TWO

4. The Liberals Emerge

RESPLENDENT IN MAJESTY, the first session of Vatican Council II opened on October 11, 1962. Although it was a gathering of officials of only one church in a world full of religions, denominations, and sects, this Council seemed to rivet the attention of all humankind. The remarkable Pope who had called the 2,700 Fathers of the Catholic Church to St. Peter's Basilica in Rome had given the proceedings a universal significance. In his papal bull *Humane Salutis*, issued Christmas Day, 1961, the Holy Pontiff had observed, "Scientific progress itself, which gave man the possibility of creating catastrophic instruments for his destruction . . . has obliged human beings to become thoughtful, more conscious of their own limitations, desirous of peace and attentive to the importance of spiritual values; and it has accelerated that progress of closer collaboration and of mutual integration toward which . . . the human family seems to be moving."[1]

Probable Council actions with regard to the revision of liturgy or the definition of Church structures would, it seemed, have a purpose larger than the reformation of but one sectarian institution. By its actions at the Council the Church would seek to inspire all men to consider how best to serve God and thus to achieve world peace and human brotherhood. Despite religious differences, men everywhere at that moment felt united in sympathy and aspiration with Catholics.

In many ways this Council was unique. Unlike Church Councils of the past, it might, one could hope, give birth to a truly new era in interreligious communication. For one thing, by papal definition, it intended to project a pastoral tone rather than a doctrinal one. As Bernard Cardinal Alfrink put it, "This Council would have a character completely different from its twenty predecessors which were generally called together to defend, to condemn specific errors. . . . The coming Council is not directed against a specific person or thing. Its objective is completely positive. . . ."[2]

This Council was also to be the first in history in which the pressures and interposition of national government would not be a threat to religious deliberation. It offered hope that a new conception of the relation of church and state, a new understanding of religious liberty, and a more creative assumption of religion's prophetic role could be expected.

The participants included Church officials in larger numbers from more parts of the globe than ever before. Certainly, therefore, the Council's actions might be expected to reflect the needs of men everywhere with greater sensitivity.

Finally, the Council would seek ways to be an instrument of human reconciliation. Without abandoning the dignity of their own uniqueness, Catholics were committed to a search for a closer fraternity with other Christians and to an investigation of a more creative relationship with Jews. The world cries out for a conception of human brotherhood that does not require, at the same moment, uniformity of temporal structures or identical patterns of economic and political organization. It is looking for a philosophy that binds men to one another fraternally without compelling any one mode of cultural expression and religious practice. Hope ran high that this Council would shed light on the path men might follow in fulfillment of that crucial human need.

POPE JOHN'S OPENING ADDRESS

The Pope's opening address intimated his own profound sympathy for many of those aspirations. Without hesitation he confessed that the Church needed to be "freed from . . . many obstacles of a profane nature such as trammeled her in the past. . . ." He proposed that the Council Fathers consider the ways by which men might fulfill their duties as "citizens of earth." But, he warned, the Church would have to "step forward," employ new "methods of research," and use "the literary forms of modern thought" if it would communicate effectively with modern man and improve its ability to shape his conscience. "One thing is the substance of the ancient doctrine of the *'depositum fidei,'* and another is the way in which it is presented."

No longer would the Church oppose error with the weapons of the past. "Nowadays the Spouse of Christ prefers to make use of the medicine of mercy rather than that of severity. She considers that she meets the needs of the present day by demonstrating the validity of her teachings rather than by condemnation." Pope John affirmed his confidence in a Church where freedom of expression and differences of opinion were to be respected. Let the Church "look to the future without fear," he counseled. "By bringing herself up to date where required and by the wise organization of mutual cooperation, the Church will make men, families, and people really turn their minds to heavenly things."

There was only one discordant note for non-Christians in the Pope's courageous message. His way of expressing the Christian's allegiance to Jesus as the Christ seemed to imply a derogation of others. "Christ is ever resplendent as the center of history and of life; men are either with Him and His Church and then they enjoy light, goodness, order and peace, or else they are without Him, or against Him, and deliberately against His Church, and then they rise to confusion and bitterness in human relations and to constant dangers of fratricidal wars."[3]

Jews can agree with Christians that when men pit themselves against God evil will disrupt human society; but we cannot agree that we fail to share in God's light and goodness simply because we do not accept this particular set of beliefs. Nor do we believe that our insistence on our own faith must necessarily put us in opposition either to the Church or to good human relations and peace.

The Pope himself had recognized the human fraternity that exists between Jews and Christians when, in his famous meeting with officials of the United Jewish Appeal in October, 1960, he asserted, "We are all sons of the same Heavenly Father. Among us all must ever be the brightness of love and its practice." Yet even on that notable occasion the Pope insisted, "True, there is a great difference between one who accepts the Old Testament and one who joins to it as a supreme law and guide, the New."[4] The emphasis on a sharp contrast between the Old and the New Testaments carries an unsettling implication that Judaism and Jews are incomplete and inferior, Christianity and Christians closer to God and His Truth and therefore superior.

The Pope's opening address, in summary, was a stirring call for Church modernization, for Catholic involvement in human need, for the development of structures of mutual cooperation with men of all faiths. It contained a rebuke against those who would stifle freedom within the Church itself; but it also was a testimony to the fact that religious differences between Jews and Christians were still quite pronounced and awkward.

A WARM WELCOME TO COUNCIL OBSERVERS

If there is to be an eventual reconciliation between Jews and Christians, it will undoubtedly be built upon much of the same attitudes of mind, understanding of human brotherhood, and regard for the method of dialogue that Pope John evoked in his effort to initiate a reconciliation between Catholics and non-Catholic Christians. On October 13, the Pope held an unprecedented meeting with the thirty-five delegate-observers and guests representing seventeen Orthodox and Protestant denominations. He assembled them before him in the Vatican's Consistory Hall in the same manner in which he was accustomed to meet with the Church's cardinals; then, as an added symbolic demonstration of his regard for their sensitivities, he sat on the same kind of chair as they, rather than on his throne. Interreligious harmony calls for such symbols of understanding and this gracious man instinctively knew how to extend his heart in love.

"I draw special comfort from your presence," he told the observers and guests seated around him. Recalling his years of service in the Vatican Diplomatic Corps and his many conversations with Christian officials, he evoked the memory of the unity he himself had experienced "on the plane of charity in the

common work, of helping those in need, which the circumstances
of time made necessary. . . . We did not haggle, we talked together;
we did not have discussions but we bore each other good will."[5]

The delegate-observers were given copies of the proposed
schemata, allotted the best seats in the Basilica, and provided
with a translation service—whereas the Council Fathers themselves had to struggle with the Latin. Most surprisingly, the
observers were also asked their opinions and invited to give
lectures (for which they were extremely appreciative), and on
the basis of their observations and suggestions many Church
Fathers prepared amendments to the various schemata before
them. Dr. James H. Nichols, a Presbyterian observer, said in
amazement, "We were taken into the deliberations of the Council
to such an extent that we were almost unofficial consultants."
He added, "I thought the Roman Catholic Church was a very
closed, complacent, and sectarian body that had nothing to learn
from anybody else. I know now that that is no longer accurate,
if it ever was."[6]

Dr. Elio Toaff, Chief Rabbi of Rome, sent greetings to the
Council Fathers on the occasion of the opening of the Council.
It was an unusual move, the first message ever sent formally
and officially by a Jewish leader to a Catholic Council. Defining
Jewish aspirations for the Council, the Rabbi said, "Jews hope
the Council will make decisions fostering peace, understanding,
cooperation, and tolerance among men. . . . Judaism and Christianity are united today in a common fight to uphold religious
freedom—one of civilization's fundamental expressions." He
further urged the Vatican Council to eliminate "all [derogatory]
expressions which are still present in the liturgy and teachings
of the catechism. . . . Jews also expect the Council Fathers to
condemn solemnly and unequivocally all forms of anti-
Semitism. . . ."[7]

This first session of the Council never took up the issue of
anti-Semitism. It had other work crucial to the Church's own
institutional needs. In fact, the original agenda was composed
of seventy-odd schemata, or draft documents, that had to be
scrutinized, debated, and voted by more than 2,500 men of
all races and of diverse cultural experience, each entitled, accord-

ing to the rules, to speak for ten minutes—a procedure that could have resulted in a Council of twenty years' duration. Many wondered how the Council would, or could, make progress at all.

EMERGENCE OF A LIBERAL MAJORITY

In dramatic fashion, however, a major issue to be resolved was confronted on the very first day. The question was whether the Council would truly represent the feelings of the hierarchy around the globe, provide them full opportunity to voice their opinions, and become the occasion for change in the Church; or would serve as a tightly controlled rubber stamp for those few administrative changes and doctrinal reaffirmations desired by the conservative group within the Curia—a group that had never favored the calling of the Council in the first place. Almost as the Council began, it adjourned. The order of business called for the election of one hundred sixty members to the ten Conciliar commissions, which were to prepare the draft schemata and consider the amendments that might be proposed in the course of Conciliar discussion. Sixteen members were to be appointed to each commission, eight by the Council and eight by the Pope.

A rebellion against immediate approval of the proposed slate of commission members was led by Achille Cardinal Lienart of Lille and Joseph Cardinal Frings of Cologne. The names that had been suggested by the officers of the Council "were unknown to many of the Bishops," and the Church Fathers wanted to have their own say as to who would run the machinery of the Council. The European cardinals thereupon suggested that regional and national caucuses consider the nominees and draw up their own slates.

Commentators on the Council later suggested that this experience of meeting each other through regional associations and deliberating across geographical lines was one of the most significant achievements of the first session. It awakened the Church to a new sense of vitality and community.

Protestant reporter Claud Nelson observed that 65 per cent of the names of the members of the Roman Curia are Italian, and 40 per cent of the Preparatory Commissions as previously drawn up were Italian; but after the bishops, by world-wide caucus, had selected the members of the Conciliar commissions, only 17.6 per cent of the 250 commission members were Italian.[8] The Council saw to it that its leadership truly represented the Church in its world-wide existence.

On Friday, October 19, the Pope elevated the Secretariat for the Promotion of Christian Unity to a status equivalent to that of a Conciliar commission, thereby indicating his intention that Cardinal Bea's staff have authority to become involved in, and to give guidance to, all Council actions that were of an ecumenical significance. American bishops, in order to prepare themselves better to participate in Council proceedings, organized twelve small study committees. One of these was assigned responsibility to maintain contact with Cardinal Bea's newly-elevated commission. The members of this American Committee on Christian Unity were Bishops Floyd L. Begin of Oakland, California; Leo A. Pursey of Fort Wayne-South Bend, Indiana; John P. Treacy of La Crosse, Wisconsin; Stephen A. Leven of San Antonio, Texas; Auxiliary Bishop Philip M. Hannan of Washington, D.C.; Charles M. Helmsing of Kansas City–St. Joseph, Missouri; and Charles A. Buswell of Pueblo, Colorado.

The increased importance granted Cardinal Bea's Secretariat, however, was not received as warmly in every quarter of the church. As Father Edward Duff has reported, from the conservative viewpoint, popularly identified with Alfredo Cardinal Ottaviani, Secretary of the Congregation of the Holy Office of the Roman Curia and Chairman of the Council's Theological Commission, Cardinal Bea's Secretariat was a danger to the Church. Until directed to do so by Council action and papal mandate, Cardinal Ottaviani had stoutly refused to consult with Cardinal Bea or to accept his assistance. Explains Father Duff, "The conservative viewpoint . . . sees the Church as the beleaguered bulwark of salvation surrounded by aggressive forces of atheism and unbelief. In such a crisis one must close ranks against the treacherous enemy and stand stalwart behind traditional policies. This conservative group, moreover, sincerely believed that the purity of doctrine was being threatened by those who

would compromise it by concessions to non-Catholics or to vis-
cerate it by false philosophic interpretations. . . . It is not for
nothing that Cardinal Ottaviani's coat of arms bears the motto
'Semper Idem,' i.e., 'Change Nothing.' "[9]

Conservatives, of course, were to be found not only among
the Italian or Spanish hierarchy. There were American bishops,
too, who gave expression to such a position. Bishop James A.
McNulty of Paterson, New Jersey, on the eve of his departure
for Rome noted that "The Bark of Peter has been picking up
barnacles from the backwash of activities by 'progressive Catholics.' Efforts to remove them will be made in the drydock of
the Council."[10] And Bishop Russell R. McVinney of Providence,
Rhode Island, reacting to changes that might have been made
in Catholicism by the Council, asked, "Why change? We have
had a flourishing institution for two thousand years and as the
saying goes, 'why break up a winning team?' "[11]

But Archbishop Albert Meyer of Chicago spoke for most of
the American hierarchy when he said, "We should not stultify
the growth of the Church by refusing to recognize the need
for change."[12]

Another key test of the power of the emergent progressive
group in the Council occurred with the presentation of the Schema
on Revelation prepared by Cardinal Ottaviani's Theological Commission. Taking the offensive, Bishop Émile Joseph Marie
deSmedt, of Bruges, Belgium, a member of Cardinal Bea's Secretariat, charged that the Theological Commission had twice rejected
the offer of the Secretariat to assist in drawing up that schema
despite Pope John's mandate. The schema, dealing with the
sources of authority in Catholic teaching, so stridently reaffirmed
narrow dogmatic principles and categories that Cardinal Bea
was moved to criticize it in forceful terms: "It represents the work
of a theological school, not what better theologians think today. . . .
What our times demand is a pastoral approach demonstrating
the love and kindness that flow from our religion."[13]

Bishop deSmedt defined what he considered ought to be the
approach of an ecumenically oriented statement: "For centuries
we Catholics thought it was sufficient to explain our doctrine
clearly. Both sides explained their own point of view using their

own terminology and from their own point of view only; but what Catholics said was not well received by non-Catholics and vice versa. . . . For several decades now, another method has been tried—the ecumenical dialogue. What does it involve? It means not being concerned with a preoccupation for truth alone but also with the way in which it is presented so that it can be made comprehensible to others. Both sides must try to explain their faith clearly and objectively and in a way that is psychologically acceptable and without engaging in controversy." He then offered these rules of behavior for Catholics: Catholics must understand the doctrines of Orthodox and Protestant Christians; know what they think, rightly or wrongly, about Catholic teaching or regard as unclear or lacking in Catholic teaching. Biblical terminology ought to be emphasized rather than scholastic terms; all useless controversy should be avoided.[14]

The Council voted by an almost two-thirds majority, 1,368 to 822, to have the schema reconsidered by a Mixed Commission that would include Cardinal Bea's Secretariat; but technically the vote had fallen short of the exact number required. It appeared as though a minority was going to overrule the clear sentiment of the majority. The Pope thereupon intervened. Interpreting the rules liberally, he remanded the schema back to a Mixed Commission to be presided over by Cardinal Bea and Cardinal Ottaviani. American prelates appointed to serve on that Mixed Commission included: Albert Cardinal Meyer, Archbishop of Chicago; Archbishop John F. Dearden of Detroit; Bishop John J. Wright of Pittsburgh; and Auxiliary Bishop James H. Griffith of New York. The Pope had confirmed the will of the majority of bishops and had strengthened the ecumenical thrust of the Council.

Finally a Schema on the Church was presented. This one too had been prepared by the Theological Commission. Joseph Cardinal Ritter of St. Louis joined Cardinal Lienart and Bishop deSmedt in another assault on the schema's triumphalist, dogmatic tones. The schema failed to acknowledge the existence of non-Catholic Christians as Christians, failed to give proper status to the clergy and laity, and lacked a clear statement about liberty of conscience.

At this point an impressive intellectual prelate, Giovanni Cardinal Montini of Milan, made his first address to the Council. He criticized the schema, emphasizing that the less Catholics insist on the rights of the Church, the more chance they have of being heard in those parts of the world that are suspicious of the Church as a paternalistic or colonial-minded institution. A week earlier Cardinal Montini, in a letter to his faithful in Milan, had also strongly criticized those Curial officials who had refused to cooperate with the various Preparatory Commissions. Their actions, he pointed out, delayed the Council. Montini urged that the Schema on the Church be returned to the Theological Commission, which ought to consult with the Secretariat for the Promotion of Christian Unity in revising the text.[15]

STRENGTHENING OF LIBERAL FORCES

Pope John then intervened in a way significant for the future course of the Council. He ordered that in the nine months between the end of the first session on December 7, 1962, and the opening of the second session on September 8, 1963, all schemata, and particularly those that had been discussed in the Council, be reworked by a Mixed Commission and sent to the bishops for their evaluation and correction. To coordinate the work of the Council, the Pope created a new Central Coordinating Commission headed by the Vatican Secretary of State, Amleto Cardinal Cicognani. To this new body he appointed many Council Fathers known to be responsive to change. He again reminded the Council that it was not necessary to reassert "the fundamental doctrine of the Church which has repeatedly been taught by the Fathers and by ancient and modern theologians, and which is presumed to be well known and familiar to all. Rather the Council in a pastoral spirit should devote its attention to the way in which the faith is articulated and presented to the world at large."[16]

Father Robert A. Graham, S.J., reported that the appointment of this new interim commission was "a definite commitment by Pope John on the side of those Fathers who have been pleading for the pastoral and ecumenical approach. . . . The new directive is a rejection of the work of the Preparatory Commission."[17]

Most liberal Catholics and most Protestants in the United States were heartened by the first session of the Council. It had achieved very little by way of actual measures adopted, yet it had traversed centuries of history; in a single two-and-a-half-month period it had set the Church on a new course. "The Roman Church is not a monolith, frozen against change. It is split from top to bottom on many major issues and the progressive wing is not a weak minority. . . . We can but give thanks," said the editors of the Protestant journal *Christianity and Crisis*.[18]

Jews followed these events with keen interest. Many presumed that the emergence of a liberal majority would assure an unequivocal statement on Jewish-Christian relations. They were cheered by the numerous liberal statements delivered on the Council floor and by decisive papal interventions on behalf of the liberal cause.

Despite the fact that there had been no assurances that a statement on the Jews would be considered at the first session, some Jews were impatient. The failure of the Council to act on a Jewish statement provoked rumors, among many not well acquainted with the inner workings of the Church, that perhaps the Jewish statement would be scuttled. Rabbi Maurice Eisendrath, President of the important Union of American Hebrew Congregations, expressed this fear. "I cannot fail to be somewhat dismayed," he said, "by reports that the Ecumenical Council does not now seem inclined to continue in those efforts at Catholic-Jewish rapprochement. . . . [It] is more than a little disheartening."[19]

Regrettably, a mood of doubt and cynicism was then fostered within the Jewish community, aggravated among American Jews when it was revealed that just a few days before the Council ended, every Church Father had found in his box a privately printed 617-page volume entitled *Il Complotto Contra la Chiesa— The Plot Against the Church*. The book was filled with the most primitive and vitriolic kind of anti-Semitism. It suggested that the liberal Catholics in the Council were a "Jewish fifth column." According to the Italian newsweekly *Vita*, the publication demonstrated "the existence of an anti-Semitic headquarters trying to exploit every occasion to rekindle blind racial hatred under the banner of a new order and to resume old and bloody schemes." [20]

Chief Rabbi Elio Toaff urged that the book be ignored "because our enemies' precise wish is that they should get publicity." [21] For most Jews, however, the incident provided evidence that Catholic anti-Semites were not inactive. Despite the fact that most bishops promptly threw such literature in the trash basket, the position of the Catholic Church on the Jewish question would not be clear until the Council, by specific action, made it clear.

5. Drama Between Sessions

THE EVENTS THAT OCCURRED between December 8, 1962, when the first session of Vatican Council II ended, and September 29, 1963, when the second session commenced, provide a case study of the fragile relations between Jews and Catholics. The election of a new Pope, the emergence of controversy over a stage play, the revelation of sources of intense opposition to a Jewish statement, innuendoes read into every press release—all of these "happenings" kept the pot boiling. Jews were sensitive and in constant need of reassurance. Catholics were uncertain and often defensive. Official contacts were minimal, and flagrant rumors circulated.

Several American Jewish delegations visited the new Pope during these months and sought his assurance that a statement on the Jews would be considered by the Council. Among the representations was one made by Dr. Joseph Lichten, Director of the Department of Intercultural Affairs of the Anti-Defamation League, who spent three weeks in Rome. But to all importuning the Pope remained noncommittal.

CONVERSATIONS WITH CARDINAL BEA

All seemed right with the world, nevertheless, early in January, 1963, when Cardinal Bea spoke to the 8th Annual "Agape of Brotherhood" at the Pro Deo University in Rome. He assured an audience that included five hundred persons representing twenty-one faiths and sixty-nine nations that a proposal to proclaim the Catholic Church's belief in freedom of conscience and worship would without doubt be presented to the next session of the Council.

In 1933 Pope Pius XII had spoken of a "positive law of religious toleration" which was to be given world-wide validity and force. In his address, however, he had allowed for the right of each state to regulate religious and moral affairs according to its own law. Critics immediately pointed out that "toleration" was a condescending, manipulative concept, particularly if no criteria were established by which to measure the morality of restrictions imposed by sectarian-dominated states. In his address, Cardinal Bea took pains to emphasize that the presentation proposed by his Secretariat was a further development of Catholic teaching on religious liberty. "I do not say 'tolerance,' which is a rather negative thing," he declared, "but religious liberty, which consists in positively recognizing a man's right to follow the dictates of his own conscience in matters of religion. It consists also in a recognition of the duties of civil society to respect and protect in practice a citizen's inalienable right to religious liberty. . . . One should always understand another man's point of view. This means putting oneself in his place and seeing things from the position from which he sees them. One should also realize that reality has 1,000 different aspects, 1,000 different facets; whereas the individual, even when very gifted and intelligent, sees only one or a few. Love of truth cautions us to bear in mind the limitations of our knowledge and also to recognize the aspect of truth which others see. . . ."[1]

In March of 1963, during a visit to the United States, Cardinal Bea addressed an unpublicized but historic meeting arranged by the American Jewish Committee. It included religious and communal leaders reflecting Orthodox, Conservative, and Reform viewpoints, although each participant attended in his own individual capacity. The American rabbis who were present at that meeting, held under the chairmanship of Rabbi Abraham Heschel, were Rabbi Louis Finkelstein, Chancellor of the Jewish Theological Seminary of America; Rabbi Theodore Friedman, President, Rabbinical Assembly of America; Rabbi Joseph Lookstein, President, Bar-Ilan University; Rabbi Julius Mark, President, Synagogue Council of America; Rabbi Albert Minda, President, Central Conference of American Rabbis.

The Cardinal assured his Jewish audience that the Council would consider the Jewish question. Then, defining what he thought ought to be included in such a statement, he asserted that the events of the Passion could not be charged against Jewry as a whole, that it was possible and indeed necessary to give the right interpretation to dogma and to clarify the true sense intended by the writers of the New Testament. Finally, he said, there was need for interreligious communication and cooperation. Cardinal Bea indicated that his views had been strongly endorsed by Pope John.

The significance of this meeting is that, in a notable display of apparent harmony, America's Jewish religious leadership, including Orthodox Jews, accepted the hospitality of a secular Jewish community relations organization, the American Jewish Committee. Thus they enabled Cardinal Bea to assess a broad range of Jewish response to his own considerations for the Jewish statement. Without doubt this meeting was influential in shaping Bea's future work in the Council.

A QUESTION OF CONTEXT

If Cardinal Bea had satisfactorily reassured Jewish religious leaders that the Council would undertake a consideration of anti-Semitism, it still remained problematical under what circumstances that consideration would take place. It was reported that a Schema on Ecumenism, prepared by the Secretariat, would probably be on the agenda of the second session of the Council. Suggestions were made that this might be the opportune time and place for the Council to deal with the Jewish issue. But many Jews were uneasy with such proposals. They did not wish to be included in a schema with theological overtones or one that defined the aspirations of the Catholic Church for the uniting of all Christians in one body. They preferred that a statement on anti-Semitism be included within whatever schema would deal with the Church's involvement in world problems.

Others contended that Jews and Christians had something more to say to each other than merely to attack anti-Semitism. A most important aspect of Jewish self-definition is the conviction that Jews have been chosen by God to serve as a unique witness people, and by the example of their lives to struggle with making His kingdom a reality in human society. One dimension of the Jewish-Christian debate is the claim each group sometimes makes for itself to an exclusive role as God's "Israel." Thus, when the Church refuses to recognize God's ongoing relationship with Jews and the salvific significance of Jewish faithfulness to His covenant, there is danger to that degree that attitudes projected toward Judaism will engender a form of group hatred. Similarly, Jews must confront the reality of the Christian's claim to be a participant in God's covenant with Abraham. They must answer for themselves the meaning of God's dealings with Christians and the nature of the Church's relationship to the Jewish people. To the degree that Jews fail to acknowledge that there can be a saving grace within the Church, and that the Church has genuinely made an effort to impart biblical values among the Gentiles, to that degree there is a danger of Jews contributing to an unspoken sentiment among their young that Christianity is an inferior religion.

A consideration of such larger aspects of Jewish-Christian relatedness made it seem opportune that a statement on the Jews be included within a Schema on Ecumenism. Yet many Jews still doubted that genuine interreligious dialogue could be fostered by the spirit of ecumenism. Further, many Orthodox Jews feared that such dialogue might lead to a weakening of the faith. In response, however, it was pointed out that the Christian has as much to gain or lose in the process of dialogue as the Jew; each needs to be willing to expose practices and beliefs to the light of God's truth. The benefit of dialogue for *both* groups could be an enriched and strengthened loyalty to God.

It later became apparent that there was also indecision among Christians over the proposal to set this question in the context of a Schema on Ecumenism. Many Protestants wished to delimit the ecumenical relationship exclusively to Christians. Officials of the World Council of Churches and some Protestant delegate-observers had expressed such views to Cardinal Bea's Secretariat.[2] Some Catholic Fathers also were against the Church's intimating in any way that the Jews are among the people of God. In their judgment, the Jews had lost their status because of their hardened resistance to Jesus as the Christ. These Catholics preferred, therefore, that a consideration of the Jews be part of a catch-all schema on world problems.

In a most confusing and paradoxical pattern of alliance, then, Orthodox Jews and conservative Catholics were joined together in opposition to a consideration of the Jewish problem in the context of a Schema on Ecumenism. On the other side, the rabbinical officials of the allegedly "secular" Jewish organizations and progressive Catholics, both of whose sincerity of faith was questioned by the "fundamentalists" within their own ranks, were agreed that Cardinal Bea should plunge ahead with the responsibility.

Controversy over *The Deputy*

Just at that moment, the play *Der Stellvertreter—The Deputy—* opened. Upon its premiere in Berlin on February 20, 1963, this drama set off an international incident. Written by a young German Protestant, Rolf Hochhuth, the play amounted to a stinging condemnation of the late Pope Pius XII for his failure to take more vigorous public action against the mass murder of Jews under Hitler. Accompanied by riots, picketing, efforts at censorship, and other disturbances, the play seemed to compel its viewers to choose one side against another, to be for or against the Pope, to condemn or to defend the Catholic Church. It was this polemic aspect of the play that led to severe criticism in both the Jewish and the Catholic press.

Fortunately, reactions to the play did not necessarily follow religious lines. Many Jews, however, wished that Catholics, whatever their objections to the play itself, could have admitted that the Church as an institution had fallen short; and many Catholics wished that more critics and playgoers, whatever their feelings about the actions of the Church, could have admitted that the play itself was unfair and one-sided. Jews wanted some bending from the Church's rigid defensiveness and Catholics wanted some recognition that there were members of their faith who had been affirmatively humane by virtue of their Christianity. Catholics also wanted some understanding of the limitations under which Pope Pius XII labored. They wished that Jews could acknowledge the genuineness of many of his actions in their behalf, particularly within the restrictions of the choices that he saw possible for himself and for the Church. Just as the reactions of some Catholic commentators fulfilled Jewish expectations, however, so some Jewish commentators demonstrated a wide breadth of understanding wth regard to humanitarian and sacrificial action of many Catholics during the war. Both communities, nevertheless, remained tense and uncomfortable with each other during the run of the play.

In the Jewish press there appeared expressions of anxiety as to how the reaction to *The Deputy* might influence the scene in Rome. Knowledgeable Jewish leaders were aware that Cardinal Montini of Milan, who had just been elevated to the papacy on Pope John's death, had been a close associate of Pius XII and had reacted vigorously to the play. In an article prepared for the *Catholic Herald* of London defending Pope Pius, who tried "so far as he could fully and courageously to carry out the mission entrusted to him," Montini accused the author of "an inadequate grasp of psychological, political and historical realities."[3] Thus, some Jews feared that whatever the accuracy of the play as history, the ill-feeling it caused might adversely affect the statement on the Jews.

THE DEATH OF POPE JOHN AND THE ELECTION OF POPE PAUL

On June 3, 1963, Pope John XXIII died at the age of eighty-one. On his deathbed he had cried out, "I give my life for the Council, for the Church and peace." Jews, with the rest of the world, were genuinely moved at his passing, and an outpouring of grief appeared everywhere in the Jewish community. Rabbis across the land in unprecedented display of affection partici- pated in expressions of respect and sympathy. Certainly no Pope had communicated as clear and consistent an attitude of friend- ship toward the Jewish people and Judaism in all of history as had Pope John XXIII.

On June 21, 1963, Cardinal Montini accepted the papal desig- nation and chose the name Paul VI. He was known as an intel- lectual and a political liberal, and had also been a supporter of Pope John. Some Jews recalled Montini's assistance in their escape from Nazi persecution. But some too were uncertain of his position on the Jewish question: It was revealed that as Arch- bishop of Milan he had written a preface praising highly a book by the Catholic exegete Angelo Alberti which at many points invoked the traditional Catholic teaching that the Jews "are a people condemned to ruin."[4] Others recalled, however, that when Montini was Archbishop of Milan, upon the request of the presi- dent of the Milan Jewish Community he had ordered the with- drawal of the imprimatur and demanded the cessation of the distribution of a confirmation book containing blatant anti- Semitic references.

Pope Paul soon made it decisively clear that he intended the Council to continue. In his eulogy for Pope John he declared, "Death cannot stifle the spirit which he has infused into our era. Can we turn away from the path so masterfully traveled? It seems that we cannot."[5]

ARAB PRESSURES AND NEW PROMISES

The Jewish community was shocked when the very respected Catholic theologian Rev. Gustave Weigel, S.J., a member of Cardinal Bea's Secretariat, pessimistically informed a convention of the National Community Relations Advisory Council that the declaration on Catholic-Jewish relations which had been pre- pared for the first session of the Council was not introduced because of Arab pressure. Father Weigel furthermore predicted that the Council would continue to avoid the issue. "Arab States would understand it [the statement on the Jews] as backing up Israel and therefore chiding and rebuffing the Arab States." In spite of "obvious sympathy among the majority of Bishops at the Council," he believed they would "rather avoid the issue than face it."[6]

The Secretariat for the Promotion of Christian Unity quickly responded that Father Weigel's statement "does not correspond to the actual state of the question involved," and "no authorization whatsoever"[7] had been given for its issuance. Father Weigel indicated immediately that he was happy to stand corrected.

An official of the Secretariat then circulated a confidential letter among a select number of world Jewish leaders, informing them that a statement entitled "Pro Judaeis," evidently dealing with the Jewish question, had been withheld from the Central Preparatory Commission prior to the first session of the Council only because of the Wardi incident. When it had been announced in the press that "Dr. Wardi, former employee of the Israel Government, had been appointed to the Vatican Council . . . it was assumed by many that the Vatican was using the religious event of the Council for indirect political purposes; as a result, some Council authorities had thought that the publicized announcement of the draft on Catholic-Jewish relations would cause, *at that time*, added bewilderment; the draft, one could imply, also had political implications. The Schema was *temporarily tabled*."[8]

The incident responsible for the delay, according to this letter, appears to have been solely the designation of Wardi as an unofficial observer. Later events were to justify the suspicion, however, that there had been sustained opposition to any Jewish statement by Arab political leaders and Middle East prelates. The Wardi incident had merely brought to public awareness an existing pressure that unfortunately continued throughout the Council's four sessions. And Father Weigel's analysis, therefore, was shown to be more accurate than the Secretariat could then afford to admit.

This confidential letter from the Secretariat went on to give the first official assurance that a statement on the Jews had been drafted and would be considered by the Secretariat, probably within the Schema on Ecumenism.

The Secretariat never intended to avoid the issue of the relations of Catholics to the Jewish people of old and of today. Nor did the Secretariat ever intend to have the Council pass over the problem of anti-Semitism, although it believed that a positive statement is far better and more beneficial than a negative one of condemnation. From the beginning we have been determined to have a strictly theological and religious statement with pastoral implications. We have been quite aware of the pitfalls of even the least of political overtones. At the same time, we wish that the statement be placed in its proper setting: the relation of Catholics to non-Catholic Christians, to the Jews, and to non-Christian non-Jews.[9]

On this heartening note, Jewish leaders looked forward to the opening of the second session.

6. Conflict and Maneuver in Session Two

PREPARATION FOR THE SECOND SESSION did not proceed as smoothly as one would have expected following "the revolution" of the first. During the late summer, bishops and *periti* (expert consultants) "had to fight word by word" to force the president and secretary of some of the commissions "to align their documents in accord with the mind of the vast majority of the Council Fathers," as expressed at the first session.[1]

When he was one of the Church Fathers, Cardinal Montini had criticized the slow pace of the deliberations and expressed displeasure at the obstinacy of the Curia. Now, as Pope, he took procedural steps intended to bring the Council to a climactic resolution. On September 15 he created a strong, small Steering Committee of four cardinals to direct the work of the second session. These were Cardinals Leo Suenens, Julius Doepfner, Giacomo Lercaro, and Gregorio Agaganian, all of whom were known for their independence of mind and their openness to the new currents in the Church.

The Council opened on Sunday, September 29, 1963. Pope Paul addressed the delegates at length, indicating his own full support of the Conciliar development. He called on the Fathers "to strip the Church of what is unworthy or defective." Then, in a moving act of ecumenicity, he turned toward the observer-delegates from other Christian Churches. Expressing his sadness at the division in Christendom, he told them "If we [Catholics] are to blame in any way for that separation, we humbly beg God's forgiveness and we ask pardon too of our brethren who feel themselves to have been injured by us."

Paul concluded with an expression of his own conception of the Church's role in the world. Let mankind realize, he said, that the Church looks on the world "with profound understanding and sincere admiration, with the frank desire not to conquer but to serve, not to despise but to appreciate, not to condemn but to comfort and save."[2]

THE CHURCH AS THE PEOPLE OF GOD

The first item on the agenda was the schema *De Ecclesia*, that is, "On the Nature of the Church." A patchwork document, it displayed the sometimes conflicting contributions of the various commissions that had participated in its formulation. The first major conflict to erupt centered upon the continued use of restrictive formalistic terms in defining the Church. The ecumenically oriented bishops called for a vocabulary clearly indicating that all who had received the Christian baptism were members of the Mystical Body of Christ, even if not members of the Catholic Church. Instead of defining the Church in juridical terms, the liberals recommended the use of the concept "the People of God"; it was biblically rooted and broad enough so that it could include within the Church all who participated in the Eucharist.

Cardinal Bea criticized the schema because it constantly spoke of the Church in its perfection. He would have had the Fathers distinguish between the Church on earth, which is in a state of pilgrimage and consists of sinners and is capable of errors, and the Church in heaven, which is assured of perfect holiness.[3]

Archbishop Seper of Zagreb, Yugoslavia, added the interesting note that the Jews also ought to be included within a schema defining the nature of the Church as the People of God. The Jews, he pointed out, stood in special relationship to the Church by virtue of their witness to Old Testament revelations and the covenant with God. The Jews, after all, were not a people who had been "rejected," as some churchmen taught. Rather, the Jews maintained a common heritage with the Church.[4]

The Bishop of Haarlem, in the name of the Dutch episcopate,

also recommended that the close bond between the Church and the people of Israel be affirmed within that schema. Despite their unbelief in Christ and despite the fact that many of them had abandoned the faith of their fathers, the Jews remain, said the Dutch bishop, "the people of faith." Until the end of time, God remains their Faithful Shepherd.[5]

These were heartwarming repudiations of any suggestion that the Jews had lost their status with God by virtue of their rejection of Jesus. The statements affirmatively supported the Jews' claim to be Israel. The belief of Jews that they are still a people of God, to whom He has remained faithful, was recognized.

"WHO IS IN CHARGE HERE?"

There were many issues to be taken up under this schema. One that exercised the Church Fathers was their own place in the governing of the Church. Under what circumstances could the bishops, as successors to the Twelve Apostles, exercise a collegial power, and how was this power to be reconciled with the supreme authority of the Pope?

Conflict also erupted over many doctrinal matters that would have important consequences for Catholic relations with other Christians. These included the role of the laity in the Church and the manner in which a statement on the Virgin Mary should be treated.

As the debate on this one Schema on the Church droned on over a period of weeks, it soon became apparent that something was awry. The Council would never complete its task if every issue was to be so fully and deliberately debated. Father Edward Duff, reporting the sentiment of many Church Fathers, asked plaintively, "Who is in charge here?"[6] One American thought the bishops might just as well "all pack up and go home." More than a thousand suggested emendations had been made to the draft document and another 350 had been submitted earlier in writing. These emendations had yet to be reconsidered by Cardinal Ottaviani's Theological Commission before a new document could be presented to the Council for final vote. It was known that Cardinal Ottaviani opposed the direction of the majority on many of the key issues. Was the infrequency of meetings of the Theological Commission a deliberate obstructionist tactic?

Curial officials in crucial Conciliar commission posts had the power to delay action endlessly. In addition to their influence in the various commissions, the Curia also controlled the presses where the new formulations and schemata were printed. In charge of the distribution process, they were capable of withholding documents from commission members for as long as twelve days at a time or longer.

Without consulting other Council leaders, the four moderators finally exercised their authority. The bishops, they decided, would vote their sentiments on several key issues even in the midst of the general debate; then the appropriate commission would be able to rewrite the schema in accordance with the clear majority's sentiment. The Council's leadership consisted of twelve presidents, a ten-man Coordinating Commission, and the four moderators. The conservatives among these authorities were outraged by the tactic of the moderators. But the Pope threw his influence behind the moderators, and by the smallest possible margin at a closed meeting of the Council leadership it was agreed to follow the new procedure.

On October 29 and 30, votes were taken on five crucial questions. On the issue of the Virgin Mary, the division was close. By a tally of 1,114 to 1,074, the Church Fathers voted to include a statement on the Virgin Mary within the Schema on the Church rather than to give it special emphasis by calling for a separate schema. The conservatives lost on this issue despite a vigorous lobbying effort that violated Curial laws concerning the distribution of unofficial material. On the remaining questions, all concerned with collegiality, the bishops overwhelmingly affirmed their legitimate authority to share in the governing of the Church. On the question defining the power of the College of Bishops to participate in governing the Church with the Pope "by divine right," the vote was yes, 1,717; no, 408.

The Pope thereupon ordered the Theological Commission to step up its schedule of meetings, convening daily, rather than once a week, as had been its custom. Debate on the central issue of collegiality could now be conducted with the majority sentiment clearly registered and could be brought to a swift conclusion. There was reason to expect that the various schemata, now revised according to the Council Fathers' wishes, would be brought to a final vote.

But the Curial recalcitrants insisted that the votes by the Council Fathers were merely advisory suggestions and not mandatory. So the debate continued sharply, with much bitterness. In response to criticism of the Curia, Ottaviani cried, to the applause of his followers, "In attacking the Holy Office, one attacks the Pope himself." Cardinal Frings called the methods of the Holy Office "a scandal," and added, "The Theological Commission has no other function but to execute the wishes of and obey the directives of the Council. . . ."[7]

While this controversy continued, a mystery surrounded the statements on the Jews and on religious liberty. Allegedly, discussion on the Schema on Ecumenism and these two matters was to be next on the agenda. But the Council would be unable to consider them unless they were available in printed form. They had been submitted to the Theological Commission in June, more than three months before the Council reconvened, yet for many months thereafter, their whereabouts were unknown. Although the first three chapters of the Schema on Ecumenism were available, the last two—Chapter IV on the Jews, and Chapter V, on religious liberty—had not yet been printed. It appeared that they were being purposely delayed.

While deliberation on the Schema on the Church was moving at a snail's pace inside the Basilica, political activity on the Schema on Ecumenism and its widely feared statements with regard to the Jews and religious liberty was mounting in pressure outside. For example, a pamphlet entitled "The Council and the Assault of the Central European Block" contained an attack on those bishops who allegedly had come under the influence of Jews and were seeking to destroy the Church by "anti-Catholic" development of collegiality. A second pamphlet, "The Jews and the Council in the Light of Holy Scripture and Tradition," drew upon New Testament sources and the teachings of Church Fathers to demonstrate that Catholic teaching clearly recognized the Jews as an accursed deicide people and a menace to the Church. The

Jews could wipe out the curse under which they lived, the pamphlet advised, only by converting to Christianity. Finally, the pamphlet insisted that the various efforts being made to update the Church were all conspiratorial attempts to destroy it, led by Jews and Freemasons on behalf of Communism.

THE CHAPTER ON THE JEWS IS LEAKED TO THE PRESS

Then a startling breach occurred in Council secrecy. On October 16 the very competent and energetic Milton Bracker revealed in the *New York Times* the outline of the contents of the official document, *"De Catholicorum Habitudine ad Christianos et Maxime ad Judaeos"*—"On the Catholic Attitude Toward Non-Christians and Especially Toward Jews." Bracker reported that this chapter now "was ready for distribution," but at that late date it seemed to him "unlikely that the Schema on Ecumenism or any part of it will be debated to a conclusion at the session."

It is not known publicly how the leak occurred. There were many Council Fathers, *periti,* and delegate-observers involved in a charade of complex maneuvers and intrigue on almost all issues. In the battle of pressure and counter-pressure, all sides employed leaks to the press, long-distance telephone calls, and the intervention of national diplomats. But why had *this* leak occurred? Bracker himself suggested that news about the statement on the Jews was made available for public discussion as a response by the Vatican to the play *The Deputy*. The passage of a Conciliar statement on the Jews, it was reasoned, would climax a long history of official Christian solicitude for the Jew. A more plausible explanation was that the leak was intended by supporters of the statement to provoke such a spontaneous and heartening response that the Council would have no alternative but to consider the document at the current session. The enthusiastic response of Jews throughout the world, merely to the news that a draft statement would be presented to the Council, was indicative of great hope and trust, despite the lack of information about its specific content. The leak to the press seemed to be part of a power play, a strategic effort to hasten and compel Conciliar action on the Schema on Ecumenism.

CARDINAL BEA'S DESCRIPTION AND JEWISH REACTION

Even while the debate over the Schema on the Church continued, the text of the statement on the Jews was at last distributed on November 8 to the Council Fathers for study. In a public communiqué, Cardinal Bea emphasized that the document was entirely and only "religious in its content and spiritual in its purpose. . . . It cannot be called pro-Zionist since these are political questions entirely outside of its scope."

Cardinal Bea recalled the "deep bond that ties the Church to the chosen people of the Old Testament" and added a reference to the coming of Jesus Christ as the culmination of the covenant made by God with Abraham and his descendants. He then dealt with the draft statement's handling of the Crucifixion account:

The responsibility for Christ's death falls upon sinful mankind. . . . The part that the Jewish leaders of Christ's day played in bringing about the Crucifixion does not exclude the guilt of all mankind; but the personal guilt of these leaders cannot be charged to the whole Jewish people either of His time or today. It is, therefore, unjust to call this people deicide or to consider it cursed by God. The sacred events of the Bible, and in particular its account of the Crucifixion, cannot give rise to disdain or hatred or persecution of the Jews. Preachers and catechists . . . are admonished never to present a contrary position. Furthermore they are urged to promote mutual understanding and esteem.[8]

Some Jews regretted that nowhere did this communiqué show the same willingness to admit Church error as had been evident in the debate over Christian disunity. Furthermore, Cardinal Bea had expressed an appreciation for the contributions of the Jewish people of *old,* but he left uncertain his view on the *contemporary* status of the Jews in relation to the Church's claim of possessing the fulfilled promises.

Despite these reservations, Jewish leaders—even the Orthodox —were so pleased by the progressive significance of Bea's communiqué that they joined in praise of it as though with one voice —even though the text of the statement had not yet been made public. Rabbi Israel Miller, Vice-President of the (Orthodox)

Rabbinical Council of America, said, "We are gratified at the proposal submitted to the Ecumenical Council. If adopted it will mark a great step forward in the betterment of inter-group relations."[9] Dr. Nahum Goldmann, President of the World Jewish Congress, exclaimed, "The Jewish people are profoundly moved and happy. . . ."[10] And Zachariah Shuster, European Director of the American Jewish Committee, predicted, "The Jews of this generation will consider themselves fortunate to have witnessed this historic step on the part of the Church."[11] One of the most enthusiastic of the responses was that of Rabbi Maurice Eisendrath, President of the (Reform) Union of American Hebrew Congregations. In an address to the U.A.H.C.'s Forty-Seventh General Assembly, November 16, Eisendrath took the occasion to consider possible steps for the Reform movement to take that would go even further in promoting interfaith understanding.

We Jews have long clamored for this indispensable change in official Catholic dissemination of facts and interpretation, but what about our Jewish attitudes toward Christendom, toward Jesus especially? Are we to remain adamant—Orthodox—in our refusal to examine our statements, our own facts, our own interpretations on the significance of the life of Jesus, the Jew? Have we examined our own books, official and otherwise, to re-appraise our oft-times jaundiced view of Him in whose name Christianity was established? . . . How long shall we continue pompously to aver that the chief contribution of Jesus was simply a rehash of all that had been said before by his Jewish ancestors? How long before we can admit that His influence was a beneficial one—not only to the pagans but to the Jews of His time as well, and that only those who later took His name in vain, profaned His teaching.[12]

PRESENTATION OF THE SCHEMA ON ECUMENISM

The Council was finally ready on November 18 to consider the Schema on Ecumenism. But only two weeks remained until the Council was scheduled to close. Would it be possible to debate, amend, reconsider, and vote on these crucial documents in such a short period?

In order to make sure that the more controversial chapters—IV and V—were at least entered in the record, the Council broke precedent. Instead of first debating Chapters I through III, Cardinal Bea was invited to make an immediate presentation on Chapter IV and Bishop deSmedt to make a presentation on Chapter V. The announcement of this new procedure was greeted by the most enthusiastic and spontaneous applause yet heard in the Council, a fitting tribute to Cardinal Bea and his Secretariat.

On November 18 Cardinal Cicognani, who was President of the Commission on Oriental Churches, made the official presentation of the Schema on Ecumenism and Archbishop Martin of Rouen added a detailed exposition of Chapters I to III. The next day Cardinal Bea formally introduced Chapter IV, the statement on the Jews, revealing that his Secretariat had undertaken the question "not on its own initiative but by reason of the express command of the Supreme Pontiff, John XXIII, of happy memory."

Bea repeated his claim that "there is no national or political question here. Especially there is no question of acknowledging the State of Israel on the part of the Holy See." He acknowledged that within Christian Scripture it is revealed that Jesus spoke "most severely about the Jews and their punishment." Nevertheless, insisted Bea, Christ's harsh words were intended only to inspire the people to be converted; most importantly, even as he was dying on the cross, he prayed, "Father, forgive them; for they know not what they do" (Luke 23:24). The Cardinal also invoked St. Paul's contention that only a "partial blindness" has befallen Israel.

Cardinal Bea then explained why a statement on the Jews should be issued now. He said it was because "some decades ago anti-Semitism . . . as it is called, was prevalent in various regions and particularly violent, in criminal form, especially in Germany under the rule of National Socialism which, through hatred for the Jews, committed frightful crimes extirpating several millions of Jewish people—we need not at this moment seek the exact number." Bea continued, "It would have been almost impossible if some of the claims of that propaganda did not have an unfortunate effect even on faithful Catholics, the more since the arguments advanced by that propaganda often enough bore the appearance of truth especially when they were drawn from the New Testament and from the history of the Church."

Bea then went on to deny that anti-Semitism drew *any* inspiration from Christian doctrine—"something which is in no way true." Rather, he said, "It is a question of rooting out from the minds of Catholics any ideas which perhaps remain fixed there through the influence of the [Nazi] propaganda."

It seemed to some Jews that Cardinal Bea was taking the Church off the hook. By contending that a valid interpretation of Christian teaching and doctrine could not be used to support anti-Semitism, he was avoiding a long, bitter history of Christian contempt for Jews. He blamed it all on the Nazis. "We do not mean," he said, "to state or hint that anti-Semitism usually principally arises from a religious source, namely, from what the Gospels recount concerning the Passion and Death of the Lord. We know very well that anti-Semitism also has causes of a political, national, psychological, social and economic nature." With regard to Jewish culpability for the Crucifixion, Bea concluded, "the Jews of our times can hardly be accused of the crime committed against Christ, so far removed are they from those deeds. Nor should the majority of the chosen people at that time be accused."[13]

Some important Jewish leaders who knew only what Bea had now twice said *about* the statement—in a communiqué to the press on November 8 and now in an introduction to the Council—but had no idea of what was *in* the actual chapter itself, were surprised and depressed. Twice Bea had failed to acknowledge any Christian roots for, or complicity in, the anti-Semitism appearing in Western civilization. At no time did he express any remorse at Jewish sufferings in the past or make any admission of Christian error. There seemed to be no realization that those distorted Christian teachings on the Crucifixion that were now to be corrected had been such lethal weapons in the hands of Christian princes and clerics. It seemed to many that Bea was bending over backward to please the Arabs and the conservatives. His remarks about Zionism were not really welcomed by the Jews. In the end it seemed as though the Church was about "to forgive" the Jews, when in fact most Jews felt it ought to be the Church that sought forgiveness.

The response of Rabbi Norman Lamm in the official organ of

the Union of Orthodox Jewish Congregations of America, though strident, was characteristic: "As Jews we object to being absolved of the guilt of killing their God. To be absolved implies that one is guilty but that nevertheless he is being forgiven. But we Jews never were guilty and we do not therefore beg forgiveness. . . . To our mind the question is not who will absolve the Jews. The question is who will absolve the Church for its guilt in inspiring and sponsoring crusades and inquisitions, blood libels and pogroms . . . the Church has expressed to the Jewish people neither apology nor confession nor regrets."[14] .

Most Jewish leaders, whatever their private reservations concerning Cardinal Bea's introductory remarks, were satisfied to withhold comment until the Church made public the official statement itself. There was reason to believe that under the pressure of contending factions Bea felt compelled to use language that would assuage opponents and win the largest possible support for the statement itself. On the wise presumption that "there is a time for everything," Jewish community leaders, schooled in patience, were happy to have the Church take a first step. There would be time enough in history to help churchmen understand what other grievances and hurts Jews might feel. Furthermore, many Jewish leaders trusted Bea and recognized that victory for his position was a victory for change and freedom within the Church. Nothing ought be done that would embarrass him or give comfort to his enemies.

CONTENTS OF JEWISH CHAPTER

With the release of the actual text of the statement, shortly after Bea's introduction, the anxiety of many Jewish leaders was relieved. It was a strong statement, and despite possible misgivings about certain words, its forward thrust received warm support (see Appendix A).

The Chapter itself consisted of only five paragraphs. Its repudiation of distorted teachings with regard to the Crucifixion was forceful. Its most radical assertion, however, was that the same principles of ecumenicity already defined in Chapters I through III dealing with other Christians "should be applied, taking differences in condition duly into account, in the matter of speaking with and cooperation with people who are not Christians, but who worship God, or at least in a spirit of good will conscientiously endeavor to observe the moral law innate in the nature of man. This applies especially in the case of the Jews, as a people who are connected with the Church of Christ in *special relationship*."[15] This last phrase was later to be attacked both by Orthodox Jews, who resented any definition of Jews that placed them in any "special relationship" to Christianity, and by conservative Catholics, for whom Jews remain, by virtue of their rejection of Jesus, a people no different from any other non-Christians.

DEBATE OF CHAPTERS ON JEWS AND RELIGIOUS LIBERTY

Following Cardinal Bea's presentation on Chapter IV, Bishop deSmedt introduced the historic and revolutionary statement on religious liberty. His words demonstrated that he knew exactly how crucial this statement would be for all non-Catholic religions throughout the world. "Many non-Catholics harbor an aversion against the Church or at least suspect her of a kind of machiavellism," deSmedt admitted, "because we seem to demand the free exercise of religions when Catholics are in a minority in any nation and at the same time refuse and deny the same religious liberty when Catholics are the majority." Furthermore, the Bishop argued, "Today in all nations of the world, men who adhere to different religions or who lack all religious belief must live together in one and the same human society; in the light of truth, the Church should point the way toward living together peacefully."[16]

Despite the enthusiasm with which Cardinal Bea's and Bishop deSmedt's introductory comments were received, the conservative minority in the Council marshaled its resources for another full fledged procedural onslaught. When the debate on the Schema on Ecumenism began, it was suggested that the Council deal first with Chapters I through III, defining the general principles of ecumenism, then consider Chapters IV and V separately. Then, in what amounted to a filibustering stratagem, the conservatives rose, one after another, to challenge the schema in totality or in its various parts. The debate was to continue for several days.

Joseph Cardinal Ritter of St. Louis, sensitive to the opposition that was emerging against placing a statement on the Jews within the Schema on Ecumenism, asserted on the Council floor, "Whether or not the fourth chapter in the strict sense pertains to the Schema on Ecumenism, such a statement clearly pertains to the proposed purpose of the Council, it exceedingly pleases us."[17] The American Cardinal was prepared to accept the statement's separation from a Schema concerned with Christian unity but he would oppose any effort to kill the Jewish statement altogether or to weaken it.

Justification for setting aside Chapter IV was provided immediately by Ignace Cardinal Tappouni of Antioch: "To treat of Judaism . . . in this schema was inopportune." If Jews are to be mentioned at all in a schema dealing with relations among Christians, it should be mentioned "by accident." If greater attention were given to the Jews, it would be understood by Arabs as an act of "discrimination," proof of a pro-Israel sentiment.[18] The Coptic Patriarch of Alexandria, Stephanos Isidarouss, warned that if the Council insisted on issuing a statement on the Jews, "We shall have to face the music" from Arab nations.[19] Ernesto Cardinal Ruffini, Archbishop of Palermo, who had been identified as one of the three most important leaders of the conservative bloc, also joined the attack. He alluded to the resistance of the Jews to conversion, and even associated them with Marxism. Objecting to the honorable mention they received in the schema, Ruffini questioned why the text should not, in that case, also take up those religions whose members are less hostile to the Church than are the Jews and more open to conversion.[20] Finally, Melchite Rite Patriarch Maximus IV Saigh of Antioch warned that the question of the Jews ought not be introduced into a schema on ecumenism, which he defined as "a striving for the reunion of the entire Christian family. . . ." He added, "It is seriously offensive to our separated brethren that they should seem to be treated on the same footing with the Jews."[21]

The chapter on religious liberty was also attacked. The Fathers were warned that it would encourage error, and the Church must always stand against diffusion of error. Religious freedom, it was suggested, would only foster "propaganda, liberalism and existentialism." By appearing to grant rights to atheism, it would strengthen the influence of Communism; further, the document failed to make a clear affirmation that there was *no salvation* outside of the Catholic Church.

Attacks were launched even on the concept of ecumenism itself. Conservatives complained that the schema had failed to delimit the right to participation in ecumenical conversation only to those Catholics who lead a holy life, devote themselves to continual prayer, have a sound knowledge of theology, and receive the approval of ecclesiastical authorities. To permit the laity to take part in dialogue was dangerous, since by Church law they were clearly forbidden to read books favoring heresy. The document semed to imply that all religions had a right to propagate their faith; opponents complained that only the Catholic Church, custodian of the true faith, had the right and duty to evangelize. Further, too much emphasis on the things that other Christians shared with the Catholic Church would blur the essential differences. Ecumenism would be furthered only by demonstrating to others what they lack, whereas complacency would be promoted by pointing out what they possessed.

To these objections, some conservatives added that the Roman Catholic Church had nothing to learn from other Christians. If mistakes had occurred, they had been due to the disobedient sons, not to the Church itself, which was infallible and indefectible. Dialogue's only use was to bring back the erring to the one true faith.

There were, of course, notable voices heard in favor of the schema and its various parts. The Archbishop of Chicago, Albert Cardinal Meyer, speaking for many American bishops, praised the schema and underscored his support, particularly for Chapters IV and V. Acknowledging that "there might be some differences of opinion on their place in this schema as another," he argued, nevertheless, that "these two chapters are intimately connected with the whole question of ecumenism."[22] Regarding religious liberty, Cardinal Meyer underscored his opposition to any Conciliar opening to a religious test for public office—a suggestion implicitly maintained in the draft schema. He urged that the document clearly declare that Catholics sought religious liberty not for themselves alone but for all men. Finally, he exclaimed,

"All should respect the religious sincerity of others and not regard differences of religious belief and practice as excuses for violating the moral obligation to treat all fellow citizens with respect, justice and charity."[23] The Archbishop of Tokyo, Peter Cardinal Tatsuo Doi, asked for an even greater emphasis on the fact that truth would be respected by the Church wherever it was found, even among non-Christian religions. José Cardinal Quintero of Caracas maintained that not all the mistakes of the past ought to be blamed on others. Many were due to the shortcomings of the Church, which must be willing to acknowledge its own guilt.

CHAPTERS ON JEWS AND RELIGIOUS LIBERTY SEPARATED FROM SCHEMA ON ECUMENISM

Despite the vigorous support that Chapters IV and V received, the issue had become complicated. In fact the Schema on Ecumenism appeared threatened in its entirety if these two chapters were to remain attached to it. The statement on the Jews was sure to be disapproved by the conservatives, the hierarchy from Arab lands, and Eastern Catholics. Arab political pressure was an ominous and not insignificant danger to the Church. Even some non-Catholic delegate-observers threw their weight behind opposition of this chapter. The Protestant delegate-observer Robert Mc-Afee Brown noted, "I am surprised by the degree to which certain observers resist the inclusion of a Chapter on the Jews. These observers who tend to come from predominantly Arab areas feel that the Jewish question inevitably has political overtones."[24]

It was reported that the World Council of Churches, although it had no objection to a statement against anti-Semitism, would have preferred that the Jews be treated outside the context of Christian ecumenism. Many Catholic bishops—even those who favored an unequivocal attack on anti-Semitism—also agreed with the suggestion that the Jewish statement be treated elsewhere by the Council. Finally, to provide added strength to this point of view, it became known that Orthodox Jews would rather have the Jewish statement appear in another context. So widespread was this argument, drawing support from Protestants, Catholics, and Jews, that the officials of the Secretariat indicated that they would not insist, after all, on having the Jewish statement a part of the Schema on Ecumenism.

The Jesuit magazine *America* took note "that some critics question the logic of including detailed consideration of the Jews in a document aimed primarily at the problem of the unity of Christians." But, the editorial continued, "there is a peculiar appropriateness nevertheless in the decision to bring up the Jewish question at this time. Without prejudice to a later study of anti-Semitism as a problem of human relations, it seems vital that the Council should establish the theological foundations of the Christian attitude toward the Jews and in the process set the stage for an entirely new perspective."[25]

At the U.S. bishops' press panel on the first day of the debate on the Jewish statement, Father Gregory Baum, Council expert from Toronto, defended the Council's treatment of the Jews in the Schema on Ecumenism. He argued that the Church can only understand itself by reference to its roots in Israel; the division produced in the people of Israel over the Messiah is a symbol of all subsequent divisions within the Christian people themselves; finally, the Church believes that Israel is part of the eschatological dimension of the Church: In the end-time the Church and Israel will be one.[26] Bishop Charles Helmsing joined himself to Father Baum's explanation. Arguing that a statement on the Jews belonged to the Schema on Ecumenism, the Kansas bishop reasoned, "To exclude all references to the Jews will be interpreted as an attempt to exclude Jews from the ecumenical dialogue."[27] Such justifications, however, seemed not to elicit great enthusiasm.

Similarly, the statement on religious liberty had its particular enemies. The combination of forces against the two final chapters appeared to be gaining ground. Evidently the Pope was persuaded either that the Schema on Ecumenism as a whole was in danger, or that it would be an embarrassment to the Church were a much larger number of bishops to oppose Chapters IV and V. On November 20 he ordered the moderators to press for a vote on Chapters I through III and set aside any vote on the last two chapters. Another possible reason suggested by some for the Pope's tactical decision was that he had decided by then to visit the Holy Land. A historic meeting with members of the Orthodox

Patriarchate would in itself give visible expression through deed and action to the principles of ecumenism. A vote on the Jewish statement and religious liberty might only complicate matters in the Middle East. A favorable vote on Chapter IV could cause ill-feeling in the Arab world, and an unfavorable vote would make impossible a visit to Israel.

On November 21, 1963, the first three chapters of the Schema on Ecumenism were approved in principle by an overwhelming vote of 1,966 placets (yes) to 86 non placets (no). The moderator promised that the last two chapters would be brought to a vote "later." Everyone presumed that "later" meant sometime before the session had concluded.

In the course of a debate nearing termination, the Council Fathers were called upon to set aside time for the nomination and election of additional members to the various Conciliar commissions. This was not an insignificant enterprise in that the election of yet a larger number of liberals on a commission might assure a smoother running of the next session of the Council. But it would also consume some of the little time remaining.

On November 21, the Pope announced that membership on each of the Conciliar commissions was to be increased from twenty-five to thirty members. Four members were to be elected by the Council and one was to be appointed by the Pope. Since the Secretariat for the Promotion of Christian Unity had only eighteen members, the Council Fathers were instructed to elect eight and the Pope would appoint four. The expanded commissions could then elect a second vice-president and secretary. The moderators were certain that by this action control of the Council would at last be decisively wrested from the Curial administrators. In an amazing feat of caucusing and communication, the fifty-nine regional and national episcopal conferences agreed on an international list of candidates. Only one Italian name appeared on the list of forty-two bishops elected. The others were from Europe, America, and Asia and were clearly committed to the progressive cause. Two American bishops were elected to serve on the Secretariat for the Promotion of Christian Unity: Bishop Charles N. Helmsing of Kansas City–St. Joseph, Missouri, and Bishop Ernest J. Primeau of Manchester, New Hampshire.

On Friday, November 29, Bishop Helmsing rose to ask the

moderator a simple and direct question: In light of the promise made nine days before to take a vote on Chapters IV and V, and in view of the moderator's authority to interrupt the debate for such a purpose at any time, why not take a vote right now? Bishop Helmsing's question remained unanswered. As the Protestant observer Robert McAfee Brown noted in his diary, there was a mounting feeling of frustration. "The seats are emptier than at any time thus far in the Council and the halls and bars are filled with Bishops who seem to realize that the debate is not going in any new directions."[28] At the press conference that afternoon the reporters queried the American bishops sharply. Why had they not seen fit to lobby and to press for a vote just as other bishops had lobbied and made representations to the Pope against the measures on religious liberty and the Jewish statement? Rynne reports that "There was no satisfactory answer except that the American bishops had not wanted to bring pressure."[29] Evidently the American hierarchy did not yet realize that many Catholic Fathers, particularly those from Italy and Spain, were capable of using varied and forceful forms of political maneuver and strategy.

On Monday, December 2, a disappointed Cardinal Bea rose to assure the Council Fathers that all their suggestions for the ecumenical schema would be seriously considered by his Secretariat; a strengthened and revised text would be ready for their consideration at the next session. Then, slowly and deliberately, he expressed regret that there had been "insufficient time" to deal fully with Chapters IV and V and to vote upon them. With unmistakable purpose, he said twice, *"Quod differtur non aufertur"* ("What is put off is not put away.")[30] The delay perhaps fortuitously would give the Fathers a chance to consider these serious issues with the care they deserved. The Secretariat would welcome any suggestions received no later than mid-February.

Although unspoken, one sensed in the American hierarchy a resolve to take on a new measure of involvement and activity in support of these two subjects, the statement on the Jews and religious liberty; issues that had stimulated such profound support from men of every faith. Certainly at the third session of the Council, these questions would be resolutely settled. They would not again be set aside.

7. Pilgrimage to the Holy Land

IN HIS CLOSING ADDRESS to the second session of the Council, the Pope made a dramatic announcement. As an expression of "prayer, penance, and renewal," he would make a pilgrimage to the Holy Land. There he would "offer to Christ his Church." No Pope had ever flown in an airplane before. No Pope in modern memory had visited biblical soil. For the moment, the Council and the world were overwhelmed. Headlines featured the eventful disclosure, and the record of the Council's second session receded into the background.

The Pope thus bought a desultory session of the Council to climactic conclusion. Through this one announcement he seemed to be willing to put into action principles that had not yet been finally promulgated by a divided Council.

The pilgrimage had its own justification and purpose. Although it was not intended to redeem a disappointing second session, it did in fact raise a glowing brand of hope. The Council had not resolved the issue of ecumenism. It had not yet faced up to the most crucial question of the Church's role in the world. But as the Pope said, "Even before the Council discusses the problems of the modern Apostolate, we can say that we already know the answers." He was indicating that a final consensus on every word was not required before the Church Fathers, on their own initiative, could provide their constituency with "a word of heartening reassurance" and the world of thought with "a shaft of truth."[1] Catholics properly recognized the pilgrimage, therefore, as an extension of the Council and a demonstration of its highest aspirations.

There is little doubt that the Pope's primary goals were in the realm of interior renewal and Christian ecumenical outreach. But he certainly must have known, too, that Jews would respond to the announcement and follow the journey to the Holy Land with keen interest. Here indeed was a moment when the Pontiff could extend a fraternal hand and serve a reconciling purpose. Would he recognize the full implications of his visit to the "cradle of the faith" of Jews and Christians? Would he seize the opportunities provided by an encounter with Israel—Holy Land and modern state?

TRADITIONAL CATHOLIC VIEWS ON THE JEWISH STATE

The Catholic Church has never looked with official favor upon the establishment of a Jewish Homeland. One measure of the Church's new direction, therefore, might be its attitude and behavior toward that State. Surely there might be expected an indication of the Pope's stance or a hint of the atmosphere that would prevail when the Council finally turned its attention to a statement on the Jews.

The dynamism required for the building of a nation contradicts any conception of the Jews as a fossilized, ghostlike people of Old Testament vintage. A 'servile people' would certainly be incapable of developing the resources required for the establishment of a thriving country. The existence of the State demonstrates that Judaism is capable of energizing the Jew; it provides him with a contemporaneity that challenges Christian hopes of converting him. Furthermore, the State supplies the Jew with a physical reality, with a corporeal nature that makes it impossible for the Christian to understand him merely by viewing him in theological terms.

When Theodore Herzl, father of Zionism, approached Pope Pius X in January, 1904, seeking his assistance for the Zionist venture, the Catholic Pontiff dismissed him with these words: "We cannot favor this movement. The Jews did not recognize Jesus, our Lord, and we therefore cannot recognize the Jewish people. . . . If you come to Palestine and settle your people there, we will be ready with priests and churches to baptize all of you."[2]

As Father Flannery has noted, "There is little doubt that the establishment of the State of Israel came as a shock, even a scandal to some Christians. They held that in punishment for the Crucifixion of Christ, the Jews would never return to their ancient homeland unless they came to believe in Him. . . . The present restoration, partial though it was, seemed a contradiction of the inspired word."[3]

Did not Jesus himself prophesy, "They will fall by the edge of the sword, and be led captive among all nations; and Jerusalem will be trodden down by the Gentiles, until the times of the Gentiles are fulfilled" (Luke 21:24)? Even those Catholics who are ready to reconsider such a prophecy of eternal Jewish wandering find it hard to accept Israel's national resurgence merely as the sign of a revitalized Judaism. Instead they interpret the event in the perspective of St. Paul's hope for the ultimate conversion of Jews to Christianity. Thus, Father Flannery concludes a discourse on the theological aspects of the State of Israel with these words: "Israel's restoration to the land of promise, even though under secular auspices, may thus be a distant preparation for her final encounter with grace. . . ."[4]

Political tensions in the Middle East would provide complication enough for the Pope's visit, and especially for his approach to Israeli officialdom. But in the light of a theological tradition antagonistic to Jewish religious vitality, there were even deeper issues.

THE SPIRITUAL SIGNIFICANCE OF THE STATE OF ISRAEL

To the Jews, the birth and growth of the State of Israel is a kind of modern miracle as well as a testimony to their faith and hope. We are not only the custodians of an ancient revelation. God is still gracious to us. He has blessed us, even in this generation. The dead bones, the remnants of Hitler's crematoria, have come alive. Jews defeated the armed might of Arab nations and established a home of refuge for the "waste products" of modern civilization. The refuse people carved out of the desert soil a

home and made it blossom. They are sharing their human and
material resources now by providing instruction and assistance
to the emerging African nations. The establishment of the State
of Israel is not just a secular political fact. The State is not merely
the result of nationalistic fervor. Israel is not just another "Balkan
entity." The hand of God is present in this enterprise.

Most Jews define Judaism in such a way that we are called
upon in the Holy Land, to exercise a corporate responsibility and
to work out our religious understanding of God's requirements
for a just society. We believe that we witness to God's existence by
the way we organize the life of community. It is not enough
to achieve an assurance of the soul's individual salvation in the
world to come. We are called by faith to create, in this world, a
society where God's presence in history is demonstrated by the
quality of justice and mercy built into the civilization. That is
why the prophets inveighed so vigorously against social injustice
and corporate evil. That is why Jewish religious law concerns itself
with the distribution of wealth, the procedures of courts of law,
the exercise of power by rulers, and the waging of peace. If our
vision of God can impel us to work toward a society and a culture
that is righteous and humane, this fact will inspire other men
and nations similarly to walk by His light. In such fashion we
wish to serve mankind and fulfill our obligation to God as His
chosen people. We do not require of all men that they become
Jews. But we hope that, whatever their denominational allegiance,
they will strive to order life in society by His word.

Wherever we live in the exile, we are instructed to build homes
and plant vineyards and pray for the peace of the city. Wherever
we live, in whatever part of the globe, we are impelled by our
faith to utilize political instruments in the effort to achieve justice.
But in the Holy Land, particularly, we are obligated as a national
entity, as a people in control of power, to translate words of
prayer into deeds of service, the lessons of the Talmudic texts into
political action, and by such behavior to proclaim our love of God.

When Christians fail to acknowledge the spiritual significance
of a Jewish State, they distort the nature of Judaism. It is as
offensive to the Jew for the Church to fail to appreciate the religious importance of the State of Israel as it would be to a Catholic

were a Jew to act as though the Church's episcopal structure had no spiritual foundation or purpose. For the Jew, the need to maintain a corporate identity in a specific geographical location carries a meaning resembling that of hierarchical institutions for the Catholic. In both cases, these are considered by many in each group to be God-given instrumentalities by which the grace of the Lord is made manifest.

Needless to say, the issue is a difficult and complicated one. The confusion of Christians regarding the religious significance of the Jewish State is compounded by the Jews' own division over the meaning of Israel and such issues as the alliance of the State with Orthodox Jewish authorities. The very task of working out patterns of religious freedom in a state burdened with such faith responsibilities continues to perplex world Jewry. Whatever the problems the Jewish State may have, however, both internally in relation to other religions and externally with Arab nations, the central significance of its existence for Jewish religious thought just cannot be ignored by any Christian who wishes to understand Jews and enter into dialogue with them.

ARAB-ISRAEL CONFLICT OVER THE TRIP

Arabs were fearful of the consequences of Pope Paul's visit to the Holy Land. They were already concerned that a Council statement on the Jews would remove the charge of deicide, undermining the basis for the punishment of exile, and would thereby provide a spiritual foundation for the legitimacy of the Jewish State. How much more fraught with danger would be the Pope's direct encounter with Israeli officials; it might be interpreted as a de facto recognition of the hated State! Most Jews realized that Arab actions to halt the trip or to urge upon the Pope an act of unfriendliness toward Israel—neither of which efforts had any possibility of achievement—would inevitably boomerang. By publicly and insistently interpreting the Pope's pilgrimage as having political significance, the Arabs would beg to be repudiated. In contrast to the Arabs' pressure on the Pope, the Israelis, by diplomatic correctness, might stand to gain. The Israeli ambassador to

Italy, Maurice Fisher, released to the press the proper disclaimer: "Any political interpretation, in a positive or negative sense, that has been given or is being given to Ambassador Fisher's contacts with the Holy See . . . is devoid of any foundation."[5]

Despite the wisdom of this strategy, however, many Jews could not restrain their hopes that the visit to Israel would presage a new and warmer Catholic attitude toward Jews. Thus, Anglo-Jewish newspapers throughout the world read into the pilgrimage, if not a political meaning, at least a significance related to the Council's declaration. The *National Jewish Post and Opinion,* for example, hopefully reported that Pope Paul's visit to Israel was "a move to smooth Jewish-Catholic relations and an affirmation that the text [chapter on the Jews] would not be forgotten at next year's session. . . . Any establishment of relations with Israel would be interpreted as another indication of the Vatican's willingness to reach some *rapprochement* with the Jewish community at large through the only Jewish diplomatic entity—Israel. . . ."[6]

ARRIVAL IN JORDAN

Press packets from Jordan's Office of Information were distributed to the six hundred journalists from around the world who were reporting on the Pope's journey. The packet contained Arnold Toynbee's 1961 assertion that the "coldblooded cruelty" of the Israeli massacre of Arabs was not unlike Nazi atrocities,"[7] and an American Catholic priest-editor's assertion that the tears of the hopeless Arab refugees cry to God as "the blood of Abel cried to God from the earth."[8]

The Pope touched down at Amman Airport in Jordan on Saturday, January 4, 1964. In his address before King Hussein he met the Arab mood by recalling Peter's reference to the Psalms in his First Epistle: "He who would love life and see good days, let him turn away from evil and do good. Let him seek after peace and pursue it."[9]

The Jordanian radio's response, in Arabic only (it was excluded from the English broadcast), recalled that "2,000 years ago the Jews crucified Christ and 15 years ago they attacked the people of Palestine. . . . The Jews are the enemies of God and of all religions in the world . . . [they] should never be forgiven for their crimes. . . ."[10]

More than fifty thousand men, women, and children crushed in on the Pope as he made his way through the Via Dolorosa. For a moment he was jolted; his glasses were broken; his party became separated from one another. The Arabs' enthusiasm, their overwhelming delight at the Pope's historic venture, made his pilgrimage a remarkable event of human communication. Without doubt he had stirred the hearts of Arab, Moslem, and Christian. This was a bridging, of almost miraculous proportions, of a gulf of centuries.

That evening the Pope met with the Orthodox Patriarch Benedict of Jerusalem and the Armenian Patriarch Derderian. It was the first encounter between a Catholic Pope and an Eastern Patriarch in five hundred years. All precedent was shattered, and the Pope could retire that evening tired and satisfied. He had indeed been a "pontiff," a bridge between men.

THE POPE IN ISRAEL

On Sunday the Pope was to journey to Israel. The government took every precaution to assure his safety, even widening the roads of Galilee in order to facilitate security measures. The authorities were determined to do all in their power to please the Vatican, for the Pope was to spend a full day in the country. Along with sites of biblical significance, he would see also a people resurrected from the ashes of destruction and a land reclaimed. Visual impressions can often speak more eloquently than thousands of the best-chosen words. The Israelis trusted that God's Shekinah (Holy Presence), hovering over this Holy Land, would be felt and acknowledged by the Pope.

By prior arrangement, the government had agreed to meet the Pope near Megiddo, about seventy miles northwest of Jerusalem in the Galilee region. An entrance from this point would enable him to see more of the historic scenes on both sides of the Jordan River. The square at Megiddo where the Pope was received was decorated with Israeli and Vatican flags. President

Shazar spoke his greeting in Hebrew. "I have come in the name of the Government of Israel," he declared, "to welcome the spiritual Father of the Catholic Church throughout the world. From Jerusalem, our capital, the City of David, I and the members of the Government of Israel with me have made our way down to Megiddo. . . ." Having thus identified himself, President Shazar continued with a classic statement of Jewish hope for the world and assurance in God's protecting care.

Surely the devastation of my people during this last generation is a bitter warning of the depths of bestiality and loss of the divine image to which ancient prejudices and racial hatreds can drag men down, if a purifying spirit does not come into being while there is yet time to extinguish the dangers forever. . . . This countryside about us is a living testimony that prophecies are being fulfilled—those of the in-gathering of our people here from all the corners of the earth and the renewal of their independent life as in days of old. . . . In very village and town of our land, that is being now built, there are signs of the fulfillment of the promise of new life. Thus our belief is strengthened that realization of our seers' vision of universal peace and social justice will come as well. Mankind shall be redeemed from its distress, the world shall be built in righteousness and this our eyes shall behold. Blessed be our illustrious guest upon his arrival in our midst.[11]

The Pope certainly could respond to President Shazar's call for a universal moral revival, but could he agree with the Israeli's religious conviction that the establishment of the State of Israel and the in-gathering of the exiles was a fulfillment of Old Testament prophecies? For if the scriptural prophecies have already been fulfilled in the coming of Christ, if the hope of Israel is to be identified completely with Jesus, if the sign of the end-time is to be an increase in Christian faith, then how interpret this revival that has occurred in the Holy Land? Would the Pope acknowledge that in the Jewish State God has provided a grace and a blessing to the Jewish people?

The Pope read his discourse in French. He did not address Shazar as president but called him "Your Excellency." He expressed gratitude "for all the kind attentions offered us by the authorities." He did not specify who these authorities were or of what land they were the authorities. He emphasized once again the religious nature of his pilgrimage: Your Excellency knows and God is our witness that we are not inspired during this pilgrimage by any other motive than purely spiritual ones. We come as a pilgrim, we come to venerate the Holy Places, we come to pray." Then he added his reminder to the Israelis that this land is sacred also to Christians. Palestine has a significance, in fact, for the entire world. The Pope continued, "Our prayers are raised toward God for all men, believing and unbelieving, and we happily include the sons of the people of the covenant, whose part in the religious history of mankind can never be forgotten."[12] The Pope climaxed his address with a petition for man's reconciliation with God and the achievement of true profound concord among all men and nations, repeating the Hebrew words for peace, "Shalom, shalom."

Many Israelis were moved. Despite differences with the Pope in religion and politics, the Pope's humanity at that moment had cut through barriers. The sincerity of his religious pilgrimage and his commitment to God were impressive.

One prominent Israeli was absent. Chief Rabbi Yitzhack Nissim had declined a governmental invitation to join the reception party. The Rabbi adhered to protocol. If, as the Chief Rabbi of Orthodox Jewry in Israel, he was to greet the Supreme Head of the Catholic Church, then he desired nothing less than the sort of dignified formal arrangements that the Pope had made with Orthodox Patriarchs. Many Jews were critical of the Rabbi for standing on ceremony at such a time. Others took his part; Rabbi Nissim should have been approached by the Pope, they said. Arrangements should have been made for an exchange of greetings. There should have been papal acknowledgment of the Rabbi's position. No such recognition or arrangements had taken place. Was it merely oversight on the part of the Pope? Or did he wish to avoid confrontation with a Jewish religious official to whom he would have to extend courtesies, as though Judaism were equal to Christianity? The Pope had proffered tokens of genuine fraternity to the Orthodox, but they are Christian representatives. Was he making a demeaning distinction, therefore, between those who have accepted a baptism of faith and those who remain apart from the Mystical Body of Christ?

Israeli government officials criticized Rabbi Nissim sharply. A display of outgoing courtesy by the Chief Rabbi, they felt, would speak even more eloquently of the Jews' moral dignity than such an act of punctiliousness. In defense of the Rabbi, the independent Israeli newspaper, *Haaretz*, commented, "The Chief Rabbi acted wisely because the faith of Israel was justified in demanding equal status with Christianity. Morals and integrity must rise above political expediency." [13]

It was widely believed that the Pope decided upon a gesture of reconciliation with the Chief Rabbi when he ordered Cardinal Tisserant to light candles and recite prayer at the Chamber of the Holocaust—as a sign of his compassion for the Jews who had been slaughtered by the Nazis. Cardinal Tisserant lit six candles symbolizing the six million Jewish victims, stood silent for a moment, and then said, "On behalf of the Pope we express our sympathy and participation in the anguish and sorrow at the terrible destruction wrought upon the Hebrew people." [14] Many Israelis were moved by this compassionate recognition of Jewish suffering.

In Nazareth, speaking of the nobility of the teachings of Jesus, the Pope surprised his hearers with the statement "It is the voice of Christ promulgating the New Testament—the new law which both absorbs and surpasses the old and raises human endeavor to the very peak of perfection. The great motive of man's labor is a sense of duty which involves the exercise of freedom. In the Old Testament it was fear and at all times, including our own, it is instinct and self-interest; but for Christ, who is the Father's gift of love to the world, the motive is love. . . ." [15]

It had been an exhausting day in Israel. The Pope had recited Mass at the Grotto of Annunciation in Nazareth, prayed at the Church of the Loaves and Fishes in Tagbha, paid homage at the rock where it is told that Jesus designated Peter as the shepherd, recited Scripture at the Mount of Beatitudes, meditated at the foot of Mount Tabor where the Transfiguration had occurred, and at last, with arms outstretched in benediction, greeted the procession that welcomed him into the Church of the Dormition on Mount Zion. Now he was ready to leave the new city of

Jerusalem and return to his Holy Land domicile in the old city in Jordan.

To this point the visit had been a success, though a qualified one. The Israelis had responded warmly to the Pope's personality and sincerity. It had been a great day in the nation's life, unmarred by the untoward incidents that some had feared. Israel was proud to have been the host to the great world spiritual leader.

But there were also dissenters whose sensitivities had been irritated at several points. Why had not the Pope entered Israel through Jerusalem—the capital? Why had his addresses avoided mentioning the name of the State and the office of its President? Why had he recalled only the *past* significance of the Jewish people, revealing no appreciation of the continuing historic meaning of Jewish survival? Why had he harked back in his Nazareth address to the age-old dichotomy between Judaism, the religion of harsh justice, and Christianity, the religion of mercy—between the Old Testament, the repository of fearful law, and the New Testament, the refinement of this law into Christian love and compassion? These were some of the questions raised by Jews, then and later. In a time of strain, when all ears were attuned to every word of encouragement or of slight, it was natural that the reaction would be mixed.

But the amenities had been maintained and the general response was positive. If Jew and Christian still remained tense in each other's presence, this was understandable. It would remain for a future time to provide the catharsis, the working through of emotional conflict, that precedes genuine dialogue. The ambivalence of kinship and alienation remained still between the mother and daughter religions.

Then, just before he was to leave Israel through the Mandelbaum Gate, the Pope surprised everyone in his parting remarks. He delivered a defense of Pope Pius XII, answering the charges that had been stimulated by the play *The Deputy*: "We are happy to have the opportunity to affirm on this day and in this place that there is nothing more unjust than this slight against so venerable a memory. . . . Everyone knows what Pius XII did for the defense and rescue of all those who were in distress, without any distinction. . . ."16

This statement caused a stir around the world. The Pope had given no intimation that there was anything in the past of Jewish-Christian relations for which he might feel some remorse. There had been no clarion-sounding repudiation of anti-Semitism. There had been no daring, progressive expression of theology with regard to the Church's conception of the Jews' role in the plan of God. But now there was a defense of Pius XII! Why such a defense on that day when he was in the Jewish State, and in that place, in Jerusalem, the capital city of Israel?

The Deputy had been written by a German Lutheran. Its popularity throughout the world was not a Jewish accusation of the Church; it was civilization's own expression of remorse that all of us, the Church, the Pope, the Western democracies, and Jews, too, had fallen short in our human responsibilities. Why did Pope Paul need to be so defensive? Was it not that he felt burdened by a Jewish presence that, even without words, even without intention, cries out to the human heart to confront its unmeasured capacity for evil?

Any defense of Pius XII or of the Church's past should at least have been accompanied by an honest confrontation with human inadequacy and evil. Jew and Christian alike—both of us—must be able to confess our confusion and our error, and then we must seek to transform guilt into responsibility. To know our human finitude is also to realize the full measure of our capacity. By God's judgment we all fall short; but by His grace we can carry our burden one step farther. The best defense of Pope Pius XII, therefore, would have been the Pope's reaching out in human fraternity to the Jew. Some assertion of his appreciation of the fact that God performed signs and wonders through the Hebrew people, or at least that Jews and Christians, both of whom call themselves Israel, share responsibility to be a light unto all mankind—some words, some act of recognition of the uniqueness and kinship of all people who claim to be covenanted with God, would have been reconciling.

Pope Paul told the Israeli Chief of Protocol as he took his

leave, "We saw today a living people at work, a calm and serene people."[17] This theme could have been expanded and elaborated in the formal address of farewell. Thus an opportunity was missed. Some Catholic observers were aware that the potency of the hour had been misspent. Thomas E. Bird wrote in *Commonweal*: "The lack of sensitivity to Jewish history and to the nation of Israel must await a happier day for rectification."[18]

Whatever feeling of discomfort the Pope may have experienced on his trip through Israel, he returned in triumph to his meetings with Athenagoras, "first among equals" of the fourteen Orthodox Patriarchs. By the gifts exchanged and the unusual courtesies of protocol, both Athenagoras and Paul demonstrated that the age-old bitterness among Christians can be redeemed in a moment, when the heart is permitted to dictate the terms of human solidarity. Athenagoras was so impressed by the encounter with Pope Paul that he declared, "There are no longer differences between us now, now that the door is open. There is only one theology, but there are many theologians. . . ."[19]

The Pope was more restrained and disciplined than the Orthodox leader. "The roads which lead to union," he observed, "may be long and strewn with difficulty."[20] Nevertheless, he and Athenagoras were able to exchange a "kiss of peace." A new page in the history of Christianity, if not in Jewish-Christian relations, had been written.

8. Crisis in the Jewish Community

By the time Pope Paul's pilgrimage ended a major crisis had erupted in the Jewish community. In two sessions of the Council the Catholic Church had done no more than present a brief chapter on the Jewish people which never even came to a preliminary vote. The Pope had visited Israel and maintained there a disciplined, noncommittal correctness. Pressures that had been building within the Jewish community suddenly found outlet. Those Jews who had involved themselves in the work of the Council and had tried to assure their skeptical brethren that all would be well found themselves embarrassed.

Orthodox Jewish leaders released a barrage of criticism. Rabbi Norman Lamm, a follower of Rabbi Joseph Soloveitchik, the leading Orthodox rabbi in America, led the attack. In the official organ of the Union Orthodox Jewish Congregations of America, Rabbi Lamm explained,

The complaint is that we have over-reacted, occasionally to the point of compromising our principles and our dignity. Jewish organizations, especially those dedicated to harmonious intergroup relations and anti-defamation as the greatest good in the universe, kept their mimeograph machines working overtime. The spirit of euphoria gripped many a seasoned Jewish spokesman, spilled over into sermons, and was reflected in the writings of various Jewish columnists. . . . The head of all Reform Temples solemnly informed a convention that the spirit of ecumenism works both ways and that, therefore, we Jews must reciprocate by accepting the central figure of Christianity "as a positive and prophetic spirit in the stream of Jewish tradition." And all of this—for a brief statement, the exact text of which has never been made public, and, in the end, which was never accepted, even in principle.[1]

Rabbi Lamm also charged that the Church had not yet repudiated its missionary intention. As a case in point he referred to the writings of Msgr. John Oesterreicher, who was assigned a prominent role in the Secretariat for the Promotion of Christian Unity. The participation in the Secretariat of this converted Jew, warned the Rabbi, is "not at all reassuring. . . ."

With similar sharpness Rabbi David H. Hill, President of the (Orthodox) National Council of Young Israel, attacked Jewish community relations officials for their failure: "These people should never have entered into any dialogues and should never have come before alien religions with hat in hand begging and pleading for recognition. We were promised that the Church would issue a statement which in effect would absolve the Jews of deicide, statements were drafted, but in the final analysis all we have received was an invitation to forsake our faith and join the Church. . . . Much of what has developed is a result of amateurish meddling. . . . The time has come for Orthodoxy to begin to assert itself. Only Torah-true Jews have the right to speak on these issues. . . ."[2]

In such attacks these Orthodox rabbis assumed a position inside the Jewish community not unlike that of the conservatives within the Catholic Church. Both feared that openness to other faiths would lead to a weakening of their own faith. Both feared that the liberals in their ranks were ready to barter away principles. Both wished to restrict participation in the dialogue to authorities whom Orthodoxy approved.

Soon other rabbis, Orthodox, Conservative, and Reform, repeated the following themes:

1. "Jews need not be grateful or overwhelmed or elated over being 'absolved' by the Roman Catholic Church of God-killing. Jews will not owe the Church one iota of gratitude if we are cleared. On the contrary, it is the Church that owes us the apology

for the centuries of their dark record toward us. . . . The charge of deicide is a blot on the Christian conscience. If this charge is removed, it will cleanse the Church's soul, not ours."[3]

2. Jewish organizational leaders, by their enthusiasm for the draft schema, by their appearance of gratitude for Catholic action, which was frustrated anyway, have acted without dignity.

3. Although the Church will invoke its own theological concepts in any statement on the Jews, it has an obligation to understand us, comprehend us, and describe us in terms of our own integrity. The Church must make the effort to recognize the uniqueness of the Jewish community, "since each religious community is endowed with intrinsic dignity and metaphysical worth."[4] Christians must confront the Jew not only in terms of his unique past, but also with regard for his distinctive present history. To relate to the Jews merely with respect to a past contribution to Christianity and to find no other saving meaning or explanation for Jewish existence is to fail to seek that which God may be communicating to civilization through Jewish survival in this day.

Many Jews could agree that there was some point in these three observations. Each had its justification.

A further assertion was made, however, that was a little more complicated!

4. "When . . . ecumenism is referred to Jews, it inevitably has proselytizing implications, and any Christian attitude toward Jews that is part of such an ecumenical context, must therefore be suspect."[5]

There is no question that evangelism ought be suspended before dialogue can take place. The attitude which seeks to learn from the other is antithetical to the attitude which seeks to convert or manipulate the other. Christians who regard dialogue as nothing but a sophisticated technique for proselytizing those of us who are without "the truth of the Gospel" are concerned with monologue, not dialogue. Dialogue presumes that there is wisdom to be gained from conversation with the other; he is potentially the custodian of a truth worth hearing. Dialogue can take place only in an atmosphere of mutual respect. It requires that both participants be ready to change as a result of the dialogic experience. In dialogue neither participant holds to a closed system of truth and both remain open to new revelation.

Numbers of Jewish leaders suspected that for some Catholics the ecumenical movement was, in fact, merely another device for luring others nearer, in order to set Catholic truth before the world. What these critics failed to see was that for many Catholics the hope of a humanity united within the Catholic Church was but a distant dream of an eschatological nature. It was a hope for the end of time. The conversion of others was a cause for prayer, but it was not justification for tract distribution, doorbell ringing, sheep stealing, or other questionable forms of proselytization. Furthermore, these Catholics recognized that the most effective missionary campaign lies in the Christian's living his own life religiously. All that the Christian can do, they felt, is to be himself. The rest is in the hands of God.

Finally, some Catholics recognized that religious pluralism was a rather enduring reality in contemporary civilization. They were ready to reconsider, therefore, the significance of diversity. They rejected the old notion that separation from the Catholic Church was necessarily a tragedy. The ecumenical movement provided a bridge enabling them to meet men of different faiths in a consideration of that which all men share together by virtue of their human condition.

Catholic Bishop Blomjous of Tanganyika, East Africa, in a revolutionary address struggled with this new appreciation of the Church's role in a world of multiple religious faiths. "We used to think that the Church was sent into the world to gain the adherence of all men to Christ," he said, "and her missionary effort was destined to convert all men to live as brothers in a single Church. . . . Today, however, we are faced with the realization that pluralism and specifically religious pluralism is established in most parts of the world and that the forces of history will eventually make it a universal phenomenon. . . . It seems that religious pluralism is part of God's plan. . . . We are forced to ask ourselves the serious question . . . what is God attempting to tell us through the multiplicity of religion?"[6]

For Jews to dismiss the ecumenical movement, therefore, as

merely a disguised missionary effort would be unjust to the complex dynamics at work in the Church. Many felt they must oppose any effort to stereotype Christian ecumenism as only a movement with proselytizing intentions. It seemed to them, on the contrary, that in contrast to former patterns of missionary imperialism the ecumenical movement was an invitation to conversation in the spirit of mutual esteem and respect.

WITHDRAWAL OF ORTHODOX JEWS FROM THE THEOLOGICAL CONVERSATION

In truth, Orthodox Jews were launching an attack on *any* form of theological exchange. We who had engaged in conversation with Church officials at that point found ourselves strongly opposed to and opposed by Orthodox Jewish rabbis.

The first intimation of a desire for an absolute withdrawal from any theological conversation with Christians appeared in a Statement of Principles adopted by the Convention of the (Orthodox) Rabbinical Council of America, February 5, 1964. "Any suggestion," the statement said, "that the historical and metahistorical worth of a faith community is to be viewed against the back-drop of another faith, the idea of a non-democratic confrontation contravening the principle of equality, and the mere hint that a revision of historic attitude is anticipated, are incongruous with the fundamentals of religious liberty and freedom of conscience and can only breed discord and suspicion."[7] The statement properly insisted that Christians ought to recognize Jews in terms of their own intrinsic worth rather than as an adjunct to or a proof of Christian worth. But it failed to acknowledge that one cannot enter into the dialogue without anticipating some change in "historic attitude" on the part of all participants— including the Christian participant. In fact, it was such a fear of change that led conservatives in the Catholic Church also to be suspicious of the ecumenical movement and to oppose any opening to other religions.

Orthodox Jews were right to insist on the spiritual independence of each religious community. But in this one world we cannot separate ourselves, ultimately, from some relatedness to

other faith communities. Christians cannot avoid confronting
and dealing with the Jewish claim to be God's Israel, just as Jews
cannot avoid considering what God intends by the strength and
growth of other religions, particularly Christianity. Without desiring
that Jews in any way diminish their loyalty to their distinctive
existence as Jews, it is likely that a consideration of our relatedness to God's other children will only deepen our knowledge
of our own faith. Such an exchange will help us to know better
how to be "a light unto the nations." Involvement in a dialogue
that concerns itself with the interrelationships among religions
does not need to weaken loyalty to one's own faith. Certainly it
is not "incongruous with the fundamentals of religious liberty and
freedom of conscience."

Some Orthodox rabbis feared that any contact with Christians would lead to a watering-down of the Jewish faith. Rabbi
David Stavsky explained, "This ecumenism calls for a lowering
of barriers and of interfaith idealism which in my opinion leads
to . . . assimilation." [8]

The famous Lubovitcher Rabbi, Menachem M. Schneerson,
was more specific:

> The brotherhood of mankind is a positive concept only so long
> as it is confined to such areas as commerce, philanthropy, and the
> civil and economic aspects of society. . . .
>
> Unfortunately, the concept of brotherhood has been misconstrued
> to require members of one faith to explain their religious belief and
> practices to members of another faith and in return to receive instruc-
> tion in the religion of others. Far from clarifying matters, these
> interfaith activities have at best added to the confusion and, at worse,
> have been used with missionary zeal by those religious which are
> committed to proselytizing members of other faiths.
>
> The alarmingly growing rate of intermarriage has a variety of
> underlying causes, but there can be no doubt that one of the factors
> is the interfaith movement or dialogue.
>
> Where one party to the dialogue is committed to proselytizing
> and the other is not, it is clear that the dialogue will be used by
> the first to accomplish its purpose and the dialogue will, in effect,
> become a monologue. . . .[9]

Rabbi Abraham Feldman, editor of the *Connecticut Jewish
Ledger* and a Reform Jewish leader, disagreed vehemently with

the Lubovitcher Rabbi. Feldman expressed a view supported by many who had participated in interreligious conversations:

When he [the Lubovitcher Rabbi] ascribes what he calls the alarmingly growing rate of intermarriage to such discussions or dialogues, he is asserting as fact that which cannot be proved and that which in our judgment, based on many years of experience, is simply not true. Judaism is not a hothouse plant. Judaism can stand exposure to the light of intellectual examination.

There are differences which exist, and exist legitimately and honorably, between the various religious faiths. It does a Jew no harm to know wherein his neighbor differs from him and it does his neighbor no harm to know why and wherein the Jew believes and practices differently. That way lies an appreciation of and the implementation of the right to be different, as well as the possibility of the protection of that right and the freedom of religious belief based on intelligence, courtesy and understanding.[10]

THE ORTHODOX ARGUMENT AGAINST INTERRELIGIOUS CONVERSATION

It remained for Rabbi Joseph Soloveitchik of Boston, acknowledged intellectual and spiritual leader of Orthodoxy in America, to provide the underlying philosophic argument in favor of Jewish isolationism. "Jews need not withdraw from mutual cooperation on social problems," Rabbi Soloveitchik explained, "but there is no value at all in theological conversation, nor, for that matter, is such conversation possible." He attacked and called "absurd" the Christian tendency to speak of Christianity as a *continuum of doctrine* revealed to the Jews, "unless one is ready to acquiesce in the Christian theological claim that Christianity has superseded Judaism."

Soloveitchik elaborated: "As a faith-entity the community of the few is endowed with intrinsic worth which must be viewed against its own historical backdrop, without relating to the framework of another faith. For the mere appraisal of the worth of one community in terms of the service it has rendered to another, no matter how great and important this service was, constitutes an infringement of the sovereignty and dignity of even the smallest of faith communities. . . . Any intimation that the community of the few is expected to shed its uniqueness and cease existing because it has fulfilled its mission by paving the way for the community of the many, must be rejected as undemocratic, contravening the very idea of religious freedom."

There could be little disagreement with that particular call to minority rights. But then Rabbi Soloveitchik offered his most controversial insight: "The language of faith of a particular community is totally incomprehensible to the man of a different faith community. Hence, the confrontation should occur not at a theological, but at a mundane human level. . . . The great encounter between man and God is a holy, personal and private affair, incomprehensible to the outsider. . . . Each community is engaged in a singular gesture reflecting the nature of the act of faith itself and it is futile to try to find common denominators."[11]

With this latter assertion there could be much disagreement. It is important to acknowledge that man's encounter with God remains surrounded in mystery; like the experience of love it is difficult to explain and describe. But even though "our hope and indomitable will for survival are non-negotiable," we are not absolved thereby of a responsibility to try to define ourselves to others. Granted that such communication is difficult, it is worth the effort. When a man can reveal to another what his encounter with God has meant for him, and how it has shaped his life, he is engaged in the most vital demonstration of his love for the other.

In making the effort to define ourselves to another we often achieve a profounder awareness of ourselves. We may also discover our relatedness to others in the most surprising and vital of terms. In truth, it is frequently in exactly such kinds of conversation that God reveals Himself, for as we confront that which is of God in the other, we are able to know and experience His image within ourselves. Contrary to Rabbi Soloveitchik, it is possible that men will discover that they share many common convictions and hopes by virtue of their humanity and their faith. But first they will have to talk to one another.

It is not necessary to minimize the Jewish conflict with Christianity in order to suggest that even in matters of faith there is much that binds us together. We are each individual and yet related; separated from each other and yet obliged to and responsible for the other; independent and free and yet called to the service of the other. No human being, institution, or religion is so redeemed and redeeming, so complete in its vision of the truth, so sufficient unto itself, that it can afford to preclude dialogue with others. God is so overpowering and overwhelming, so full of love, that none of us can encompass Him totally, fully, and completely. We can learn from the other.

Rabbi Soloveitchik attacked those of us who had participated in conversations with the Church and who had responded to the churchmen's request for assistance. He intimated that we seemed to be willing to trade favors pertaining to fundamental matters of faith and (heaven forbid!) "reconcile some differences." He suspected that we were about to bargain away the Jewish faith.

There was no evidence at all, no cause for this suggestion that any of us had the power or even the desire to water down Judaism. No responsible Jewish leader had in any way suggested for any reason that Jews give up, revise, or tone down any basic Jewish belief. Rabbi Soloveitchik, by casting aspersions and doubt on other Jewish leaders, was leaving the impression that the only authentic Jews and the only responsible Jewish leaders were Orthodox rabbis.

Furthermore, Rabbi Soloveitchik had no grounds for charging that the assistance and suggestions given to the Vatican Council were an intrusion. He had failed to realize how profoundly and sincerely many Church Fathers desired such helpful honesty on our part. Whether ultimately agreeing with us or not, they wanted our opinions so that they could see themselves as we saw them. Only then could the Church fulfill the Pope's mandate to reformulate its teachings in such ways that they might be understood by the other.

There was also the implication in some of the Orthodox Jewish criticism that "secular" Jewish agencies had no business at all in dealing with the Vatican. The Orthodox were pressing their own institutional purposes. As I have earlier pointed out, considerations of "religious" versus "secular" are artificial when applied to the Jewish community. The so-called secular Jewish organizations all have religious leadership and membership. They are secular only in the sense that they are not under Synagogue jurisdiction or control and that not all their members are Synagogue-affiliated. The Jewish people never centered all of their communal structure and responsibilities within the Synagogue. It should also be appreciated that whenever matters of faith were under discussion these community relations agencies consulted the best religious scholarship and rabbinical leadership available to them.

The action or non-action of the Council would significantly affect the relationship of all Catholics to *all* Jews—not just "Torah-true Jews." Thus, all Jews, laity and rabbinate, secular and religious, being subject to the consequences, good or ill, of the Vatican Council's work, had the right and the obligation to give notice to their concern. The Council was a religious gathering of Christians, to be sure, but its definition of religious teaching would have implications for the public order. No one could be arbitrarily excluded from interest in its proceedings.

Finally, some Orthodox Jewish leaders suggested that interreligious dialogue was only a waste of time anyway, since the Church would never change—a suspicion long ingrained in Jewish thought by the tragic events of past history. Yet there was evidence everywhere that the mere announcement of a statement on the Jews had set in motion a fundamental revision of Church teaching. As Rabbi Marc Tanenbaum, in an interview for the *London Jewish Chronicle* observed, "So widespread is the movement among Christians towards eliminating anti-Semitism in texts and liturgy, including the deicide charge, that even if a Statement on the Jews is not approved in Rome, the revolution has now begun and it would take a counter-revolution to stop it." Then Rabbi Tanenbaum pointed out the irony that "the statements of the Rabbinical Council of America were used by anti-Semitic elements in the Vatican and by the Arab States to prove that religious Jews were hostile to Christians, that they were not interested in the Jewish chapter, and that, therefore, Cardinal Bea and those who share his viewpoint were unnecessarily getting the Catholic Church into trouble."[12]

RESPONSE OF CATHOLIC CLERGY

As though responsive to this complicated disturbance, at least a dozen Catholic bishops in the United States sought the opportunity to address Jewish audiences. A conciliatory message was heard from all. If the reaction of many Jews was based on hurt and impatience, these messages contained a healing word that gave promise for the future. It was pronounced perhaps most eloquently by Richard Cardinal Cushing, Archbishop of Boston. Speaking before the National Conference of Christians and Jews February 20, 1964, Cardinal Cushing said,

The whole world is eager for a statement. . . . The voice of the Church on religious liberty and our relations to Jewish people is being awaited in universities, in national and international organizations, in Christian and non-Christian communities, in the press and elsewhere, and it is being awaited with urgent expectancy. I am convinced we shall not be disappointed.

To my great personal disappointment, the Council did not make this part of its finished business at the last session, but I am confident that eventually it will. However, we do not have to wait for the Council to speak officially before we undertake the fraternal dialogue and theological confrontation encouraged in this chapter. On this level of the scholar and the man of the street there must be a closer meeting of minds and, above all, of hearts.

As a matter of fact, it was not a set-back for the ecumenical movement when the second session of the Council failed to discuss item by item the statements about religious liberty and about Catholic-Jewish relations. . . . The delay could be useful in giving further time for a fuller and deeper understanding of these problems. It could even help to ensure that when adopted, final decrees will not be empty gestures, but will reach down into every phase of religious instructions and practices. . . . We live in an atmosphere that is new and good. We have a sense among Christians and between Christians and Jews of the common heritage which we share in various ways. We are in the springtime spirit of new discovery of one another and of wonder at the myriad lengths which bind us together after centuries of separation.[13]

PART THREE

PROGRESS TOWARD A STATEMENT IN SESSION THREE

9. Rumors Between Sessions

ONE AFTER ANOTHER, at precedent-setting report meetings, the bishops of the United States found the occasion to assure the American Jewish community that a statement on the Jews would be adopted at the third session of the Council. Archbishop William E. Cousins of Milwaukee, Wisconsin, for example, accepted for the first time an invitation to address the members of a Jewish congregation. Before an enthralled audience of four hundred he predicted that at its next session the Council would endorse a statement condemning anti-Semitism by a vote of 1,000 to 300. The Archbishop confessed that "Christians had made many mistakes through the centuries including false imputations of guilt in the death of Christ."[1] Archbishop Lawrence J. Shehan expressed his hope that the Council would "condemn all expressions and attitudes which can justly be regarded as offensive."[2] Francis Cardinal Spellman of New York exclaimed, "It is simply absurd to maintain that there is some kind of continuing guilt which is transfered to any group of people and which rests upon them as a curse for which they must suffer."[3]

But in the meantime the Arab League Council meeting in Cairo decided that all its thirteen member nations ought be officially represented at the Holy See. Only five had maintained accredited diplomatic missions to the Vatican. This announcement prompted the Catholic magazine *America* to comment, "The sudden Arab interest in the Vatican does not proceed from any deeply spiritual motive. The Arabs are seeking closer relations

133

in order to spike what they consider a Zionist movement to enlist Catholic sympathy for Israel."[4]

Then two major events occurred that were once again to provoke anxiety and recrimination among Catholics and Jews. The first was Pope Paul's announcement on Pentecost Sunday that he was forming a new, special Vatican Secretariat for Non-Christians. It would have, he told the twenty Cardinals and five thousand seminarians in St. Peter's Basilica, a very different role but would be analogous in structure to the Secretariat for the Promotion of Christian Unity. The second was a rumor, from deep inside the Vatican, that the Curia had managed to win the Pope's approval for a revision and weakening of the Jewish statement.

NEW SECRETARIAT FOR NON-CHRISTIANS

In his Pentecostal announcement, the Pope indicated that the veteran sixty-nine-year-old diplomat Paolo Cardinal Marella, Archpriest of St. Peter's Basilica, was the designated head of the new Secretariat. He failed to mention, however, which non-Christians groups would come within Marella's concern and whether he would have responsibility for the statement on the Jews.

Some Jews would have welcomed such a move. They were uncomfortable within the theological structures of "Christian Unity" and denied any special relationship between Judaism and Christianity. In fact, they preferred that Jews be considered merely one among the other non-Christian religions. But many other Jews were convinced that the issue of Jewish-Christian relations belonged within the context of the Church's ecumenical concern because Judaism is not like other religions. Being Israel, we are not Gentiles. In addition, those who had some knowledge of personalities and positions in the Vatican had great confidence in Cardinal Bea as a liberal and grave reservations about Cardinal Marella, who was known to be a "Romanist" and a conservative. At the end of the second session of the Council, he was reported to have jokingly reassured his colleagues, "Have no fear, once the talk ceases and the bishops depart, we will change everything back the way it was."[5]

Vatican officials were caught by surprise at the establishment of Marella's Secretariat and speculation abounded. I was then in Rome and heard some Council officials suggest that the new Secretariat could play a "reconciling role" if both Moslems and Jews were included within its activities. But others contended that it would be difficult for a Secretariat to function if it tried to foster close relations with both the Jewish and Islamic faiths. The smoldering Arab-Israel tension and antagonism could well mar the Secretariat's work.

Finally, in an unsigned front-page story in *L'Osservatore Romano*, rumored to have been written by Cardinal Marella himself, it was explained that the new Secretariat would not be tied officially to the Vatican Council. This meant that the statement on the Jews—like any other matter that had been brought before the Council—would remain within the appropriate Conciliar jurisdiction. In the case of the statement on the Jews, this would be Cardinal Bea's Secretariat.

The article stressed the fact that the new Secretariat would seek "understanding" with other faiths and not their conversion. "Proselytising," it said, "should be left to mission work." Nevertheless, the article explained that the new Secretariat would have the duty of "exposing the Gospel to the eyes of all men and recalling the true notion of the good neighbor."[6] The establishment of this new Secretariat was the first hint that Pope Paul intended to have the Church open the way for a consideration of the truths espoused by adherents of many religions throughout the world.

RUMORS OF A WEAKENED JEWISH STATEMENT

As the reader will recall, Session Two, during its last days, had witnessed the presentation of a five-paragraph chapter on the Jews but no vote had been taken. Between sessions, therefore, Cardinal Bea and his Secretariat had put their hands to drafting another statement, fuller and stronger than the original.

Meeting in secret session between February 27–March 7, 1964, the Secretariat had agreed not to place the Jewish statement within the Schema on Ecumenism, "since strictly speaking, ecumenism deals only with the relations among Christians," but to keep it as an appendix to the Schema. In addition, the new appendix would be expanded to touch upon the relationship of Christians with non-Christian religions, including Islam.

But now there was a most disturbing rumor: The Secretariat had completed its draft and had submitted it to the Pope for review but had received no reply. Other theologians, conservative in orientation and closer to "political realities," were using the interval to draft a weaker version. According to this report, the new version would omit any reference to deicide and would include an expression of hope in an eventual Jewish union with the Church—a hope that could only be interpreted as a call to Jewish conversion. Amid all this confusion lurked the fear that there would be no statement on the Jews at all. At that very time Dr. Joseph Lichten, the Anti-Defamation League's expert on Catholic affairs, and Rabbi Marc Tanenbaum of the American Jewish Committee were invited to address the 54th Annual Convention of the Catholic Press Association in Pittsburgh, Pennsylvania. In an emotionally charged presentation both called on the editors of Catholic publications to let their "editorial voices be heard" in a vigorous protest "against the reported effort to abandon the Jewish Decree . . . or to empty it of meaning by removing the explicit condemnation of the false deicide charge."[7]

Msgr. John Oesterreicher, Catholic respondent at that session of the Catholic Press Association Convention, revealed that the Jewish statement definitely was to be removed from the Schema on Ecumenism and that it *might* be incorporated in a larger statement dealing with all other non-Christian religions. Agreeing that "apprehension and disappointment" were replacing the initial optimism, he expressed his own fear that there would be a "shortening of its message" and "a loss of substance."[8] The response of Catholic editors was immediate and, with but few exceptions, overwhelmingly sympathetic: "This generation which has seen the Nazi genocide should, by historic right, be the one to look into its own conscience and from this contemplation bring forth a thoroughly Christian answer to a problem too long left unattended," said the Boston *Pilot*."[9]

Father John Sheerin in his widely syndicated column declared, "This is an instance in which public opinion in the church ought to make itself felt. It is time for the official church to renounce forever the big lie on which anti-Semitism is based—the lie that the Jewish race is guilty of the murder of Christ. . . . Christendom has inflicted a terrible injustice on the Jews and the scales of justice must be righted."[10]

A contrasting response was made by Msgr. Paul H. Hallett in the *Denver Catholic Register:*

> The very vehemence with which Rabbi Tanenbaum pleaded for a decree of the Vatican Council absolving Jews from a crime no one said they committed [sic] testified to his keen awareness that Christ is not a dead historical character but the most living person in the world.
>
> There is only one explanation for this obsessional insistence on the part of a Jewish leader like Rabbi Tanenbaum for the removing of a teaching that does not exist. That explanation is a feeling lying either deep inside or near the surface of the Jewish mind that the Jewish nation which conveyed Christ to the world must accept him before they can find peace. . . . *The Jews must accept Christ before they will feel fulfillment.* No decrees of the Vatican Council can change that external fact.[11]

But such a regression was not typical. Not only did most Catholic spokesmen in this country express strong opposition to any watering-down of the Jewish statement, but so did many Protestant churchmen who had been delegate-observers to the Council. In a letter to the Pope, Robert McAfee Brown, representing the World Alliance of Reformed and Presbyterian Churches, joined John C. Bennett, President of Union Theological Seminary, in warning: "In view of the remarkable reception given to the original statement in the Jewish world last Fall, we are concerned that if this material [dealing with deicide] is removed, the rest of the world, particularly our Jewish brethren, will be able to draw only the unfortunate conclusion that the Council Fathers do in fact wish to stigmatize the Jews as a deicide race. The negative import of such an action on Jewish-Christian relations is incalculable."[12]

On May 30 the Pope received a delegation of leaders from the American Jewish Committee. He had an opportunity to allay Jewish anxiety. His remarks were friendly, but he said nothing specifically of the issue before the Council. "We are glad of the opportunity you offer us of confirming what is already well-known concerning the attitude of the Catholic Church and that in particular of the Holy See toward the Jews. . . . We again strongly deplore the horrible ordeals of which the Jews have been victims in recent years. We wish you every favor from God whom we invoke with all our hearts on your behalf, and that of all those who are near and dear to you." [13]

On June 11 Robert C. Doty of the *New York Times* wrote an article supporting the feared rumors. All reference to the issue of the Crucifixion had been deleted and the declaration was drastically watered down, he said. The decision to amend the text came from "the highest levels of the church and is based on a combination of political and theological considerations."

As a member of the Central Coordinating Commission and as one of the presidents of the Council, Cardinal Spellman was urged by Jewish leaders to act at once. In an intervention, dated June 13, 1964, the New York Cardinal protested changes in the Jewish statement. He warned, "It is desirable that the word deicide be reinstated." Cardinal Spellman added, "I hope that this reinsertion can be so submitted as to compensate for the adverse tendency of the published accounts of its suppression." [14]

Arab sources meanwhile also maintained their pressure on Rome. The Arab Evangelical Church Council endorsed a statement opposing attempts by "Christian heads in the West" to absolve Jews of the responsibility for the crucifixion of Christ. Given extensive publicity by the Arab radio network in the Middle East, the Arab Council expressed its "firm adherence to the clear teachings of the Gospels, as dictated by divine revelation, that the Jews are indeed guilty for the death of Christ." [15]

Reaction to all these reports in the Jewish community was mixed. The Anti-Defamation League and the American Jewish Committee, both of which had committed personnel to work with liberal Catholic officials, decided to intensify their program of consultations. Throughout the United States, South America, and Europe, Jewish delegations under the auspices of American

Jewish Committee and Anti-Defamation League staff paid visits to their local bishops, alerting them to the situation in Rome. Most prelates assured their Jewish callers that they would remain vigilant to achieve a strong statement. Anti-Defamation League and American Jewish Committee leaders were optimistic that the obvious majority inside the Vatican Council supporting the Jewish statement would ultimately prevail. On the other hand, leaders of Orthodox Judaism—now joined by some Reform officials—issued sharp attacks on the Council and renewed objections to any Jewish contact with the Vatican. Rabbi Bernard Rosenberg, writing in *Orthodox Life*, warned that the Church's only interest was to "induce" Jews over the threshold of the church.[16] Rabbi Leon Feuer, President of the (Reform) Central Conference of American Rabbis, argued that a Vatican statement concerning the Crucifixion was a Christian problem and that Jews need not press for its adoption. "An obsequious appeal for a statement by the Ecumenical Council can only be revolting to the Jewish spirit and an insult to the memory of Jewish martyrdom; such an act of atonement on the part of the church is long overdue and should need no special pleading on our part."[17]

POPE PAUL'S FIRST ENCYCLICAL

The mood of apprehension was not improved when, on August 10, 1964, Pope Paul issued the first encyclical of his thirteen-month-old pontificate, entitled *Ecclesiam Suam (His Church)*. This 15,000-word document set forth the Pope's views on the relation of the Catholic Church to the various "circles" of humanity surrounding it, including not only believers in God but even professed atheists.

The encyclical left many people bewildered and it received a mixed reaction. The language included courageous phrases of a progressive thrust and at the same time a cautious holding back. There were in it some assertions of doctrinal position that were sure to set obstacles on the path of any reconciliation between the Catholic Church and the non-Catholic world.

Archbishop Iakovos, voicing the disappointment of Orthodox Christians, charged that the Pope was "withdrawing the advance guard" and "reenforcing old positions." He termed Pope Paul's conception of conversation with other Christians "the monologue type of dialogue."[18] The *Christian Century* noted "dangerous ambivalences" and "disturbing moods." The editors heard the "creaking of closing windows" and "the silencing of dialogue."[19] Dr. W. A. Visser 't Hooft, World Council of Churches executive, complained, "According to the encyclical, dialogue is mainly in the form of communication of truth which the Roman Catholic Church holds whereas we understand dialogue, above all, as the process of sharing in which all receive and give and in which all are enriched and transformed."[20]

The most celebrated portions of the Pope's encyclical were his statements concerning world peace. The Catholic Church "shall be ready to intervene where an opportunity presents itself in order to assist the contending parties to find honorable and fraternal solutions for their disputes. . . . Wherever the Council of Nations come together to establish the rights and duties of man we are honored when they allow us to take our seat among them." Such sentiment was later to lead to the Pope's invitation to address the United Nations.

The Pope also indicated that the Catholic Church "recognizes and respects the moral and spiritual values of the various non-Christian religions, and we desire to join with them in promoting and defending common ideals of religious liberty, human brotherhood, good culture, social welfare and civil order. . . . We will not fail to take the initiative where our offer, in genuine mutual respect, would be well received." But then he added his belief that it was only in the Catholic Church that God "has revealed the perfect and definitive form [of religion], free from all error in which He wishes to be known, loved and served. Indeed, honesty compels us to declare openly our convictions that there is but one true religion, the religion of Christianity."

Projecting an evangelistic conception of dialogue, the Pope called upon the Church to strengthen its proclamation of that truth "which is both indisputable and *necessary* for salvation. The dialogue is, then, the method of accomplishing the apostolic mission. . . . Anything that makes known the teachings of which the Church is both custodian and dispenser receives approbation."

A reconciling note in this encyclical was the assertion that "the spirit of dialogue is friendship, and even more, is service.

. . . Before speaking it is necessary to listen not only to a man's voice but to his heart. . . . We must make ourselves their brothers." The Pope pledged that the salvation mission of the Church "will not be introduced with the armor of external force but simply through the legitimate means of human education and of interior persuasion . . . with full respect for personal and civic freedom." Dialogue, he added, "excludes a prior condemnation, the offensive and time worn polemic." By making us "discover elements of truth also in the opinions of others it will force us to express our teachings with greater fairness. . . . The dialogue will make us wise."[21]

Depending on which phrases of the encyclical they wished to stress, non-Catholics could emerge from a reading of the document either cheered by its advances or stunned by its seeming regressions. Clearly, without necessarily inhibiting a progress that would be constructive, Pope Paul intended to dampen any runaway exictement for reform that might have been engendered by Pope John's openness.

Jews recognized that Paul was not Pope John. But they remained uncertain as to exactly what difference that would make with regard to the Church's relation to the Jews. They did not have to wait long for their answer. On September 3, 1964, the *Herald Tribune* disclosed the text of the secret watered-down statement on the Jews.

CONTENT OF NEW JEWISH STATEMENT

The new statement refrained from absolving Jews *of the past* from a collective responsibility for the Crucifixion. It placed discussion of the relationship to the Jews within a context of hope for their eventual "entrance . . . into the fullness of the people of God established by Christ," a union awaited "with great desire." It avoided any mention of Christian involvement in past Jewish suffering. It failed to reassert Christian convictions concerning the reconciling significance of the Crucifixion. While it defined the Church as "the continuation of that people with which at one time God, in His ineffable mercy, desired to conclude the ancient pact . . . ," it dealt not at all with the contemporaneous significance of the Jewish people.

Although deficient or objectionable in all of these features, the statement did contain strong language both deploring and *condemning* hatred and persecution of the Jews. It repeated the earlier draft's call to Catholics not to present the Hebrew people *of present times* as an accursed people.

If some Jewish leaders had been dissatisfied with the earlier statement prepared for the second session of the Council, the version to be submitted now for discussion at the third session provoked a unanimous outcry. Morris B. Abram, President of the American Jewish Committee, explained, "Any declaration, no matter how well intended, whose effect would mean the dissolution of the Jewish people as such, and the elimination of Judaism as a religion, will be received with resentment by Jews throughout the world." [22] Dore Schary, National Chairman of the Anti-Defamation League, acknowledged the "good faith of the American Catholics in wishing the Church to be free of anti-Jewish sentiments as a quasi official document. . . . But it should be clearly understood that Jews will not pay the price of conversion." [23] Rabbi Abraham Heschel, interviewed by the *Herald Tribune* the very next day, recalled his past remonstrances with Vatican officials on this exact issue. He said, "As I have repeatedly stated to leading personalities of the Vatican, I am ready to go to Auschwitz any time, if faced with the alternative of conversion or death."

The Israeli press, that had heretofore been rather moderate and restrained in its references to the Council, now unleashed a full barrage of criticism. And Jewish leaders, involved in deliberations with the Council as well as the Church Fathers, received the full brunt. *Hamodia* (September 30, 1964), organ of the extreme Orthodox Agudath Israel Party, charged that the Catholic Church was examining its Jewish document "from a lofty platform as though the Jewish people sat before them accused at the bench, begging for a favorable opinion. There is no greater insult to the Jewish people. . . ." Attacking Jewish leaders involved in the Council, the Orthodox editors added, "They stand as beggars before the gates of Rome pleading for a crust of bread at the hands of persecutors . . . this groveling blemishes the whole of the Jewish nation." *Lamerhav* (September 13, 1964), publication of Israel's Achdut Avodah—left Socialist party—exclaimed, "No ecumenical spirit has created this new version. Odors of the Middle Ages rise from it. Jewish leaders . . . must divorce themselves from all dealings and all activities related to the Jewish document." The Independent, non-Party alligned *Haboker* (September 14, 1964), alone of Israeli papers, urged Jewish leaders to continue their "diplomatic activities." The paper expressed the hope that a vote on the Jewish statement might now be postponed until the fourth session of the Council so that the Church Fathers might by then be persuaded to adopt the original version.

American Catholic reaction was also critical of the new version. "The Council's work on the problem of anti-Semitism," said one diocesan editor, "is already a failure, and one that can never be wholly repaired."[24] "I doubt that so hearty a plant [as anti-Semitism] will be uprooted by the mincing words of the Council draft," warned Catholic columnist John Leo.[25]

America reported that some of the prelates in Rome viewed the press leak of the statement as "an unhappy pressure tactic."[26] It seems probable, indeed, that the leak was such a purposeful device on the part of an insider disturbed over the dilution of a statement on the Jews. By revealing the text of the statement, even before the Council session, he and his sympathizers forced the issue into open debate at a moment when expediency seemed to be winning out over principle behind closed doors in the interval between sessions. In fact, this is how the editors of *Commonweal* understood the situation. In a stirring editorial they explained, "If we are serious about erasing Christian anti-Semitism, we cannot settle for the mild form of lip service now before the Council. The needs for diplomacy and the political sensitivities of the Arab governments must not be granted the sort of weight that bring a parliamentary compromise. In one sense the history of Christian anti-Semitism is a history of expediency winning over principle. Even now when anti-Semitism itself is being confronted, the danger is that expediency will win out again."[27]

Thus alerted to the resistance they were to meet, American prelates entered the third session of the Council ready to do vigorous battle. The liberals were determined to take charge and fireworks were anticipated in Rome.

10. A Vote at Last

By VARIOUS SYMBOLIC ACTS at the opening of the third session in mid-September Pope Paul sought to allay the doubts of liberals in the Church. Upon entering St. Peter's, for example, he descended from his throne to join twenty-four prelates at the altar and concelebrate the Mass with them. Thus he acknowledged his regard for collegiality even before the concept had come up for a vote.

In his opening address the Pope called upon the Council "to describe" and "honor" the prerogatives of the episcopate.[1] He seemed to be giving a "go" signal to those who were ready to press for the speedy approval of the Schema on the Church. Similarly, he recognized the Protestant and Orthodox auditors present as members of Churches "that are so far and yet so close to us." He dedicated the Catholic Church to strive "to understand better all that is genuine and admissible in the different Christian denominations that are distant from us." Thus he appeared to be encouraging those prelates who were ready to adopt the Schema on Ecumenism.

The Pope was later to warn his hierarchy and theologians against "a temptation that sometimes works its way into good souls"—namely, a desire "to hide, weaken, change, deny if need be those teachings of the Catholic Church which are not acceptable today by the separated brethren."[2] In this his opening address he stressed the importance of the centralized authority of the papacy and made it clear this was not one of the issues up for dialogue or discussion.

Enheartened, nevertheless, by the Pope's obvious gesture of sympathy for their progressive intentions, the Council Fathers entered immediately into debate. The first schema to be considered was that on the Church. Votes were taken separately on each chapter, and the liberals won by margins even larger than they‹ had expected.

PROGRESS DURING THE FIRST TWO WEEKS

Council work moved swiftly. Within the first week it was announced that debate would be scheduled on religious liberty and the statement on the Jews. Votes had already been taken on the crucial sections of the Schema on the Church. By the second week debate had been scheduled for schemata dealing with revelation and the apostolate of the laity, and votes were scheduled for the Schema on Ecumenism. The Catholic columnist John Cogley reported with obvious satisfaction, "The conservatives . . . have been chastened and are in a mood for a compromise on many positions which were once unthinkable to them. . . . There is less anxiety all around."[3]

Rabbi Abraham Heschel in New York, however, was still anxious over the fate of the weakened statement on the Jews. He decided to accept another invitation to visit Rome. Arab pressure on the Pope had been insistent and continuous. As late as September 3, Patriarch Maximos IV Saigh of Antioch had requested the Pope on behalf of the bishops of his patriarchate to withdraw the Jewish declaration. At the end of September the Syrian Prime Minister called a meeting of bishops in union with Rome and urged their continuous action in that regard.[4] Rabbi Heschel had every reason to be concerned.

A friend of Cardinal Bea's and a distinguished scholar, Rabbi Heschel carried with him into an unprecedented audience with the Pope on the opening day of the Council the authentic credentials of American Jewish religious leadership. Details for the meeting had been arranged through The American Jewish Committee and Rabbi Heschel was accompanied in the audience by Zachariah Shuster, A.J.C.'s European director. The two men left satisfied that the statement on the Jews could be strengthened

and repaired by Conciliar action and that the Pope would at least
not oppose such an effort. It remained then for liberal Council
Fathers to reject a weakened statement, to replace it with a
stronger one, and to delete any reference that could be interpreted
as missionary. Heschel had good cause to believe that American
bishops would take the initiative in this progressive move.

Some in the Jewish community criticized Heschel's "solo
diplomacy." They interpreted it as a form of pleading, unbecom-
ing to Jewish dignity. It was no such thing. Rabbi Heschel had
come at the request of Catholic dignitaries and particularly
Richard Cardinal Cushing. His purpose was to offset misconceptions with regard to Jewish attitudes toward the Council. Conservative prelates had used public Orthodox Jewish expressions
of disinterest as an argument against a strong Jewish statement.
"The Jews really aren't concerned one way or the other," they
contended. "Why offend the Arabs when the Jews don't give a
hang anyway?" Rabbi Heschel verified for the Pope the Jews'
profound expectation that the Church would do justice, in this
case, to their own noblest Christian heritage.

Dr. Joseph Lichten, staff member of the Anti-Defamation
League, had already been in Rome for several weeks consulting
with Catholic prelates from every continent and sharing with
them his concern that a Council statement on the Jews that failed
to deal specifically with the charge of deicide would be a blunder.
Dr. Lichten carried with him the then unpublished findings of an
exhaustive survey conducted for the Anti-Defamation League by
the Survey Research Center at the University of California.

Under the direction of the Lutheran sociologist Dr. Charles Y.
Glock, the Research Center sought to discover whether "modern
Christians still typically blame the historical Jew for the crucifixion
and hold the Jew guilty for the crimes of his ancestors." The survey
also tried to ascertain whether such negative religious conceptions
predisposed the Christian to accept secular anti-Semitic stereotypes
of the Jews. The preliminary findings revealed that 61 per cent
of the Catholics surveyed named Jews as "the group most
responsible for crucifying Christ." Forty-six per cent agreed with
or were uncertain about the statement that "the Jews can never
be forgiven for what they did to Jesus until they accept him as
the true Savior." Close to a third of American Catholics also

maintained hostile stereotypes of the Jews, such as: The Jews dominate international banking; they cheat in business; they are likely to be less loyal to their country.[5]

Summarizing the findings, Dr. Lichten reported, "Perhaps as many as 5,000,000 American Catholics, out of a total of 44,874,-371, see the Jews as principally responsible for the death of Jesus, and they are led thereby to a negative assessment of the contemporary Jew. The fact that those who believe and feel this way tend to go to church more frequently, underscores the need for the Catholic Church to intensify its efforts, if it hopes to win all Catholics to the principles of brotherhood, which it espouses."[6]

So troubled were Catholic leaders by this startling revelation of "Christian" anti-Semitism that the Dutch Documentation Center for the Council volunteered to publish the findings and distribute it to every Council Father since the debate on the Jewish statement was shortly to commence. Therefore, on September 17, the findings were placed in the mailbox of each Church prelate with a note by the Center director expressing his hope that the document would "serve the Council, the Church and the love between Jews and Christians."

DEBATE ON RELIGIOUS LIBERTY

A prior order of business, however, was the debate on the important statement on religious liberty. It began on September 23 with an introduction by Bishop deSmedt, who recalled that the statement had been presented but not debated at the last session of the Council. In the intervening months the Secretariat had worked diligently, reviewing more than 380 amendments. The statement, he believed, was now improved and strengthened. Bishop deSmedt once again argued the case for religious freedom.

The counterattack was immediate. Cardinal Ruffini explained that the Catholic Church is the one and only Church and therefore should be supported by the state. Those in error have no claims on the state, he said: "Only truth has rights and truth is one."[7] It is simply for prudential reasons, and not as a matter of principle, that the state eschews force in compelling anyone to profess a religion. Cardinal Ottaviani, too, joined in arguing for the right of the state to intervene in religious matters in support of Catholic truth. "Those professing revealed religion," he said, "have rights over and above those deriving from the natural law. . . . It is not true that the state is incompetent to choose a religion. If this were so we would have to suppress all the concordats made by the Holy See with national governments."[8]

The response that followed was impassioned. Bishop Cekada of Yugoslavia warned that to allow the state to intervene in religious affairs would be to grant it freedom to suppress religion, as in the Communist world. The Church hierarchy had to make it clear that freedom of conscience was a universal and absolute principle. Several African bishops similarly cited their minority status in most countries as reason enough for a statement supporting religious freedom. Bishop Columbo of Milan, the Pope's special consultant on theological matters, warned that a statement on liberty was the necessary precondition for Catholic participation in dialogue with men of good will.

Several American prelates joined the debate—Cardinals Albert Meyer of Chicago and Joseph Ritter of St. Louis, Archbishop Alter of Cincinnati, and Bishop John Wright of Pittsburgh. Richard Cardinal Cushing of Boston rose to deliver, on this subject, his first address to the Council. "The Church must become the champion of religious freedom," he cried out. "We must insist on this declaration because it is so important for all nations. . . . It is something the Catholic world and the non-Catholic world have been waiting for."[9]

DEBATE ON THE JEWISH STATEMENT

Immediately following the debate on religious liberty, but before a vote was taken, Cardinal Bea introduced the Jewish statement (see Appendix B). It is "absolutely impossible," he pleaded, "to do what some of the fathers have asked, namely to remove the question completely from the agenda." Then at great length he once again dealt with the historical and theological factors involved in the alleged Jewish culpability for the Crucifixion. It was clear that he was dissatisfied with the changes made in the text between Sessions Two and Three by officials of the Coordinating Commission. His presentation, in effect, was an invitation to the Council to offer amendments that would allow the Secretariat to revise the text and strengthen it.

Cardinal Bea questioned whether even the leaders of the Jewish Sanhedrin, the ruling Jewish body in the days of Jesus, were aware of the identity of Jesus when they approved the Crucifixion, and therefore whether even that group could be accused of "deicide." "Certainly the words from the Cross, 'Father forgive them, for they know not what they do,' supported the view that they did not knowingly execute the Son of God," Cardinal Bea reasoned.

The aged German Bible scholar and friend of Pope John acknowledged, as the University of California studies had demonstrated, that blame for the death of Jesus had caused the Jews to be despised and persecuted. Nevertheless, he rejected as false any idea that the deicide charge against the Jews was the "principal basis of anti-Semitism." Hatred of the Jews, he maintained, has many other sources of a political-national, psychological, social, and economic nature.

Cardinal Bea also told the Council that his Secretariat had had nothing to do with the omission from the text of its original passages dealing with the charges against the Jews as a "deicide people." Without explaining how or under what circumstances the changes had been made, Bea assured the Council that "this was accomplished without the Secretariat's cooperation."[10]

American bishops had caucused on September 16 at the Pontifical North American College and pledged themselves to united action in order to strengthen the statement on the Jews. Present at the meeting were one hundred seventy out of the two hundred forty American prelates in Rome. They agreed to restore to the statement an unequivocal declaration that the Jews "even in the times of Christ," as well as those who live today, "could not be held responsible for the Crucifixion." They also decided to seek restoration of the language that the "Jews are not a deicide nation." At least six bishops volunteered to prepare to speak up in the general debate.[11]

At the American bishops' press conference on the afternoon of Cardinal Bea's presentation Father Thomas Stransky, C.S.P., an officer in Bea's Secretariat, revealed that Amleto Cardinal

Cicognani's Coordinating Commission, not the Secretariat for the Promotion of Christian Unity, had been responsible for releasing the weaker Jewish statement. Father Stransky urged on the Americans his conviction that "the renovation of the Church" was of such supreme importance that "the Church must be ready to expose itself even to the accusations of pursuing political ends in its declaration on the Jews."[12]

In contrast, Msgr. John Oesterreicher at that same press conference spoke "in defense of the new version." He told the press panel, "It meets many of the concerns of Jews today. If the original had not been revealed to the press then the present version would have been quite satisfactory to many." He then attacked the "many wrong conclusions and mis-statements that had been made concerning the missionary intent of the statement." The Latin word *adunatio* ("drawing together"), he pointed out, is "a supple and tender one," implying "an eschatological hope for the final union of all people in the people of God, and is an exact counterpart of the Jewish hope for the same union envisioned by the prophets."[13]

Stating it bluntly, Oesterreicher said, "both Christians and Jews believe in a final oneness, for the Christian a Christian oneness, for the Jew a Judaic one."[14] In this assertion Oesterreicher blurred a significant theological distinction: A Christian oneness requires that all men accept Jesus as the Christ, whereas a Jewish oneness does not oblige all men to become Jews. Many Jews were disappointed that Oesterreicher had failed to understand or sympathize with their unhappiness over the statement's implication that Jews would achieve the fullness of their destiny only when they became Christians. Fortunately, not many of the American bishops were ready to follow Msgr. Oesterreicher's defense of the weaker version; Archbishop O'Boyle particularly would later call for a deletion of the objectionable phrases regarding conversion, and all of them urged a stronger attack on anti-Semitism.

SMOOTH SAILING

Following Bea's presentation, the liberals were surprised and gratified to find that the Jewish statement encountered but a

minimal resistance in the debate. Only a few token speeches in
opposition were delivered by the conservative Cardinal Ruffini
and by two representatives of the Arab world, Cardinal Tappouni
and Archbishop Tawil. All other speeches, including masterful
declarations by such leading personalities in world Catholicism as
Cardinals Lienart, Frings, Lercaro, Leger, and Koenig, supported
the Jewish statement and urged its strengthening.

Ernesto Cardinal Ruffini of Palermo, Sicily, defended the aban-
donment of the term "deicide" since "no one can kill God." He
also urged that the Jews be exhorted to love Christians and he
called for the removal of anti-Christian passages from the Talmud,
in which, he charged, Christians are held in contempt and despised
as animals. Finally he charged "Jewish masonry" with being
responsible for the anti-clericalism in Europe.[15]

Ruffini's arguments went far beyond a conservative theological
defense of a literal interpretation of the Gospels. His talk was
an outright attack on the Jews and Judaism, as hostile as it was
uninformed: There are, for example, no anti-Christian passages
in the Talmud. At one time some passages of a veiled derogatory
nature could have been interpreted as referring to Jews who had
become Christians, but these passages were excised from the
Talmud centuries ago by Church authorities operating under the
guidance of Jewish converts. Church authorities did not rest even
after such violence had been perpetrated on the freedom of
Jewish conscience; they rounded up thousands of Rabbinic and
Talmudic texts and cast them into the fire. The whole sad story
of Church suppression of the Talmud is precisely one of those
thoroughly documented Church-sponsored sins against Jews for
which Christians ought to feel remorse.[16] Ruffini was doing no
more than parroting a stock canard in the anti-Semite's wares.

During this period of debate two more anti-Semitic pamphlets
were distributed to all the bishops. One, entitled "According to
Jesus, the Jews Are Deicides," was written by one "Father Marcel
Mauclair," alleged to be a priest. The thirty-page document
charged that the Jewish statement was written by Msgr. John
Oesterreicher and Father Baumunder (sic) sponsored by
"the foremost Judeo-Masonic organization, the omnipotent B'nai
B'rith." Quoting liberally from the New Testament the pamphlet
sought to demonstrate that the Catholic Church would "destroy

its prestige" by issuing a statement on the Jews "contradictory to the word of Jesus." The second pamphlet, suggesting that two of its authors were Council Fathers, neglected to supply their names. Twenty-two pages in length, it was entitled "Jewish-Masonic Action in the Council." It repeated the outlandish canard that Cardinal Bea himself was the son of a rabbi and the agent of a Jewish plot to overthrow the Church. Its reference to a Jewish Masonic conspiracy seemed to provide factual support for the charge already uttered by Cardinal Ruffini.

There then followed two presentations by prelates representing Arab concerns. Speaking for himself and five other Middle East Patriarchs, Ignace Gabriel Cardinal Tappouni, Patriarch of Antioch, offiered his "solemn opposition to the document on the grounds that *any* Council statement on the Jews would open the Church to the charge of having "political tendencies."[17] In addition, the Middle East prelate warned that the Council might be considered "pro-Jewish," and "this does us much harm." The Melchite Patriarchal Vicar Joseph Tawil of Damascus, Syria, also called for the rejection of the document since "the benevolence it shows to the Jews might alienate many Arabs expelled from Palestine."[18]

As an article by Rev. Gregory Baum explained, such strong Eastern opposition to the Jewish statement was not "simply due to Arab pressure"; but "we must admit that anti-Jewish sentiment is ancient and deep in the life of the Church. In particular, certain Eastern liturgies perpetrate the deicide myth and pronounce dreadful curses on the Jews. Some of the Eastern Bishops have declared that if their faithful were suddenly told that the Jews were not guilty of deicide, and not an accursed people, they might falter in their faith, feeling that the teaching of their liturgy is no longer to be trusted."[19]

With these presentations the opposition had stated its case. Now came the defense of a Jewish statement. Cardinal Cushing was the first of the American hierarchy to speak. He cried out, "Our respect for the Jews and our love for the sons of Abraham must be made clear. . . . The Jewish people cannot be accused of deicide." Then, referring to "crimes committed in our own times," he called upon the Church Fathers "to confess humbly before the world, that Christians too frequently have not shown themselves to be true Christians . . . in their relations with their Jewish brothers. How many have died because of the indifference of Christians, because of silence!"[20] The Boston prelate concluded, "If not many Christian voices were lifted in recent years against the great injustices, yet let our voices humbly cry out now!"

In the course of the debate many ranking Fathers re-echoed this note of confession and contrition. One of the most far-reaching speeches was that of Bishop Leon Elchinger of Strasbourg. "We cannot deny," he declared, "that not only in this century but in past centuries as well, sons of the Church—not infrequently in the name of the Church—committed crimes against the Jews. Certain facts of the inquisition should not be denied either, nor the fact that in our own days mistakes were being made in sermons and catechetics which clashed with the spirit of the New Testament. Why should we not find in the spirit of the Gospel the courage to ask forgiveness in the name of so many Christians for so many serious injustices?"[21]

Albert Cardinal Meyer of Chicago in a similar spirit exclaimed, "Justice demands that we give explicit attention to the enormous impact of the wrongs done through the centuries to the Jews. The particular afflictions which the Jewish people have undergone make it imperative that we add a special condemnation of every form of anti-Semitism, as was done in the earlier text. . . ."[22]

Cardinal Ritter of St. Louis objected to the apparent missionary phraseology of the weakened text. Referring to passages that hoped for a "gathering together" of the Jews and the Church, Ritter pointed that these words sounded as though the Church aspired to converting the Jews. He noted that the text did not speak to Moslems and pagans in the same evangelical tone. But then he urged that the call for conversion be placed at the end of the declaration, a suggestion disappointing to Jews who believed that any reference to conversion was ill suited to a statement of ecumenical significance.[23] Archbishop John Heenan of Westminster, England, agreed with the Jewish objections: "The question of conversion whether of individuals or of whole communities has no place in the context of ecumenism. The object of ecumenism is not the conversion of either non-Catholics or of non-

Christians. Ecumenism sets out to break down barriers between religious denominations in order that each may come to know and better understand the other. Ecumenism is an essay not in polemics, but in charity. Its intention is not for one side to score a victory, but for each side to emerge with a deeper understanding of the other." [24]

On the second day of the debate Bishop Stephen A. Leven of San Antonio, Texas, speaking in the name of almost all United States bishops, launched a strong appeal for the insertion of a clear statement that the Jews should never be called deicides or killers of God. "The Fathers must make sure that the term God-killer is never again used against the Jews. Any silence on this would be an offense against justice." He called for two textual changes: A clear repudiation of the charge of deicide and a return to the earlier text. "The word deicide," Bishop Leven pointed out, was, after all, "a word of infamy and execration invented by Christians and used to blame and persecute the Jews. For so many centuries, and even in our own times, Christians have hurled this word against Jews and because of it, they have justified every kind of horrible excess and even their slaughter and destruction. It is not up to us to make a declaration about something philosophical, but to reprobate and damn a word which has furnished so many occasions of persecution through the centuries." [25] Then adding another word "in his own name," the Texas prelate insisted that the Council include "an expression of our eschatological hope that all men of every race and people, Jews and Gentiles, will be gathered together with God . . . in the universal Church." [26]

Archbishop O'Boyle of Washington, D.C., demurred. He rose to insist that the statement be "ecumenical"—that is it must be "intelligible to the Jews." Therefore, he explained, "any reference to an ultimate joining together of Jews and Christians must be omitted. For it brings to the minds of Jews the memories of past persecutions, forced conversions, and forced rejections of their faith." [27] Thus, "When a Jew hears of the desires of Catholics for his conversion, he thinks of the renewal of the 'proselytism' which for many centuries violated his rights and personal dignity. . . . When we express our hope in words which lead the Jews to interpret them as a definite and clear intention for their con-

version, we construct another high wall separating us from a holy
and fruitful dialogue with the Jewish people."[28]

There seemed to be no doubt in anyone's mind that the statement on the Jews had been well presented and amply defended.
It was confidently anticipated now that within a few weeks Cardinal Bea would resubmit for preliminary voting a statement much
strengthened in its attack on anti-Semitism. Undoubtedly the
reference to "deicide" would be reinstated. But it was still not
clear how the Church would handle the question of its hopes
for Jewish conversion.

Arab protests, directed and coordinated by the Egyptian ambassador in Rome, were intensified. Arab newspapers warned that
the matter of the Jewish declaration would be raised at the
Conference of Non-Aligned Nations then meeting in Cairo. The
Syrian government and Christian members of Jordan's parliament
publicly protested the passage of such a declaration.

Patriarch Kyrillos VI of Alexandria called for an Orthodox
"summit conference" to oppose the Council's action. "No Ecumenical Council, whatever its level," he said, "can change the
text of the Holy Bible. The New Testament convicted the Jews
and their children of Christ's crucifixion and to absolve them
of that crime would be an open refutation of the Bible. If the
Jews are so eager to rid themselves of the charge of Christ's
crucifixion, let them declare their belief in Christ."[29]

The Arab League instructed its ambassadors in many countries to make plain to Catholic authorities the "political significance of any Council action." The ambassadors were instructed
to seek contacts with cardinals and bishops and then report
back on the results of their conversations.[30]

World Jewish leaders, in contrast, decided that they would not
now be drawn into a campaign of counterpressure. The Jewish
statement seemed to be in good hands within the Council. In an
unprecedented display of international Jewish harmony the leaders
of every major Jewish organization, religious and secular, in
the United States, England, France, Australia, South Africa, and
Argentina issued a declaration directed to the entire Jewish community. "It would be improper for the Jewish community which
is not a part of the church or its ecumenical movement to offer
suggestions concerning religious doctrine" to the Vatican.[31]

The debate had moved so smoothly that a wave of optimism swept over the Council. It was expected that forthright statements on religious liberty and on the Jews would be voted on in this session. But unbeknown to most Council Fathers a movement was afoot within the Coordinating Commission to remove both statements from the sole jurisdiction of Cardinal Bea's Secretariat.

Efforts to Destroy the Jewish Statement

About October 8–9 Cardinal Bea received instructions—allegedly from the Pope but in reality from Cardinal Cicognani—to send the religious liberty statement to a new special Mixed Commission (among whose members were known enemies of the statement) in order for it to be reconsidered and reformulated. It was also rumored that Cardinal Bea had been directed to submit the Jewish statement to Cardinal Ottaviani's Theological Commission for incorporation—in what would obviously be a truncated form—in the Schema on the Church.

Cardinal Bea was outraged. Ascertaining immediately that the instructions had not been sent directly by the Pope but were a ploy by the conservatives, Bea rallied the support of seventeen leading Council prelates, including Cardinals Albert Meyer of Chicago and Joseph Ritter of St. Louis. They addressed a sharp letter to the Pope beginning with the new historic phrase *Magno cum dolore,* "With great sorrow." The cardinals deplored the apparent violation of Council rules by this maneuver. The seventeen prelates warned that if the effort to change jurisdiction in violation of the Council's rules were to become "public knowledge," it would be "extremely prejudicial to the whole Church in the light of world opinion."[32] Cardinals Cushing and Spellman also intervened with the Pope on this issue.

On October 16 the Pope ordered Cardinal Cicognani to write Cardinal Bea suggesting that the religious liberty statement be submitted to a Mixed Commission "according to Council rules." Under the rules, the Mixed Commission would have power to make *advisory* proposals only to Cardinal Bea's Secretariat—not "reformulation." A Mixed Commission had no power, in itself, to rework the document.

No word was heard on the rumors concerning the Jewish statement, however, until a rule-breaking disclosure was made by
Gaston Cruzat, Director of the Latin American Information
Center for the Council, for which disclosure he was later censured.
According to Cruzat, the Pope had assured the seventeen liberal
prelates that the main assertion of the Jewish statement—notably
an examination of Jewish responsibility for the Crucifixion—
would remain intact even if the statement were made part of the
Schema on the Church instead of standing as a separate text or
appended to the Schema on Ecumenism.[33] It was apparent that
the Pope had not yet determined his own preference on how the
Jewish statement should be handled. The options were many:
The statement could be included within the Schema on Ecumenism
as originally intended. It could be presented as a resolution on its
own merits. It might be attached to a new statement defining
Catholic attitudes toward all non-Catholic religions. In shortened
form the theological aspects of the statement could be mentioned
in the Schema on the Church. Or the purely social dimension of
the problem of anti-Semitism could be confronted in the all-
embracing Schema on the Church in the Modern World. Obviously, then, even at this date there was no final or fixed text,
since the exact wording of the statement would have to depend
on the context of the schema in which it would be placed.

SCHEMA ON THE CHURCH IN THE MODERN WORLD

On October 20 the Council turned to a discussion of the
Schema on the Church in the Modern World. Within this schema
the Council planned to offer its opinions regarding economic and
political matters, social justice, race relations, war and peace,
overpopulation, and birth control. In his introductory report,
Bishop Guano exhorted, "The Church cannot remain closed up
within herself as in a fortress, intent only on defending her own
interests and members. The Church recognizes that she is living
in the world sharing the life of men in order to give them the
life of God, existing among men and for men."[34]
Despite some criticism of the language and several omissions,
Protestant observers and Jewish commentators noted with satis-

faction that the document resolutely assured all men of "the sincere intention" of the Church "to cooperate in the building of a truly fraternal city." Christians "practice in the world the love of God," it asserted, "by alleviating the living conditions and suffering of their brethren. . . . Nor can there be true peace which is the fruit of charity and justice, truth and liberty, so long as many men are deprived of due liberty, or others are suffering from hunger or some other disability because of an inadequate distribution of the goods of the earth."[35]

Race relations, just political and economic organization, the maldistribution of the world's physical resources, the primary significance of conjugal love as distinguished from the functional purpose of procreation, the consolidation of peace, and the rights of conscientious objectors—all these were among the many important and official issues debated on the Council floor. A new day seemed to be dawning in the openness with which such issues were discussed, setting an example of relevance and freedom for all religious groups to admire and emulate. On Monday, November 9, when the debate came to a close, many felt reasonably assured that, while the Council might not yet have answers for the world's most pressing problems, it had at least responsibly asked the right questions.

For the next several days the Council discussed the schemata on missionary activity and on the adaptation and renewal of the religious life; it considered the declaration on Christian education and the problems involved in mixed marriage.

As exciting as these discussions were, the fact remained that debate was eating away at the calendar. The Council session was now in its final week. The Fathers still had to consider amendments to the Schema on the Church, including the controversial matter of collegiality, and to vote upon it for the last time. They had to consider amendments to the Schema on Ecumenism and to vote upon it for the last time. They had to discuss the revised declaration on non-Christians and a statement on religious liberty

THIRD SESSION BOGS DOWN IN FINAL WEEK

On November 17 the Council at last gave full attention to the complex issue of collegiality. By an overwhelming vote the Church

Fathers affirmed the right of bishops by the "act of consecration" to share with the Pope in the ruling of the Church. This action was hedged, however, by a significant intervention. In an effort to pacify the conservatives and to win their approval for the revolutionary insistence on collegial power, the Pope suggested that an "explanatory note" be introduced into the deliberations. The note made it absolutely clear that the bishops could exercise their power only "according to norms approved by the Supreme Authority." Furthermore, the authority of the Episcopal College could be exercised only *with* the Pope and never without him. Nor did the Pope's position as head of the College preclude his acting alone.

On Tuesday of that last week the revised text of a declaration on religious liberty was at last distributed to the Fathers, to be voted on first in its individual parts and then, on Thursday, as a whole. On Wednesday a new version of the declaration on the Jews and non-Christians was distributed, with a final voting sched uled for Friday, the last day of the session. It was now entitled Declaration on The Relationship of The Church to Non-Christian Religions. It was no longer an appendix to the Schema on Ecumenism but was to be considered on its own merits as an independent Declaration. Votes were intended to register the will of the Church Fathers on the documents "in principle." Council rules permitted thereafter only slight changes in the text within the spirit of the document as approved. In the next session the Fathers would vote again conclusively, and the Pope would promulgate the final text. A favorable vote in the third session would effectively block any possible maneuver behind the scenes between sessions to abandon these statements or empty them of their content.

On Wednesday Archbishop Felici announced that two hundred prelates had petitioned that the voting on the statement on religious liberty be held off since the document now before the Council Fathers had been so substantially amended and revised, since its first appearance, that it was "a new document." According to Council rules, a new document required debates and discussion once more before voting could take place. Complying with this argument, Cardinal Tisserant, on what has become known as "Black Thursday," announced that after Bishop deSmedt's introduction of the religious liberty statement there would be *no vote*. The Fathers would then be able to examine the "new" document at their leisure and send in their observations to the Secretariat by January 31, 1965.

Consternation gripped the Council hall. The bishops could hardly believe their ears. Within a few hours a petition was circulated eventually signed by more than a thousand bishops calling upon the Pope, "with reverence but urgently, very urgently, most urgently," to permit a vote before the end of the session of the Council, "lest the confidence of the world, both Christian and non-Christian, be lost."

When Bishop deSmedt finished his presentation the Council Fathers acted out their sentiment. Violating procedural rules they clapped vigorously. The applause was loud and sustained. It became rhythmic at points and evidenced a protest against any effort to inhibit it or cut it off. The bishops were demonstrating.

The Pope responded to the liberal delegation who had rushed to his chambers by saying that he could not interfere with the Council's procedures. He promised—a promise that he repeated twice—that the statement on religious liberty would be the first order of business at the next session of the Council.

That afternoon two American cardinals in audience with the Pope intimated that if a similar attempt were made to put off a vote on the Jewish declaration they would absent themselves from the closing session as a public protest.[36] Had it not been for the protest mounted by the Council over the mishandling of the religious liberty statement, a similar tactic might have been utilized to put off the Jewish statement.

LAST-MINUTE CHANGES IN THE SCHEMA ON ECUMENISM

The anger of many of the liberals over the fact that the Pope had refused to intervene against a maneuver that obviously ran counter to majority sentiment in the instance of religious liberty was exacerbated when they learned that he had also personally suggested forty changes in the text of the Schema on Ecumenism. Cardinal Bea and his Secretariat felt obliged, with the approval of the Pope, to accept nineteen of these revisions. So late in the hour had the changes been made that they were presented to the Council Fathers orally and circulated in mimeographed form.

Most of the nineteen amendments were not of momentous theological significance, although they tended to cool the warmth of the document, particularly in its relation to Protestants. The point is, however, that there was no time for the Council Fathers to discuss the changes. They had either to accept them or to abandon the Schema on Ecumenism.

One of the amendments in wording most irksome to the Protestant observers was the deletion of the original statement that the "separated brethren *find* God in Jesus Christ through the guidance of the Holy Spirit in Scripture," and the substitution of the statement that the separated brethren *"seek God."* "The difference between 'finding' and 'seeking,' " said Protestant theologian Robert McAfee Brown, "is a pretty monumental difference and the new wording . . . jeopardizes many of the gains in ecumenical understanding that have been made in recent years."[37] Another Protestant observer, commenting on the Pope's arbitrary exercise of authority, exclaimed, "We have seen the naked face of what we have always feared in Rome."[38]

On Friday, the last business day of the third session, the Council Fathers in a final vote approved the amended Schema on Ecumenism. Then they voted on the declaration on the Jews.

VOTE ON THE JEWISH STATEMENT

By overwhelming majority, 1,651 yes, 242 yes with reservation, and 99 no, Cardinal Bea's much strengthened draft of a statement on the Jews (see Appendix C), as part of a separate "Declaration on the Relationship of the Church to Non-Christian Religions," was accepted. It provided the basis for a final schema to be presented at the very next session. The statement had dropped the reference to the conversion of the Jews. It both deplored and condemned anti-Semitism. It contained a specific warning against considering the Jews both of former days and of the present time as a people guilty of deicide. It marked a decisive liberal victory over the conservative effort to change the statement.

The response of the Jewish community was generally favorable, although some, recognizing that the vote was still only preliminary, restrained their enthusiasm. Zachariah Shuster, European Director of the American Jewish Committee, for example, remarked, "The Catholic Church is taking a new direction . . . ," whereas the Chief Rabbi of Rome, Elio Toaff, said, "We shall see what effect the requests for amendment will have on the final text." [39]

In Tel Aviv Dr. Isser Unterman, the Ashkenazi Chief Rabbi of Israel, "warmly welcomed" the statement. He stressed, however, that the document ought also express "remorse for past wrongs against Jews," and he articulated the hope that the Church would ultimately "view sympathetically the growth of the Israel State as an historical event, which in our firm belief is a fulfillment of the divine promise mentioned in Holy Writ." [40]

The reaction in the Arab world was predictably hostile. Foreign Minister Kadri Toukan of Jordan charged that the Roman Catholic document would encourage Israel to "continue its aggressive policy." [41] In Jordan ten Christian members of Parliament denounced the statement in a message to Pope Paul VI. They said the Council's vote was "tantamount to a stab in the heart of Christianity" and would "cause a rift in the Catholic Church and prevent unity with other Christian Churches." Catholic prelates representing Melchite, Armenian, Chaldean, Maronite, Syrian, and Latin rites sought to purchase advertising space in the Jordan newspapers in order to explain and defend for Eastern Christians the true significance of the statement. Their full statement was not accepted for publication. The Jordan papers forced the deletion of two critical paragraphs, one of them denying that the statement was guided by political motivation and the other deploring the campaign against the Vatican Council by the press and charging that the press "sowed confusion and the spirit of false information." [42]

In an effort to placate the Arabs Pope Paul arranged to meet with the President and Premier of Lebanon. President Charles Helou of Lebanon, the only Christian Arab head of state, had been a former Ambassador to the Vatican and was officially charged by the Arab League with responsibility for making a diplomatic protest. *L'Osservatore Romano,* the Vatican newspaper, also carried a front-page editorial over the signature of Cardinal Bea restating the purely religious significance of the declaration and rejecting "arbitrary and twisted" interpretations that read "political intention and aims into it."[43]

The Council session concluded on Saturday with an official promulgation of the Constitution on the Church, the Decree on Oriental Churches, and the Schema on Ecumenism. During that historic session the Church Fathers also approved a text on non-Christians and engaged in significant discussion of a wide variety of Church problems as well as the role of the Church in dealing with the world's major social problems. Finally, the Council had been assured that religious liberty would be the first issue for discussion at the next session. This was indeed a fruitful session. The promulgated documents evidenced a continued openness within the Church toward men of good will. But the power of the conservatives to delay progress, their ability to manipulate and maneuver, and to control the administrative machinery of the Church remained strong.

A haunting uncertainty touched the hearts of many friends of the Catholic Church. Obviously the majority spoke the voice of the Church but the minority wielded much power. How would the Pope deal with this impasse? What administrative regulations would he encourage that would give all men a reasonable assurance that the Catholic Church meant to live up to the promises of its promulgated declarations? In a word, the consequences of the display of Curial power on the religious liberty issue, as well as the Pope's arbitrary exercise of authority in revising the Schema on Ecumenism, planted a doubt that the Catholic Church was capable of as radical a reformation as some had dared hope when Pope John originlly set the Council on its course.

Protestants and Catholics in America both freely communicated their apprehension. Father John Sheerin confessed, "The Americans are heartsick. The temporary defeat of the religious liberty document rankles."[44] Father Gregory Baum, commenting on the papal interventions, warned, "The Pope has certainly the authority to do this. But whether he does not ultimately lose prestige and weaken the Bishops' attachment to him is a question one may well ask. Since the coherence of the hierarchy and the entire church is ultimately based not on juridical bonds, but on faith, love, good will, cooperation and the readiness to make sacrifices, the insistence on authority at the wrong moment can destroy the ties of loyalty and thus produce the very opposite effect."[45]

Robert McAfee Brown, respected Protestant observer at the Council, acknowledged that "much has been accomplished, many formerly closed doors have not only been pushed ajar, but actually entered." Yet, he concluded, "there is mounting apprehension . . . a tiny handful was able to thwart the overwhelming majority of the Council Fathers. . . . It does not mean that good can no longer emerge out of the Council but it does mean that Protestants will be watching with a new kind of anxiety. . . ."[46]

PART FOUR

SESSION FOUR AND THE FINAL STATEMENT

11. Anxious Interlude

THE PRELIMINARY APPROVAL at the third session of a forthright condemnation of "hatred and persecution of Jews" enabled Catholic officials in the United States immediately to plan for the first formal theological conversation with Jewish scholars. For several years the National Conference of Christians and Jews had been considering the convening of such a colloquy in cooperation with the American Benedictine Academy. When the statement on the Jews was shunted about at various Council sessions, it was thought wise to postpone the meeting. In truth, the emotional situation had become tense. If the Council had not acted, American Catholics might have felt defensive and Jews sullen.

The Council's action cleared the air. With the issue of "deicide" seemingly set to rest and official Catholic opposition to anti-Semitism manifest, it was possible to engage in dialogue on those issues that were really more central. Even after the distorted conception of the Jews as an accursed people is eliminated, the fact remains that Jews and Catholics hold to convictions that call for clarification and understanding. Both claim title to the role and destiny of being God's chosen people, Israel. Both claim fidelity to the true revelation of God's word as contained in Jewish Scripture; yet both attribute different meanings to the same scriptural words. It was to such questions of agreement and disagreement that the theological colloquy directed its attention.

A HISTORIC COLLOQUY

This was to be a historic theological encounter on the relations of American Jews and Catholics. Representatives from each group were invited to discuss together basic issues of religion in a spirit of mutual esteem, eschewing any polemic intent to demonstrate error in the other's most cherished faith commitments. Twenty-six Bible scholars, historians, theologians, and community relations experts gathered for a week-long conversation at the end of January, 1965, at St. Vincent's Archabbey in Latrobe, Pennsylvania. As one of the Benedictine Fathers put it, this first exchange was "an ice-breaker which plowed into an indistinct frozen mass and at last upturned and set free huge pieces of material which later can be chartered and explored."[1]

For many, the most significant achievement of the colloquy was the realization that we knew so little about each other. We had viewed each other from the perspective of our own misconceptions and stereotyped categories. The scholars soon realized that a lot more intergroup talking was required.

Another notable aspect of the colloquy was the realization that there was division within both groups along very similar lines of scholarly judgment and theological predisposition. For example, some Jews wished to define the concept of the chosenness of Israel in exclusivist terms, whereas others sought ways of being inclusive enough to allow for those Christians who might also find themselves, by God's grace, within "His castle." Similarly, some Catholics wished to define the concept of the Church so as to delimit it only to those who were juridically Christian, whereas others recognized that Jews properly could consider themselves still "the Congregation of God" and that the Church gained in wholeness when it maintained a dialogue with the Jew. With regard to Bible studies, Jews and Catholics differed among themselves and with each other as to whether scholarship could ever truly rediscover the meaning of the biblical word in its "pristine purity"—as, for example, in the exact sense in which the prophets may have used the word. Even if that were possible, there was disagreement over whether such an understanding was "truer" than the meanings and interpretations that had been provided by tradition and historic experience. We were discussing, in other words, the binding nature of the biblical word as revealed through contemporary scholarship as against the authority of traditional interpretations given to the words by Church or Synagogue. This led us into a discussion of how we made the Bible relevant, in any event, to life's changing conditions and why and how it was that we could both have revered the same words and yet read them so differently.

In all of these discussions division rarely occurred strictly on religious lines. The scholarly exchange sharpened our own conceptions of self, opened our eyes to the other in new perspective; the dialogue brought us to a more poignant realization of the tragedy of human alienation from unity with God and separateness from each other. Vatican Council II seemed already to have worked its magic. Rarely had Jews and Catholics been able to discuss matters of faith together in such an atmosphere of acceptance and mutual respect. We were eager now to explore the possibilities for a second colloquy. For many who took part, that week's experience had helped to redeem hundreds of years of painful history.[2]

FURTHER REVISION IN THE GOOD FRIDAY PRAYERS

Pope Paul then cheered all Jews by making further revisions in the Good Friday prayers. Pope John XXIII had earlier ordered that the description of the Jew as "perfidious" be stricken from the Holy Week prayers, but the prayers still contained references to "the conversion of the Jews" and to the fact that the Jews suffer from "a veil over their heart" in that they do not accept Jesus as the Christ. The prayers also concluded with an assertion that Jews needed a deliverance "from their darkness." Not only did Pope Paul direct that all such references be omitted, but he amended the prayers to acknowledge that as the "people of Abraham" the Jews were "beloved by God."[3]

In the United States Bishop Ernest L. Unterkoefler of Charleston, South Carolina, assured the Anti-Defamation League at its Fifty-second Annual Convention that the Catholic Church was committed to a revision of "every document, textbook and instructional manual which does not conform to the spirit of the Vatican Council's declaration on the Jews."[4]

A warm breeze stirred across the land.

NEW CHILL IN JEWISH-CATHOLIC RELATIONS

Just as there had seemed to be a thaw in the frozen relationship between Jews and Catholics, the spring of the year 1965 witnessed a new chilling blast of interreligious misunderstanding. Pope Paul in a Lenten homily made a reference to the Jews as a people who had killed Christ. Several important Church Fathers issued full-blown theological arguments in defense of the traditional interpretation of the Jews as an accursed people. Rumors from Rome intimated that the statement on the Jews had once again been drained of its strength.

Pope Paul's Lenten Homily

Early in April Pope Paul extemporaneously addressed an outdoor service at a parish church in suburban Rome, the Church of Our Lady of Guadalupe. Appealing to his faithful to renew their faith in Jesus, the Pope recalled the story of the Crucifixion. He pointed out to his listeners that the tragedy of the rejection of Jesus reoccurred in every generation. It "repeats and perpetuates itself even today in all those who by word or deed deny Christ, offend him and renew his passion." In his reference to the original Crucifixion the Pope fell into the pattern of blaming the Jews collectively for the killing of Jesus. According to the text of the homily published in *L'Osservatore Romano*, the Vatican City newspaper, the Pope said, "It is a grave and sad page. It describes in fact the clash betwen Jesus and the Jewish people. That people predestined to receive the Messiah, who awaited him for thousands of years and was completely absorbed in the hope . . . at the right moment when Christ came, spoke, and presented himself not only did not recognize him, but fought him, slandered him, and injured him; and in the end killed him."[5]

Jewish reaction was immediate. "The Pope's Revival of the Deicide Charge Shows the Need of the Council Schema," exclaimed one Anglo-Jewish newspaper in bold headlines.[6] Many wondered aloud whether the Pope's homily was not intended, after all, "to undermine the Council Schema and render it worthless." Rabbi Balfour Brickner, Director of Interfaith Activities for Reform Judaism, expressed his amazement: "It is difficult to believe." He called on the Pope to explain the meaning of his words, "particularly in light of the Vatican's statements and admonitions that preachers and teachers in the Church do nothing to acerbate anti-Jewish attitudes through reference to the old falsehood of deicide."[7]

Not all Jews reacted with such distress. The Anti-Defamation League maintained a discreet silence. The *London Jewish Chronicle* editorialized, "Jewish leaders and organizations should retain a sense of proportion before they rush into public expressions of 'dismay' or 'concern.'"[8]

The Vatican itself, as the Catholic press reported, "immediately tried to tidy up the affair as best it could."[9] Vatican Radio announced that the Pope did not say that the Jewish people "killed the Christ"; he merely said that the Jewish people "finally repudiated him."[10] Other Vatican sources denied that the Pope had intended to imply a collective Jewish guilt. He was merely using this historical fact of the killing of Christ to illumine a human phenomenon in today's world. He meant that mankind in general—Christians and non-Christians alike—continue to reject Christ.

The Greek Orthodox daily *Falastin,* published in Jerusalem, Jordan, on the other hand, hailed the sermon for "confirming just in time before Holy Week the Gospel truth regarding the killing of Christ by the Jewish people."[11]

Catholic press action in the United States ran a wide gamut: *The National Catholic Reporter* commented, "Barring further explanation . . . the Pope made a blunder; this one was serious enough not to be ignored or defended or glossed over."[12] Some Catholics tried to defend the homily. Msgr. John Oesterreicher explained that the Pope "had no intention of torpedoing the Council's declaration on the Jews. . . . Ignoring, rebelling against, even hating Jesus is not typically Jewish, but, alas, a typically human and universal phenomenon."[13] Father Stephen Schmidt, secretary to Cardinal Bea, urged Jews to understand that "had the Pope been addressing a meeting of scholars he would have used more theologically precise language that would have conveyed the sense of the Conciliar document. The statement must be seen as an address to the simple faithful who would not have understood its sophisticated explanations."[14] This supposed clarification, coming from Cardinal Bea, perplexed Jews. Who else, after all, were we hoping to enlighten through a Conciliar statement other than "the simple faithful"?

The *Catholic Review*, newsweekly of the Baltimore archdiocese, annoyed at the Jewish reaction, warned in more aggressive language that "His duty as the Supreme Teacher in the Church may well have prompted the Pope to make it clear that the Council has no intention of denying what the Gospel tells us about the role which sons of the Old Testament regrettably played in the redeeming death of the Founder of the New Testament. . . . The Church can scarcely be expected to repudiate the Gospel witness about the role of Jews in the crucifixion. . . . Nor can she be true to her own divinely imposed mission to bring all men to Christ without praying that the Jews and all non-Catholics may freely find in Catholicism the fullness of God's will for them."[15]

Conservatives' Attack on Jews

At the very moment when Jews and Catholics were embroiled over the Pope's homily and its alleged meaning, reports reached New York concerning major pronouncements by two important Catholic prelates boldly defending the old teachings that the statement was designed to revise.

The first was a communiqué issued by the distinguished and respected Melchite Patriarch Maximos IV Saigh of Antioch. Obviously intending to allay the anger of Arab Christians and to explain how such a statement could have been adopted by the Council, the Patriarch asserted that "personal interest" had evidently guided the vote of many Council Fathers and particularly the American cardinals and bishops. "The personal reasons are dictated by a sentiment of pity due to the massacre of millions of Jews by Nazism and . . . the fact that the greater number of

Americans have commercial interests with the Jews." Maximos defended the Council's denial of Jewish collective guilt for the Crucifixion. "It is not permitted to pursue them [the Jews of this day] with our vengeance and to exterminate them by hatred, oppression and death." But to soften the radical consequences of this Church teaching the Patriarch added, "There certainly remains on the forehead of the Jewish people as long as it is far from Christ the Redeemer . . . the stain of shame." Thus, the collective Jewish crime, according to Maximos, was not our involvement in the murder of Jesus but rather our continuous rejection of him as the Christ. This is a stain that can be remedied only when the Jews convert to Christianity. In any event, whether for killing Jesus or repudiating him, Maximos intended that Jews be characterized as a shamed and reprobate people.

Finally, the Patriarch accused the Jews of always trying "and by all devices not to differentiate between the heavenly Jewish religion which gave the prophets and criminal Zionism in order to attract the world's sympathy." Finally, speaking forth a combination of religious moralizing and political intrigue, the Patriarch exhorted his followers, "Israel can be defeated . . . by the devotion, the solidarity, and the unity of the Arab ranks in compelling the nations who support Israel to endorse the Arab point of view as well as their sacred rights. One·cannot defeat Israel by becoming an enemy of the Holy See because everyone knows the strength of the Vatican's power in the balance of the forces of the world."[16]

In Rome, in a weekly magazine, *La Palestra del Clero* (*The Training of the Clergy*), written by and for the Italian Catholic clergy, Msgr. Luigi Maria Carli, Bishop of Segni, charged that the Council's declaration was a "historic distortion" and "injustice." He explained, "I hold it legitimate . . . to affirm that all of the Judaic people of the time of Christ were responsible *in solidum* (the whole) for the crime of deicide even though only the leaders followed by a part of the people had consummated the crime. . . . In this sense and according to the biblical mentality Judaism, after the time of Jesus, is objectively participating in the responsibility for deicide by the measure in which this Judaism constitutes the free and voluntary continuation of the Judaism of those times. For these same reasons Jews can be called reprimanded and cursed by God."[17]

Rumors Again: Jewish Statement to Be Weakened or Killed

In late April reports reached New York that, with the Pope's permission, the specific reference to deicide would be deleted from the Jewish statement. Upon hearing this, Rabbi Heschel angrily responded, "The deicide charge is the most dreadful calumny ever uttered. It resulted in rivers of blood and mountains of human ashes. . . . It is absurd, monstrous, and unhistorical, and the supreme repudiation of the Gospel of love. The weakening of the document in any of its aspects—which was inspired by a grandeur of consciousness and the spirit of love invoked in the third session—would remain for all times as one of the major contributions to anti-Semitism."[18]

I could not myself believe that the Council Fathers would permit anyone to tamper with a statement that had already been approved so overwhelmingly. But I must admit to being personally quite shaken when in mid-May I shared the platform with Rev. John Courtney Murray, S.J., at the annual meeting of the World Congress of the Catholic Press.

In an act of extreme graciousness I had been invited to address the editors of Catholic newspapers throughout the world on "Religious Liberty and the Freedom of Conscience." I used the occasion to speak as well on the issue of anti-Semitism and urged the Council to repudiate for all time such distorted theological conceptions as had been articulated by Patriarch Maximos and Bishop Carli.[19]

Father Murray had just that afternoon flown in from Rome. He spoke in general terms about the final version of the religious liberty statement. He was optimistic, and he outlined its contents beautifully, saying nothing, however, about the Council's position with regard to the Jews.

After the formal presentations Father Murray asked permission to put some questions to me. He explained that he had never heard of the charge of Jewish accursedness for deicide until he was forty years of age. He did not believe that it was a

current problem in contemporary Catholicism and wondered why
Jews were so insistent on a statement specifically dealing with
"deicide." "What will such a statement accomplish?" he asked.
Then he recalled how an Israeli radio commentator had predicted
that the Vatican Council's approval of a statement on the Jews
would be but the first step in the recognition of the Jewish State.
"What can you do," he asked, "to get the Israelis off our back?
We are tired of the Jewish pressure being put on us."

I was stunned and taken completely off guard. It was a moment
of such high tension that I cannot now recall all that I said
in response. I poured out my heart. How could Father Murray
not know after all these years of debate and in view of the vigorous defense of the doctrine of accursedness—how could he not
realize that the issue was a live one for Christian theology? Had
he not read in history how Jews had suffered at the hands of
Christian princes and prelates? Was he not aware of recent studies
of Catholic catechisms demonstrating that Church teachings with
regard to the Jews were still offensive?

I acknowledged that Jews had been concerned with the statement and had lobbied perhaps to excess, but I pressed Father
Murray: Could he honestly say that Jewish pressure on the
Vatican had approached in any degree that which had been
brought by the Arabs? He nodded his agreement with my
evaluation.

When I finished these remarks, the editors' response indicated
their emphatic support for my position. But doubt gnawed at my
innards. Could it be that the issue of deicide was still not settled
in Rome? Were Father Murray's questions, after all, not a statement of his conviction but rather a warning that there had been
yet another tampering with the statement?

On June 20 and 21 Jewish leaders throughout the world were
startled by news accounts in the *London Observer* and the *Frank-
furter Allgemeine Zeitung*, repeated by the Associated Press,
that the Pope had instructed the Vatican Council's Coordinating
Commission "to drop the Declaration from the agenda." There
was an immediate stern denial from the Vatican. "The entire
report is deprived of any basis," said Cardinal Bea.[20]

The June 24 issue of Hamburg's *Welt* explained, "The alarmist news had been circulated deliberately by some especially concerned and zealous champions of the Declaration, with the aim of provoking a forthright denial from Vatican Council circles; and in this way counteracting the opposite pressure on the Pope." The Jesuit magazine, *America*, demurred: "This explanation is plausible if bizarre; but even more puzzling is why professional newsmen . . . became pawns in a questionable manner."[21]

The truth, as we later learned, despite all the denials and assurances was not far removed from these rumors. In between sessions, behind closed doors, the conservatives were wielding a sharp scalpel.

EXTENSION OF THE JEWISH-CHRISTIAN DIALOGUE

If these springtime episodes were disconcerting, there were other signs that comforted. Msgr. John S. Quinn of Chicago, an expert retained at the Council, addressing a conference co-sponsored by St. Xavier Catholic College and the B'nai B'rith Women's Council of Chicago, recalled a remarkable prayer that he said had been composed by Pope John. The statement had been written, he said, "as an act of reparation and a prayer for forgiveness to be read in Catholic churches." He noted that it was finished just before Pope John died in June, 1963. The prayer read:

"We are conscious today that many, many centuries of blindness have cloaked our eyes so that we can no longer see the beauty of Thy chosen people, or recognize in their faces the features of our privileged brethren.

"We realize that the mark of Cain stands upon our foreheads across the centuries. Our brother Abel has lain in the blood which we drew . . . by forgetting Thy Love.

"Forgive us for the curse we falsely attached to their name as Jews. Forgive us for crucifying Thee a second time in their flesh, for we know not what we did. . . ."[22]

Whatever the situation in Rome, American Catholics were intent on developing a more fraternal relationship with their Jewish neighbors. The Anti-Defamation League's National Chairman, Dore Schary, announced that at least twenty Catholic-Jewish clergy and lay dialogues were to be sponsored jointly that year. The discussions held at various Catholic conferences would cover a wide range of subjects, including social justice, race relations, anti-Semitism, church-state relationships, and family life.

The American Jewish Committee revealed that the Henry Regnery Company, Catholic publishers, would publish Catholic high school level textbooks on religion stressing "ecumenical fairness" toward Jews and Protestants. The publishers had engaged a rabbi to serve as their consultant; they had made changes in the manuscripts consistent with their own theology, so as to present Jews and Judaism in a fair and sympathetic light. Catholic children's books published by Allyn and Bacon of Boston contained illustrations of Jesus as a lad in a synagogue. Hebrew letters and the Star of David were prominent, thus making sure that Catholic children would recognize Jesus' origin as a Jew and their own indebtedness to the Jewish religion.

Sixty theologians from sixteen Catholic and twelve Protestant seminaries met in Chicago under the auspices of the Anti-Defamation League, Loyola University's Bellarmine School of Theology, and the University of Chicago's Divinity School. Particular attention was paid to the spirit and the manner of the presentation accorded Jewish tradition and theology in the seminary curriculums.[23]

Reacting to all these and similar developments, Richard Cardinal Cushing at a general workshop on Christian unity told his Catholic audience that in his opinion the Jewish-Christian dialogue was ecumenism's most "dramatic gain." This should not surprise us, he commented, "since we share with the Jewish people common roots, an ancient covenant and a common destiny. . . . Jews are witnesses, too, to the promises of God in a world which has not received Him in their suffering. . . . The suffering of Jews is a sign of their election and their greatness; a sign that the Holy Spirit rules over them. . . . They are a people of great destiny and great promise and have added a rare and precious dimension to our dialogue with the world. We owe our religious lives to them as to the root."[24]

12. Reconsideration and Promulgation in Session Four

"THE FOURTH SESSION is a test of the Council's sincerity. The mood that is already forming is, frankly, one of jitters."[1] Thus Father Thomas Stransky, an official of Cardinal Bea's Secretariat, characterized the mood as the Council Fathers prepared for their final and climactic session.

Well might the Council Fathers feel jittery. In three sessions over a three-year period, accompanied by much fanfare, the Catholic hierarchy had finished and made public only five documents. In this last session, to begin September 14, 1965, action would have to be concluded on eleven schemata, including the important documents on Religious Liberty and the Church in the Modern World, both of which still needed rewriting, and the controversial schemata on Divine Revelation and on the Relation of the Church to Non-Christian Religions, both of which still required final voting. Rumor had it that the declaration dealing with the Jews might not even be presented for vote—or in any event, that it would be further amended in order to dispel any possible political interpretation or conservative objection.

At the Pope's request, Msgr. Jan Willebrands, an official of Cardinal Bea's Secretariat, journeyed to the Middle East. His was the final effort in an intensive campaign on the part of the Pope to win the support of Arab and Orthodox prelates to an amended declaration. The Pope was concerned with the reaction of Arab leaders, but even more so with Orthodox theological opinion for it was with the latter group that the Catholic Church had established its closest relationship during this period of ecumenicity. The Pope would not want *rapprochement* with the Orthodox to founder over a statement on the Jews.

DELETION OF THE WORD "DEICIDE"

Both Arabs and Orthodox, each group for its own reasons, insisted that the word "deicide" be deleted. The Arabs explained that biblical punishment for the Crucifixion included Jewish dispersion. If the Jews were now to be cleared of the guilt of deicide, the punishment of exile and dispersion would also be lifted and Jews would be morally justified in gathering in one place, that is, in re-establishing their nationhood in Palestine. By acquitting the Jews of deicide, the Church Council, *de facto*, recognized the State of Israel as religiously legitimate.

The Orthodox churchmen argued that to include the word "deicide" would give the impression that the Gospel account of Jesus' crucifixion was inaccurate or renounced by Council action. Finally, it was said, the word "deicide" itself created confusion by suggesting that it was possible to kill God. There was no point in the Secretariat's fighting for a word that had become a magnet drawing dissent; the concept could be adequately handled through the use of other less-loaded phrases. The Secretariat recognized that deleting the word "deicide" would satisfy both Orthodox and conservative Catholic theologians.

Catholic conservatives in addition wished Cardinal Bea's Secretariat to make it clear that at least *some* Jews were implicated in the Crucifixion and were punished on this account: Jerusalem was, after all, destroyed and brought to shame. Further, the New Testament clearly and unequivocally recalled Jewish enmity toward the Gospel and the consequent displacement of the Jews as the people of God.

The Pope himself was persuaded that the section on Judaism should be rewritten in the light of these objections. It was the unhappy task of Cardinal Bea's Secretariat to prepare a text that would meet the objections of Arab statesmen, Orthodox hierarchy, Catholic conservatives, and Jews and at the same time articulate clearly the Secretariat's liberal convictions. The

Secretariat met in March and May 1965 and examined the text
in minute detail, making whatever changes they felt would leave
the declaration intact in spirit, yet capable of achieving a wider
degree of support.

The reason for "jitters" on the part of the Church Fathers was
now quite evident: Despite all contortions to satisfy the anti-
Semitic bloc in the Church they remained dissatisfied; Jewish
reaction to rumors of the statement's amendment, on the other
hand, indicated that Jews would look upon a rewritten document as a retreat. No matter what the Council did, it was sure
to leave some element in the Church, or in the Jewish community,
or among the Arabs, unhappy.

On September 11, just three days prior to the opening of
the session, the Secretariat publicly revealed its capitulation. The
words saying the Jews were not "guilty of deicide" had been
deleted from the text "in order to clear up any eventual misunderstandings arising from differing interpretations by the
Israelis and Arabs," and lest it lead to the idea that "Council
declarations were negating all that was said in the writings of
Evangelists." The Secretariat hastened to assure the press that
other words would be substituted in order not to change the
meaning of the text. Furthermore, the Secretariat pointed out
that such a change would have to be approved in voting. The
Italian wire service, ANSA, queried, "Was this 'leak' from the
Secretariat intended to prepare the way for acceptance of these
changes or to arouse a public sentiment against it?"[2]

Father Stransky explained to the American bishops that "deicide" was, after all, an "emotional word" and the declaration
would, in different words, spell out clearly the Church's conviction that the Jews could not be held collectively responsible for
the Crucifixion.[3] In response, Max Lerner, columnist and sociologist, voiced the sentiments of many Jews on this issue: "If the
specific reference to deicide is omitted, it will show that the
revolution which Pope John XXIII started has sputtered and
fizzled out. The reference to deicide may be only a symbol, but
we all live by symbols. And of what can that be more truly said
than of a great and powerful Church?"[4] *America* stated in an
editorial, "Since amendments are still possible we may hope that

the fixed form of the text will reflect the Council's further deliberations. . . ."[5] If eight hundred bishops could be persuaded to
vote against the new wording, the original text of the Jewish
statement, with its condemnation of any consideration of the
Jews as guilty of deicide would be restored.

THE SESSION BEGINS

When the Council opened on September 14, the Pope announced
that in accordance with the mandate given him by the Constitution on the Church, he would establish a "Synod" of bishops. He
promised that the Synod would be assembled "according to the
needs of the Church for consultations and collaboration when,
for the greater good of the Church this would seem opportune
to the Pope."

In his opening address, the Pope also announced his forth-
coming trip to the United Nations in New York on October 4
to plead for peace. This notification raised the hope that the
Council would conclude its debate on religious liberty, consider
its attitude toward the Church's role in the modern world, and
initiate a satisfactory action with regard to the Jews before the
Pope landed in New York City, for all of these were issues in
which Americans were deeply interested and world political
leaders had a vital stake.

On September 23 the Council Fathers voted 1,907 to 224
to accept, provisionally, the Schema on Religious Liberty subject
to its final amendment. It was also announced that the Declaration on the Relation of the Church to Non-Christian Religions
would be distributed for final vote sometime during the week
of October 4. Thus the two "American issues" were shaped up
administratively prior to the Pope's historic journey. Touching
all bases, the Pope also granted an audience to a four-member
delegation from the Palestine-Arab Liberation Organization. He
assured them that the Council had no intention of taking any
action "detrimental to legitimate Arab interests."[6]

On September 29 the text of the revised declaration on the
Jews was at last circulated to the Council Fathers (see Appendix
D). Not only had the new document dropped the word "deicide";

it also deleted the word "condemnation" when referring to hatred of the Jews—although it "decried hatred, persecutions and displays of anti-Semitism against Jews at any time by anyone." It specified clearly that *some* Jews had been implicated in the Crucifixion. In addition, it implied that Jews collectively had lost their status as the Church of God, in punishment for their failure to accept Jesus as the Christ, and that Christians were now "the people of God."

Administration spokesmen all insisted that the statement had been made more forceful. Father Stransky, for example, termed it a "stronger" document. He pointed to the fact that for the first time it mentioned anti-Semitism by name and deplored it. Msgr. John Oesterreicher argued in its favor, asserting also that "the new wording was stronger than the former even with the omission of words."[7]

Other Catholic officials charged immediately that this was not a stronger document at all; *it was an emasculated one.* Rev. George Tavard, one of America's foremost Catholic theologians on ecumenical affairs, confessed, "The text is not as advanced as it once was. . . ."[8] Abbé René Laurentin, a Council *peritus* and journalist for the Paris newspaper *Figaro,* began work on a brief calling upon the Council to restore the original language. Bishop Leven of San Antonio similarly sought to stir up an American campaign to vote down these new changes from the text approved by the bishops at the third session.

In a bristling memo to the American hierarchy, Bishop Leven criticized particularly reference to the displacement of Jews by the Church as the new people of God and deletion of the word deicide. On this latter point, he reiterated, "the word deicide was invented by Christians and has been hurled at Jews for centuries to justify persecutions and pogroms. It seems fitting that this Sacred Council should specifically reject it." He asked the Church Fathers to vote "non-placet" so that "the former and *approved* text may remain."[9]

Israeli press reaction was almost universally critical of this altered version of the statement. The independent *Haboker* (October 17, 1965) charged that the Council had "capitulated not only to its internal prejudices but to the political pressures of the enemies of Israel." *Davar* (October 5, 1965), official publication of Israel's majority party Mapai, sadly concluded that the Council statement could never correct the existing evil of anti-Semitism. This version, it asserted, "is a clear cut retreat . . . the minority has succeeded in emptying the document of its ethical content."

In the United States Jewish reaction ranged from the American Jewish Committee's restrained judgment that the new version, though "less decisive and satisfactory," was nevertheless "a forward step in Jewish-Catholic relations," to Professor Abraham Heschel's dramatic charge: "Not to condemn the demonic canard of deicide . . . is a defiance of the God of Abraham and an act of paying homage to Satan."[10] Heschel was much closer to the actual sentiment in the Jewish community than was the American Jewish Committee. One evidence of dissatisfaction was indicated by the way Pope Paul was received in New York a few days later.

POPE PAUL'S RECEPTION BY AMERICAN JEWISH LEADERS

Jewish religious leaders in the United States accorded the Pope a civil but cool reception when he came to America. Jewish religious and organizational leaders agreed not to solicit any official meeting with the Pope or to greet him in any fashion other than that required by protocol. Certainly they would in no way violate or compromise their own religious integrity.

The executives of the New York Board of Rabbis resolved not to accept an invitation to participate in the Catholic Mass at Yankee Stadium or to distribute invitations to rabbis. They stood on the solid grounds of Orthodox religious teaching that prohibits participation by Jews in a Christian religious service. The fact that Reform rabbis joined in boycotting the event, however, was indication that it was not Halacha (religious law) alone that prohibited Jewish participation—actually, a few rabbis were present at Yankee Stadium—but that Jewish leaders were just not eager to cheer this particular Pope.

If the New York Board of Rabbis was being stern in its refusal to cooperate with the diocesan committee planning for the Mass, it must also be acknowledged that Catholic leaders in New York were not entirely diplomatic in their dealings with Jews. On two successive days announcements were made from the New York City Hall press office that the Protestant Council of New York and the New York Board of Rabbis had agreed to distribute the tickets for the papal Mass to non-Catholic officials. Yet at no time had any diocesan official been in touch with the New York Board of Rabbis. When word got back that the rabbis "did not know anything about such cooperation," a telephone call was finally placed from the Chancery Office. Rabbi Harold Gordon, efficient executive of America's largest communal interdenominational rabbinical association, then explained that the rabbis were religiously prohibited from participation in a Christian religious service. They welcomed an opportunity, however, to greet the Pope and they would be glad to do so in a neutral setting outside the context of a religious service. The rabbis never received an answer. Instead, the next day the Protestant Council in the name of the Religious Leaders' Committee of New York City circulated a fifty-man rabbinical list with tickets of invitation.

The Religious Leaders' Committee of New York City is a quasi-official group appointed by the Archdiocese, the Protestant Council, and the New York Board of Rabbis. Its function is to maintain contact and cooperate with city officials, and particularly with the New York City Youth Board in its fight against pornography and juvenile delinquency. This time the Religious Leaders' Committee acted without the approval of its Jewish constituency. The officers of the New York Board of Rabbis were infuriated.

The biblical text for the Mass drawn from the Book of John—the regular reading prescribed in the office for that day—describing the disciples' "fear of the Jews," suggested to New York's Jewish leaders that the service was not "ecumenical" after all and they were right to have stayed away. Allegedly the whole debate in Rome was an effort to end such wide-sweeping references to a corporate Jewish enmity toward the Christian Founder and his followers. Had not Cardinal Bea taken pains to indicate that it was not "the Jews" in a collective sense who were to be considered guilty but only the princes and leaders of the people and those who followed them? The difficulty and complexity of this whole enterprise was here disclosed: How does one explain away every one of the harsh references to "the Jews" to be found in the New Testament? How will the Church instruct her faithful so that hereafter, when Scripture says "the Jews," they will know that such a reference does not really mean all Jews?

On one earlier occasion during his day-long stay in New York, the Pope had an opportunity to meet religious leaders across faith lines—at a reception at the small Catholic Center for the United Nations. Unfortunately, Catholic officials again made mistakes in their dealings with the Jewish community. Instead of working out arrangements with the accepted Jewish coordinating agencies, an approach was made to a single congregation located near the United Nations. Leaders of the major organizations were thus put into an embarassing posture when invitations arrived from such an unrepresentative source. Although a significant and powerful group of Jewish leaders attended that reception, several of them subsequently apologized publicly to their Jewish constituents for their appearance.

Fortunately, the public press had no inkling at all of this wrangling. Newspapers throughout the world reported only the ecumenical glow of the occasion. The three religious groups, they were told, in obvious harmony of spirit, declared that their coming together highlighted "present cooperative trends" and "previous instances when representatives of various faith groups worked together in the cause of peace."[11] Television viewers saw the Pope walk over to greet non-Catholics who attended his Mass, and Rabbi William Rosenblum, one of the few rabbis in Yankee Stadium, was recognized and identified.

It was good that the misunderstandings and acrimony behind the scenes had not then been disclosed. This day had been given over to the quest for peace, and man's need for rededication to that fleeting ideal should not have been marred in any way. The Pope placed the prestige of the powerful Catholic Church behind the United Nations, which institution, though faulty, remains the best peace-making instrumentality man has yet devised. When the Pope cried, "Never again, never more. Not the one against the other," he spoke for men of all races and creeds.

Although there would yet be much strain and misunderstanding in the relations between Jews and Catholics, and we would make many mistakes in our dealings with each other, surely, with so much good will in evidence, we could aspire to a more harmonious understanding. When a Catholic friend who had used my ticket returned that evening from the Mass and telephoned her exaltation—the Mass had been for her the pinnacle of a life of devotion and sacrifice for her faith—I was certain that out of such personal and individual experience Jews and Catholics could build a life together in this one world. Whatever may happen in Rome, nothing can stop American Jews and Catholics, who want to be brothers with each other, from forging the most solid links of fraternal respect.

FINAL STATEMENT DEFENDED AND CRITICIZED

In accordance with Council procedure, Cardinal Bea distributed to the Church Fathers a booklet describing the Secretariat's action on their many suggestions for revision of the text that had been adopted in principle the year before. Alongside the original text was the newly revised version and an explanation justifying each change. It was a thick booklet and a very revealing document (see Appendices D and E).

What had started out in Session Two to be a short chapter on the Jews within the context of ecumenism had become in Sessions Three and Four a lengthy separate Declaration on the Relation of the Church to Non-Christian Religions. The original intent to speak directly and particularly to the Jews had been abandoned. Yet in some ways this could be considered a gain. The Church had been inspired to address itself in a deeper way to the condition of all men who were not Christians. In truth, the document contained a revolutionary openness to that which "men have in common" and which "leads to mutual fellowship." It acknowledged that "from ancient times, continuing up to the present, there is to be found among various peoples a recognition of a Supreme Being and even of a Father." This perception and recognition "penetrates their lives with a profound religious sense."

A Church that had once characterized other peoples as living in darkness was ready now to acknowledge that God had revealed

Himself not to Christians alone. Many other peoples, too, are custodians of God's truth: "The Catholic Church rejects nothing that is true and holy in these religions. She regards with sincere reverence those ways of action and life, those precepts and teachings, which though differing in many aspects from the ones She holds and sets forth, nevertheless often reflect a ray of that truth which enlightens all men."

But then, having made such a splendid affirmation of inter-religious understanding, the Church felt it necessary to satisfy its traditionalists; so Cardinal Bea, in the name of the Secretariat, was placed in the position of having to explain and defend crucial changes.

In speaking of "The Variety of Non-Christian Religions," for example, the earlier text had simply affirmed that "other religions found everywhere *counter* the restlessness of the human heart, each in its own manner, by proposing ways . . . teachings, rules of life, and sacred rites." The newly revised text read, "Other religions *try to counter* the restlessness of the human heart. . . ." While thus casting some doubt on the efficacy of other religions, the declaration added a new phrase expressing its own conviction that "the Church must ever proclaim Christ 'the way, the truth and the light,' *in whom men find the fulness of religious life. . . .*" Despite its original intent to underscore that which men hold in common, the Secretariat, under pressure from the supporters of the "One True Church" doctrine, now tempered the moment of reconciliation with an assertion of Christianity's superiority.

On other issues, however, Cardinal Bea's Secretariat stood firm. They would permit no compromise. One such was contained in Section 3 of the declaration, dealing with the Moslem faith.

THE RELIGION OF ISLAM

The Secretariat spelled out at some length those concepts that Catholics and Moslems shared together. In a paragraph on the Moslem faith, the statement took note of the fact that "In the course of centuries, not a few quarrels and hostilities have arisen." It called on the Holy Synod "to forget the past and to work sincerely for mutual understanding." Cardinal Bea reported that some Church Fathers wanted to amend this text, specifically suggesting " 'Christian states, to safeguard the faith have valiantly resisted the Mussulmans as they assaulted Europe'—so that it did not seem that the quarrels and hostilities arose from the fault of the Christians." The Secretariat held its ground and rejected that amendment.

AMENDMENTS TO THE CHAPTER ON THE JEWISH RELIGION

The chapter on the Jewish religion was revised in several significant ways. As Father Thomas Stransky, a staff member of the Secretariat, later acknowledged, "phrases and qualifications had to be introduced or omitted in the final text and these have changed the document from a bold proclamation to that of bold argument. The shift was regretfully thought necessary . . . for Roman Catholics." [12]

One change was simply an attempt at clarification. A word was added to make it plain that the Church's link to the Jews was of a spiritual nature only; there must be no thought that the Christian Church possessed corporeal identify or kinship with the Jewish people. The old text read, "As this Holy Synod searches into the mystery of the Church, it remembers the bond that ties the people of the New Covenant to Abraham's stock." The revised text made it specific: "the bond that *spiritually* ties. . . ." Insisting that God's purpose of salvation is served by maintaining their own particularity as a corporate people, the Jews are assured now that the Church makes no pretense of being linked to them in any direct sense as a people.

This passage had a significance, however, beyond mere clarification. It asserted that, after all, the Church, in its very definition of self, must take note of its spiritual indebtedness to the Jewish religion. There is, then, a core of belief, a body of values and practices, that Jews and Christians do share together, and this shared spiritual heritage provides our relationship with its special character and enables us to communicate with each other at a more profound level of understanding. This shared heritage makes it possible for us to work together for social justice, assured that we maintain similar conceptions of human dignity.

But, as though to inhibit the very warmth with which such a common patrimony would be imbued, the Council withdrew its original expression of gratitude: "with *a grateful heart,* the Church of Christ acknowledges . . . that the beginnings of her faith are found among the Hebrew patriarchs and prophets." The new text deleted the "grateful heart"—"lest it be understood as if we had to give thanks to the Jews of today," the Secretariat's explanation held. There is the rub! The Church seemed unwilling or unable to explore or even mention the possible significance of the ongoing faith of the Jews, despite the fact that all the other chapters in this decree discussing non-Christian religions dealt directly with their contemporary practices and beliefs. The Church was ready to acknowledge its indebtedness to the Judaism of old, but beware of any thought that the Church should have anything to be grateful for from contemporary Jews or Judaism! When this fixation upon the past is accompanied by a definition of Judaism as a religion worthwhile because it prepared the way for Christianity, the statement's inadequacy becomes clear.

Lest the Jews miss the point, the Secretariat added a few more polemic notes: "As Holy Scripture testifies, Jerusalem did not recognize the time of her visitation (Luke 19:44) . . ." "the Church is the new People of God. . . ." The Secretariat's *Modi* (explanation of amendments) asserted, "It is true that Israel is not now a sacrament of Salvation for the world. . . ." It must be made clear that "according to the Catholic faith the Jewish people after the rejection of Jesus on the part of Jerusalem and the Synagogue was no longer the Church (Assembly) of God it had previously been."

So the document implied that a Jew, merely on the basis of his membership in the Synagogue, cannot be assured of salvation. Nor do the Jews have status with God as His holy people. Jews' fidelity to their faith, their sufferings through the centuries, their loyalty to God seemed to have been granted no contemporaneous significance.

Given such concessions, some conservative Catholic prelates felt free to press Cardinal Bea through their written "interventions" (suggested amendments) to account for words in the New Testament that seem to designate Jews as a reprobate people,

collectively, to be punished for their rejection of God. One, for
example, cited the words of St. Paul in 1 Thessalonians: ". . . the
Jews, who killed both the Lord Jesus and the prophets, and drove
us out, and displease God and oppose all men by hindering us
from speaking to the Gentiles that they may be saved—so as
always to fill up the measure of their sins. But God's wrath has
come upon them at last."

The Secretariat held firm at this point. The memorandum re-
plied: "It is impossible to explicate the significance of a single
text apart from the total biblical doctrine on Israel." Cardinal
Bea then offered a different exegetical approach: "Many of the
harsh words were intended not as specific judgment, but as
prophetic-type admonitions or threats calling the people to
repentance. . . ." "Many of the harsh judgments relate to leaders
of the Jews and to that section of the inhabitants of Jerusalem
who followed their leaders in the rejection of Jesus. For this
'wicked generation' Christ foretold chastisements and punishments.
. . . But we are not to apply what is contained in these judgments
to all the generations of the Jewish people."

The Secretariat then cautioned the bishops: "Such terms as
deicide (Gottesmord, Christ killer, Peuple déicide and other
such expressions) should be proscribed entirely from the Christian
vocabulary." Thus the Council statement effectively and strongly
made it clear that no Catholic should hereafter interpret Scripture
in such a way as to suggest that the Jews are "rejected by God,"
or "accursed," or that all the Jews then alive or of today are
responsible for what happened to Jesus in his Passion. The word
"deicide" itself was omitted.

Along with this repudiation of a distorted form of Christian
teaching, Cardinal Bea's Secretariat felt compelled to add words
explaining the historical context of the Crucifixion. The revised
text reads, "The Jewish authorities and those who followed their
lead pressed for the death of Christ." The reader is then directed
to a source text, the Gospel of John, where it is recalled that
Pilate could find no crime in Jesus and so he handed him over
to Jewish authorities for crucifixion. This addition may have been
motivated by a desire to delimit responsibility to a relative few
and thus preclude blaming present-day Jews. But many Jewish

scholars will deny vigorously that the account in John (the least historical of the Gospels) is an accurate rendering of the exact historical situation. A strong case can be made that Rome, and Rome's priestly Jewish vassals, misread Jesus' intentions and looked upon him as a political threat and so did away with him for political reasons. Not a *legitimate* Jewish religious authority, therefore, but Roman political rule was most threatened by Jesus and his followers.

Without debating this point, however, it is disturbing to find the repeated assertion that responsible *Jewish* leaders were the most culpable for the crucifixion of Jesus; it undoes much of the good that the statement intended to achieve, for it would seem that the Jewishness of the participants is irrelevant. The persons responsible for the Crucifixion were acting out a drama of cosmic proportion—that is, they were demonstrating the consequence of evil in the heart of man. It is of no special significance that they were *Jewish* authorities since the *whole scene* was set in Jewish surroundings. Jesus and his followers were Jewish, as were his enemies. Throngs of Jews cheered Jesus in Jerusalem. And those who wept at his death were also Jewish. Furthermore, the drama, properly interpreted, demonstrates that prototypes of all mankind participated in the execution. Among those implicated in the conspiracy were members of a corrupt Jewish priesthood, a cruel and tyrannical Gentile ruler, and the followers of Jesus himself— Judas, who betrayed Jesus, and Peter, who denied him. Thus Jew, Gentile, and Christian were all involved. It was evil in the heart of man—not some Jews—that laid Jesus low, the same kind of evil that corrupts civilization even to this day. The addition of a passage underscoring Jewish enmity to Jesus not only undermined its reconciling purpose but betrayed the best in Christian theology!

If such revisions tended to weaken the text, others strengthened it. It was decided to attack "anti-Semitism" specifically and by name. The former document read, "This Synod . . . *deplores, indeed condemns,* hatred and persecution of Jews, whether they arose in former or in our own days." Although the new text deleted the word "condemns," it contains phrases that are powerful and specific: "The Church . . . moved . . . by the Gospel's spiritual love decries hatred, persecution, displays of anti-Semitism, directed against Jews at any time, or by anyone." In its concluding passage the revised text repeats this admonition: "The Church thus reproves, as foreign to the mind of Christ, any discrimination against man or harassment of men, because of their race, color, condition in life, or religion." [13]

Unfortunately this forthright attack on prejudice was minimized in the minds of many Jews because the Church had failed to confess its own efforts in the making of anti-Semitism. Unless the Church could also display a spirit of contrition, its own attack on hatred of Jews might be misunderstood as but mere sentiment without serious intention.

ADOPTION AND PROMULGATION OF THE DECLARATION ON NON-CHRISTIAN RELIGIONS

For the three days prior to the voting a letter calling upon the Fathers to reject the schema was distributed in the Council hall—in violation of rules of procedure. The letter was distributed and signed by Italian Bishop Luigi Carli of Segni, Archbishop Marcel Lefebvre, superior general of the Congregation of the Holy Spirit, and Archbishop Geraldo de Proençe Sigaud of Diamantina, Brazil. The letter charged the schema as being "unworthy" of the Council and criticized, particularly, the passages dealing with the role of the Jews in the death of Christ. [14]

The letter claimed that the text failed to respect Gospel teachings regarding the responsibility incurred by Jews in the death of Christ. Holy Scripture and tradition, it said, uses exactly such concepts as "reprobate" and "accursed" with regard to the Jews, while the Council declaration avoids them. Finally, the declaration is unacceptable since it fails to express hope for the eventual conversion of the Jews. [15] A four-page tract, signed by twenty-eight Catholic organizations from fourteen countries, three of them based in the United States, was also circulated to the Council Fathers. It charged the declaration to be an "outrage" and declared that "only an anti-Pope or a secret conspiracy could approve a declaration of this kind." [16]

On October 14–15 the Council voted on the entire declaration. Eight votes were taken in all:

Vote 1—on the Schema's introduction—Yes, 2,071; No, 110; Null 4.

Vote 2—on non-Christian religions in general with special mention of Hinduism and Buddhism—Yes, 1,953; No, 184; Null, 6.

Vote 3—on the Islamic religion—Yes, 1,910; No, 189; Null, 6.

Vote 4—on the first section dealing with the Jews, setting forth the spiritual relations between the peoples of the Old and New Testaments—Yes, 1,937; No, 153; Null, 9.

Vote 5—on rejecting the collective guilt of the Jewish people for the death of Christ—Yes, 1,875; No, 188; Null, 9.

Vote 6—declaring that the Jews must not be represented as "accursed" or "rejected" by God—Yes, 1,821; No, 245; Null, 14.

Vote 7—on rejecting anti-Semitism, persecutions against the Jewish people, and the spreading of anti-Jewish sentiments through preaching or teaching—Yes, 1,905; No, 199; Null, 14.

Vote 8—a summary on universal brotherhood excluding all discrimination—Yes, 2,064; No, 58; Null, 6.

After these votes on the schema section by section, the Fathers voted 1,763 to 250 in favor of the declaration as a whole.[17]

It should be noted that despite all of Cardinal Bea's careful planning and a studied effort to win a wider support for the document, the absolute opposition remained adamant and even increased in size between sessions three and four. The antagonism toward the Jewish statement was larger than that directed toward any other religious groups, although in fairness it should be observed that when the chips were down many of the bishops who had earlier expressed reservations regarding the statement now finally agreed to favor it. The size of the affirmative vote also increased considerably when on October 28 the measure came to a final public vote prior to its promulgation: 2,221 in favor, 88 opposed, 2 with reservations, and 1 null. But the favorable vote was still nine to thirteen votes fewer on this declaration than on the other schemata to appear before the Council.

Henri Fesquet, the French correspondent of Le Monde, who

covered the Council at all of its sessions, reported the mixed feelings of many. "Roman diplomacy carried the day over total frankness. Many Fathers are saying this quietly to each other." Fesquet added, "When the details of the various attempts to abort or water down the Conciliar declaration are known, we will be stunned, by such passion, aberration, hatred, and to put it bluntly, ignorance and stupidity . . . it is above all a pity that the real reasons for the changes were screened behind pious clichés."[18]

The world's newspapers immediately headlined the action in Rome as an act of clearing the Jews, absolving them of guilt, finding them innocent. Needless to say, Jews breathed a sigh of relief that a sad chapter in history had ended. But they were also annoyed at the way the news was stated. For Jews felt no guilt and needed no absolution. When the Church's action was put in such terms, Jewish anger countered, "It is not for the Jew to beseech the Church for forgiveness. After two millennia of ignoble persecution of the Jew and the Synagogue, it is not the Christian prerogative to pardon. We are the ones who should forgive, and they plead with us for forgiveness."[19] Catholic commentators hastened to assure the Jewish community that the statement was not an absolution; rather it was addressed to Catholics and it was a corrective on Catholic teaching.

Other church actions coincident with the Pope's promulgation of the text, on October 28, 1965, however, maintained the symbolic imagery that an absolution was being granted. Once again an irritated Jewish reaction was provoked. The Church declared "innocent" the Jewish residents of the City of Trent, all of whom had been burned to death nearly five centuries ago for the alleged ritual murder of a two-year-old child, Simon, and the child's status as a "martyr" was withdrawn. The Congregation of Rites forbade any further veneration of relics or saying of Masses in the child's name. In the light of the widespread suffering of Jews caused by wild charges of ritual murder through the centuries, this absolution of Jewish victims seemed too mild an action.[20] The editorial response of *Reconstructionist* was representative: "It is always easier to pronounce others innocent and absolve them of responsibility for a crime than to confess one's own guilt and admit one's own culpability. The Vatican Council's Jewish statement was a reminder of this fact. . . . Surely the Vatican can do more . . . than absolve the Jews of Trent and declare one murdered child no longer fit for veneration. The time has come for the Church to admit who the real murderers were and to declare the true martyrs of more than a thousand years of ritual murder worthy of admiration, respect and peace."[21]

Jewish religious and communal leaders in the United States met for two days following the Vatican Council's adoption of the declaration in order to ascertain whether they could agree on a common statement. They could not. Orthodox Jews, on the philosophic basis that no comment ought be made about the religious views of another's faith, urged the Jewish community to silence. Conservative Jews wanted to write a blisteringly critical analysis of the document. The American Jewish Committee wanted a statement that would emphasize the affirmative. The Jewish organizations decided to go their own way, each to issue its own statement. Interestingly, many of the Jewish statements that were later released combined aspects of all three of these attitudes:

The World Conference of Jewish Organizations, for example, chose to make "no comment" on the definition of Catholic doctrine (on the theological implications of the declaration), but then it expressed "appreciation for the evident goodwill and the sincere feeling for human brotherhood which impelled so many distinguished leaders of the Catholic Church to strive for a public repudiation by their Church of the movement which seeks to distort Catholic teachings and to exploit these distortions in the service of anti-Semitism."[22]

The American Jewish Committee uncritically called the declaration "a turning point in 1900 years of Jewish-Christian history" and "the climax to an unprecedented effort to bring about a new era in relations between Catholics and Jews."[23] In contrast, the editors of *Reconstructionist* asked, "One wonders, in light of this statement, whether the Church will ever succeed in reforming itself unless it comes to grips with the cruel, even barbaric aspects of its own history and literature . . . acknowledges its own sins and repudiates them in the sight and hearing of all men."[24]

The English language Israeli publication, *Jerusalem Post* (October 17, 1965), urged its readers to recognize that the Church

Fathers had been asked "to reconsider some of the Church's most venerable and venerated doctrines and to ask themselves whether for eighteen centuries the Church has not been misleading its followers." Although critical that the Council had not gone as far in revising Catholic teaching as some of the Council Fathers had urged, the *Jerusalem Post* noted, the Council "has shown that it is prepared at least to begin to recognize its historic errors. The real test will now come, of course, in the practical application of the document. Its spirit and sentiments have, happily, already found a wide echo."

The American Catholic press hastened to emphasize that which was affirmative in the declaration and to assure Jews of Catholic good will. Bishop Francis P. Leipzig of Baker, Oregon, who had been appointed chairman of a new subcommission on Catholic-Jewish Relations for the United States' Bishops' Commission on Ecumenism, confessed, "It is true that the declaration has a few . . . imperfections," but, he added, "so have some other documents issued by the Council. What counts is the over-all text and the over-all spirit." This text, he suggested, expresses the Church's "reverence" for the Jews and its wish to "honor" them. "I look forward to the time when the Council's wish for a more deepened conversation with our Jewish brethren will be implemented and I pledge my wholehearted support toward that important purpose."[25] Bishop Leipzig's pledge was significant; his subcommission has already set in motion programs for implementing the American Church's ongoing dialogue with Jews.

Bishop Leipzig's warm and sincere assertion was characteristic of most of the Catholic reaction, despite a few disturbing exceptions. Father Raymond Bosler of Indiana sounded a keynote to the importance of the statement and the need for further work: "One thing these four years of struggle over the document made clearly evident is the frightening amount of anti-Semitism in the Christian Church. Here is proof enough for the need of a declaration on the Jews."[26]

13. Catholic Teachings on the Jews and Judaism

SHORTLY AFTER THE close of Vatican Council II, Cardinal Bea published in the important *Civiltà Cattolica* a summary of the Catholic Church's teachings on "the role of the Jewish people in the Divine plan of salvation."[1] His tightly reasoned twenty-page article was intended to contrast the formulations of the Council with the traditional positions held by the many conservative Catholics who had unsuccessfully opposed the Council's declaration. Cardinal Bea used the device of setting forth his own view against that of Msgr. Luigi Carli's on the grounds that the Italian Cardinal had "gathered and restated most recently those arguments which are usually used to support the concept of collective responsibility of the Hebrew people for the crucifixion of Jesus with all its related consequences."[2] Cardinal Bea's article, therefore, provides us with a significant interpretation of the Council's statement on the Jews in historical perspective. And it helps us see how far the Church has progressed in its teachings on the Jews and, at the same time, how far removed it remains from many of the expectations held by Jews.

For the sake of clarity, the teachings of the Church may be examined both from the perspective of its significance for Christian theology and also with a concern for its practical or sociological implication. It must be remembered, of course, that references to the Jewish people and Judaism are not only to be found in the statement on non-Christian religions. The Church also defined her relationship to the Jews in the Constitution on the Church and in the Dogmatic Constitution on Divine Revelation. And the sociological dimension of the Church's relation to the Jews will be influenced by its Decree on Ecumenism, the Declaration on Religious Freedom, and the Pastoral Constitution on the Church in the Modern World. In this chapter I shall try to assess briefly the implications of all these documents for the formation of contemporary Catholic teachings on Jews and Judaism.

THE THEOLOGICAL DIMENSION

The teaching of conservative Catholics, as we have already noted, consists of the following well-known components:

1. The Jewish people failed to recognize Jesus as the promised Christ because of spiritual blindness, "hardheartedness," or wickedness. In rejecting Jesus as the Christ, Jews turned their backs on God and voluntarily abandoned His promises to them as a people.

2. The enmity of the Jewish people toward God is particularly revealed in their unjust condemnation of Jesus and in the fact that the Jews exhorted Pilate to crucify him.

3. As a result of their collective involvement in the guilt of deicide, the Jews became a reprobate and accursed people. They are no longer the people of God.

4. Jerusalem was destroyed and the Jewish people were driven into exile. They were made to endure, through the decades, the most grave punishment. These facts are evidence of their condemnation as a people.

5. The Jewish people are no longer an instrument of salvation for mankind, and Judaism itself, hardened in opposition to the Gospel, is an inferior religion.

6. The Church no longer has any relationship to the Jewish people except that which it has toward all peoples—the obligation to confront them with the truth in Christ.

7. The Church, the New Israel according to the spirit, replaces the Jewish people as the chosen people of God and as the instrument of God's plan of salvation for mankind.

8. The Jewish people will be forgiven their sins only upon their repentance and acceptance of Jesus as the Christ.

Vatican Council II clearly confronted many—but not all—of these teachings and repudiated those that were most damaging. It made it clear that such assertions are contrary to the spirit of the Gospel by insisting, to begin with, that the Church finds its roots and has its beginnings in the religion of the Jewish people. This historic fact itself provides a "special tie" between the Jewish people and the members of the Church. As the Dogmatic Constitution on the Church asserts in its first chapter, the Church was "prepared for in a remarkable way through the history of the people of Israel and by means of the Old Covenant."[3] And in its second chapter, defining the people of God, the Constitution describes the role of the Jewish people in God's plan of salvation: "He [God] therefore chose the race of Israel as a people unto Himself. With it He set up a covenant. Step by step He taught the people by manifesting in its history both Himself and the decree of His will and by making it holy unto Himself."[4]

In the Declaration on the Relation of the Church to Non-Christian Religions the Council elaborated this theme: "In truth, the Church of Christ acknowledges that, according to God's saving design, the beginnings of her faith and her election are already found among the Patriarchs, Moses and the prophets. . . . The Church, therefore, cannot forget that she received the revelation of the Old Testament through the people with whom God in His ineffable mercy concluded the Ancient Covenant" (see Appendix D).

The Council has created a basis for the Christian's sense of relatedness to Judaism, and an attitude of respect for Jews. As Cardinal Bea put it in his *Civiltà Cattolica* article, "If we visit with reverent awe the Holy Land where Christ lived, walked, worked and suffered, we shall encounter with all the more respect, even veneration, the people from whom Christ was born and by means of whom the church received so great a wealth of doctrine and example." Cardinal Bea then confessed "It is a fact that often *Christians do not profess such veneration* and they do not realize the relationship that they, as members of the church, very clearly have with these people or, at the very least, are indifferent or remain aloof from them (not to say worse)."[5]

This primary teaching of the Council, then, is intended to make clear the Church's indebtedness to Judaism of old, its spiritual tie to the Jewish people, and its desire to awaken an attitude of respect for Jews. Furthermore, as the Council asserted, the Church still benefits from its connection to Judaism: "Nor can she forget that she feeds upon the root of that cultivated olive tree into which the wild shoots of the Gentiles have been grafted (Rom. 11:17–24)." The Council Fathers wished to suggest that its Old Testament heritage remains a vital, sustaining, revivifying, and inspiring element of Christian faith, even to this day. In an address before the Council, Cardinal Lercaro elaborated: "The Jewish people have [in the eyes of the Church] not only a value and a supernatural dignity in time past, and in connection with the origins of the Church, but also in the present."[6] And in its Constitution on Revelation the Council, referring to Jewish Scripture, explained, "These books, therefore, written under divine inspiration remain permanently valuable. . . . The same books, then, give expression to a lively sense of God, contain a store of sublime teachings about God, sound wisdom about human life and a wonderful treasury of prayers. . . ."[7]

With this affirmation of the continuing importance of the biblical heritage, the Council was in a position to confront the reactionary argument that the Jews had become a reprobate people by their collective participation in the guilt of deicide. It is here that the Vatican Council took its strongest position. The Church acknowledged that "the Jewish authorities and those who followed their lead pressed for the death of Christ. *Nevertheless,*" it declared, "what happened to Christ in his passion cannot be attributed to all Jews without distinction, then alive, nor to the Jews of today."

Cardinal Bea explained that, according to the New Testament itself, even the Jewish authorities who are implicated in the Crucifixion are to be excused to the degree that they had a "certain ignorance" regarding the divinity of Jesus. This ignorance, he suggested, was not the result of hard-heartedness or malevolence but a legitimate and understandable consequence of their Jewish education. "In fact, these people had been educated for centuries to the strictest monotheism and a spiritual conception of God. Therefore, it does not surprise us that to a Jew a God 'who became flesh' and 'a Son of God' was a concept extremely difficult to understand (so that even Peter did not learn by himself, but by revelation from the Father) [cf. Matthew 16:18]. Therefore, if the formal guilt of deicide cannot, with certainty, be charged even to the leaders of all the people who directly participated in the trial of Jesus, much less can it be charged to those who were absent, scattered throughout the world, and still less for those living in subsequent ages."[8]

In conformity with this more sophisticated understanding of the Crucifixion events, the Council's statement urged, "May all see to it, then, that in catechetical work or in preaching the word of God, they do not teach anything that is inconsistent with the truth of the Gospel and with the spirit of Christ." Since this exhortation concluded the paragraph repudiating the collective guilt of Jews for the Crucifixion, it corrected forthrightly and without equivocation a most damaging interpretation of Christian Scripture, and it directed that a correct interpretation ought now to be brought to any reading or lesson from the New Testament.

Conservative Catholic theologians, however, were able quickly to retreat to a new ground. Granted, they said, that the Jews are not collectively guilty of the Crucifixion, yet "as long as Jews remain far from Christ the Redeemer, there certainly remains on the forehead of the Jewish people a stain of shame."[9] The Council's response to such argument was to invoke once again and thus to restore to a position of centrality Paul's teaching that the Jews remain dear to God. The Council's statement acknowledged that "Jerusalem did not recognize the time of her visitation, nor did the Jews for the most part accept the Gospel; indeed, many opposed its spreading. *Nevertheless,* according to the Apostle, God holds the Jews most dear for the sake of the Fathers: his gift and call are irrevocable (Romans 11:28–29). The Church keeps ever in mind the words of the Apostle about his kinsmen: 'Theirs is the sonship and the glory, the covenants and the legislation, the worship and the promises' (Romans 9:4–5)."

Thus the Church teaches that in some way Jews still possess a cherished place in God's plan for salvation. God's revelation came first to the Jews and to them belongs the promise of a fullness of faith in the end-time. The Council asserted, "In company with the prophets and the Apostle [Paul], the Church awaits the day known to God alone on which all peoples will address the Lord in a single voice and serve him 'shoulder to shoulder' (Zephaniah 3:9)."

Despite this clear statement of the Jewish people's right to the status of "election," the Council emphasized in several of its documents that there was a guilt in Jerusalem and a dire consequence for the Synagogue by virtue of its opposition to the Christian claim. As Cardinal Bea explained, Jerusalem was destroyed, the inevitable result of a "millennial history of infidelity and opposition to God,"[10] and "the Jewish people are no longer the people of God in the sense of being the instrument of salvation for humanity."[11]

Cardinal Bea was careful to delimit the consequences of these judgments. He explained that Jerusalem was destroyed not "solely and simply" because of the Crucifixion; rather its destruction was the prototype of "that terrible reality of the judgment with which the history of mankind will be concluded. . . . The cause and the motive of it is not a presumed collective guilt of the chosen people. . . . The Judgment on Jerusalem strikes at moral evil, pride, rebellion against truth, and the pursuit of injustice."[12] Cardinal Bea acknowledged also that while "generally speaking . . . a guilt does exist for the inhabitants of Jerusalem, since they directly witnessed the preaching, the miracles, the solemn entrance of Jesus, it is not possible that those who lived far from the events [should be] sharers in the guilt."[13]

Similarly, Cardinal Bea warned that the Jews lost their status as an instrument of salvation "*not* because they had been completely rejected as a punishment but simply because their function of preparing the Kingdom of God terminated with the coming of Jesus and with the foundation of the Church. Henceforth, the very nature of the 'people of God' and manner of joining them changes completely. The people of God of the New Testament are no longer confined to one people alone nor are they propagated by descent through the flesh, but by faith. This does not at all admit of the disavowal of the divine election of Israel 'according to the flesh.' The Jews will remain dear to God for the sake of the Fathers for all times and to all eternity." [14]

Having clarified its position on these crucial points, the Church went on to repeat its claim that Christians are the new People of God, an affirmation appearing in several of the Council documents. Unfortunately, this Christian self-definition was in several cases accompanied by a critical or negative judgment on Judaism, both ancient and contemporary. For example, the Constitution on the Church asserts that God's election of the Jews was "by way of *preparation* and as a figure of the new and perfect covenant which was to be ratified in Christ and of that *more luminous* revelation which was to be given through God's very word made flesh. . . . For those who believe in Christ, who are reborn, not from a *perishable* but from an *imperishable* seed . . . are finally established as 'a chosen race, a royal priesthood, a holy nation, a purchased people' (I Peter 2:9–10)." The Constitution continues: "Though there may be many nations, there is *but one people of God* which takes its citizens from every race, making them citizens of a kingdom which is of a heavenly rather than an earthly nature." [15]

The Constitution on Revelation, too, judges the books of the Old Testament to "contain some things which are *incomplete* and *temporary* . . . ," and adds, "The principal purpose to which the plan of the Old Covenant was directed was to prepare for the coming, both of Christ the universal Redeemer and of the messianic kingdom. . . ." Then the Church Fathers proclaim, "The word of God which is the power of God for the salvation of all who believe, is set forth and shows its power in a most excellent way in the writings of the New Testament." [16]

In summary, Catholic teachings on Jews and Judaism, as now articulated in Council documents, have the following components:

1. The Church acknowledges its spiritual ties to the Jews through that which is Hebraic in the Christian faith, or a prefiguring of Christianity in Judaism.

2. Despite the enmity of some Jews toward Christianity, Jews remain dear to God and their election will never be revoked.

3. Neither the Jews of the past nor those of this day can be held collectively accountable for the Crucifixion. Their inability to recognize the divinity incarnate in the person of Jesus may have been the result of a steadfast but limited conception of monotheism and not the consequence of any intentional moral weakness. They are not an accursed or reprobate people.

4. Although there was guilt among some Judaeans in the death of Jesus, Jerusalem was destroyed not on that account alone. Its destruction was the conclusion of a long period of inner corruption and fratricide, a warning to all men who would rise up in violence against their brothers.

5. The promises made to the patriarchs are now fulfilled and perfected in the Church. The Synagogue, therefore, is no longer a vehicle of salvation.

6. The Church, the New Israel according to the spirit, replaces the Jewish people as the perfected sacred instrument of God's plan for redemption.

7. However, since the spiritual patrimony common to Christians and Jews is of such magnitude, the Catholic Church recommends biblical and theological studies and fraternal dialogues with Jews in order to achieve mutual knowledge and respect.

8. The Church continues to hope that all men may one day be united as one people in love of God. It is the burden of the Church's preaching "to proclaim the cross of Christ as the sign of God's all-embracing love and the fountain from which every grace flows."[17]

A CRITICISM OF THE CHURCH'S NEW APPROACH

The new theology of the Vatican Council without doubt corrects a distortion in Christian doctrine that had caused enormous harm to the Jewish people. For this alone it is to be praised. It also invites theological conversation and scholarly study in the hope that respect and understanding will result. Finally, it affirms that, in ways not yet fully defined, the Jews remain dear to God and possess a divinely mandated destiny in history.

Despite these progressive teachings, most Jews will remain dissatisfied with the Church's theological formulations for a variety of reasons. The following three considerations, at least, are uppermost:

1. Jews will deny that the purpose of Jewish history or the meaning of Jewish Scripture is by way of "preparation" for a more perfect or luminous Christianity that allegedly fulfills and completes the prophetic word.

2. Jews will insist that their refusal to accept the Christian claim is in no way an act of sinfulness, a blindness, or a turning of their backs on God. Nor does it demonstrate a "certain ignorance." To the contrary, Jews interpret the persistence of their particularity as an act of fidelity and a testimony of their love for God.

3. Jews will claim still to have a divine mission to be a witness to God and a blessing for mankind. Jews have not lost that responsibility by virtue of the emergence of Christianity. Furthermore, Jews are satisfied that through the Judaism developed in the Synagogue, particularly in the post-biblical period, they still experience God's presence. Judaism in its contemporary form reveals itself as a dynamic and vital faith, certainly as relevant to the problems of modern man as Christianity.

Fortunately, Jews will not be without allies in defending their position on these issues. There are individual Christians who have already sensed the inadequacy of the Conciliar decrees, and who are sympathetic to Jewish dissatisfactions. They have spoken out, calling for further developments in the Church's teaching.[18]

Jews take particular umbrage when Christians suggest that God's dealings with the Hebrews were only preparatory, and that His relation to Israel was imperfect or incomplete. Jewish commentators note, with some irony, that throughout its Constitution on the Church the Vatican Council continued the presumption that the symbols and imagery applied to the Jews in the Hebrew Bible now adhered instead to the Church. According to Jewish self-understanding, such scriptural references to the Hebrews of former days still describe the Jews of this day. For example, Scripture evokes images suggesting that the Jews are like a Flock of which God is the Shepherd (Ezekiel 34:11), the Chief Cornerstone (Psalm 118:22), the Congregation of God (Numbers 20:4). In the Constitution on the Church, the Vatican Council recalled all of these images and then appropriated them for the Christian Church.

The Constitution on the Church also referred to the famous passage in Jeremiah, where the prophet speculates upon the nature of "the days that shall come." He expresses his faith that the Lord will make "a new covenant with the house of Israel" (Jeremiah 31:31). Invoking that passage, the Council suggested that the Church's right to the name, privilege, and responsibility of Israel thus had its roots, after all, in Jewish prophecy. Needless to say, Jewish Bible scholars are astonished by what they contend is a plucking-out of context of such prophetic passages. The contrasting Jewish and Christian interpretations brought to this particular text are a good example of how it is possible to read the same words differently; they explain why, even if Jews and Christians acknowledge that they share together a Scripture, some degree of tension and conflict will still remain in their relationship. Each group cherishes a particular and different understanding of the meaning and significance of the biblical heritage.

In chapter 31 Jeremiah sought to kindle a spark of hope among his people in a time of sorrow and tragedy. They had disgraced the dignity of their national integrity and were exiled. Jeremiah spoke of a new day, of a time to come. He hoped thereby to maintain the remnant in their faith and to revivify their flagging spirits. His Messianic vision remains in its essential outline still the dream of contemporary Judaism: The exiles of the Jewish people will be restored in their land (31:8–9). "Again I will build you and you shall be built, O virgin Israel! . . . Again you shall plant vineyards upon the mountains of Samaria; the planters shall plant, and shall enjoy the fruit" (31:4–5). In that marvelous time also God will put His law into our inward parts and write it into our hearts (31:33). In a climactic promise of great emotional import, considering the despair and distress of the Hebrews, Jeremiah then declared that God will "forgive their iniquity" and "will remember their sins no more" (31:34). Never, he cried out, will God cast off the seed of Israel! Only when the sun no longer lights the day and the moon and stars fail to shine by night will the seed of Israel cease from being a nation (31:35–37).

The Catholic theologian Rev. Gregory Baum, O.S.A., a consultant to Cardinal Bea's Secretariat, caught the sense of that particular Jewish unhappiness with the Council's statement. In an address at Brandeis University he observed that "most Christians who respect Jews today respect them as 'precursors of Christianity'—as potential Christians—not for what they are, but for what they may become. Such an attitude is inadequate and insulting." Father Baum added, "God continues to operate in the Jewish people. Christians must regard the Jewish religion as an authentic God-Inspired, supernatural worship of the one true God."[19]

As we have noted, the Council affirmed the Pauline doctrine that the Jews remain dear to God and that their election is not revoked. On the other hand, the concept "the people of God" was defined by the Church in such a way as to exclude the Jews, and, as I have noted, Cardinal Bea maintained several times that the Jews were no longer an instrument of redemption for mankind. How can one reconcile this contradictory and ambivalent attitude toward Judaism?

The first part of the Council's paradoxical affirmation unfortunately is not clearly defined. The Council does not tell us in what way the modern Jew "remains dear to God," nor does it explain the contemporaneous meaning and significance of the election. And the second part of the affirmation is a gratuitous judgment on the Synagogue. Jews will find it offensive—particularly in light of the Church's consistent assertion of the superiority of its own faith. Such a coupling of derogatory judgments on Judaism with a claim to Christian perfection is bound to be irritating. In fact, it is this that caused Jewish dissatisfaction with the otherwise remarkable Schema on Ecumenism.

The statement of Catholic principles on ecumenism deservedly aroused a widespread enthusiasm among non-Catholic Christians. For the first time the Catholic Church had acknowledged that other Christian communities "can be rightly described as capable of providing access to the community of salvation." It defined the nature of Christianity in such a way as to confirm the right of these separated brethren "to be honored by the title Christian and properly regarded as brothers in the Lord."[20] In a moving passage the schema confessed that Catholics by their past sins may have been responsible for the rupture in Christianity—for which at times men of both sides were to blame."[21] Thus the schema recalled Pope Paul's prayer at the second session, begging God and the separated brethren for their pardon, "just as we forgive their trespasses against us."[22]

The "ecumenical movement" was defined to refer specifically to "those activities and enterprises, which, according to the various needs of the church and opportune occasions, are started and organized for the fostering of unity among Christians."[23] In order to encourage Catholic participation in this movement the schema called upon the faithful "to avoid expressions, judgments and actions which do not represent the condition of her separated brethren with truth and fairness, and so make mutual relations with them more difficult." It called for dialogue between competent experts, intensive cooperation in carrying out duties for the common good of humanity, and common prayer where this is permitted. "We must get to know the outlook of our separated brethren. Study is absolutely required for this. . . . Most valuable for this purpose are meetings of the two sides—especially for discussion of theological problems—where each can talk to the other on an equal footing." The schema also called for the training of future pastors and priests in an ecumenical approach to theological differences "and not polemically."[24]

The schema acknowledged that in the process of dialogue with other Christians the Catholic Church herself may gain new insight and be enriched in her own understanding of Catholicism. Ecumenism, therefore, was not to be feared as a force that weakens the Church; quite the contrary, it should be welcomed as a means of enabling Catholics to express their faith in a fuller way. "Nor should we forget that whatever is wrought by the grace of the Holy Spirit in the hearts of our separated brethren can contribute to our own edification."[25]

It is clear that the spirit that permeates this schema is revolutionary. It views the other as brother in the service of God, not as antagonist or inferior. It evokes an attitude of humility and a willingness to listen and to learn from the other. To the degree that such an approach to the interreligious dialogue will also be brought by Catholics to their dealings with Jews—and in America such an intention has been formally declared—then the schema can be read with some measure of joyous expectation. But obviously, because of its Christian sectarian formulations Jews could not respond as warmly to it as did Protestants. Although the ecumenical *"spirit"* engendered by this document— as contrasted with the official ecumenical *movement,* which has as its purpose the achievement of Christian unity—has in fact been extended to the Jewish community, the schema nevertheless, expresses Christian priority in such exclusive terms as to evoke inevitably a competitive and defensive Jewish retort. The schema asserts, for example, that the Christian Church is "God's only flock." [26] It repeats the continuing Catholic conviction: "It is through Christ's Catholic Church alone which is the all-embracing means of salvation that the fullness of the means of salvation is attained. It was to the Apostolic College that God entrusted all the blessings of the New Covenant. . . . The Catholic Church has been endowed with all divinely revealed truth, and with all means of grace. . . ." [27]

Some Catholic scholars have already made efforts to soften the exclusivist implication of such assertions and to demonstrate their appreciation and respect for the vitality of Judaism. In a revised introduction to his book on anti-Semitism in the Gospels, Father Gregory Baum observes, "So much development has taken place [since the New Testament era] in Judaism and Christianity, that the Christian Church today facing modern Judaism cannot really regard itself as it was 1,900 years ago as the fulfillment and replacement of the Jewish religion contemporary to it." [28] Father Baum concludes his book with these words: "We may confidently assert that according to scriptures God continues to make Himself known in the synagogue and worshipped there by men who believe in His covenant." [29]

Father John Sheerin concluded his widely published analysis of "the story behind Vatican II and the Jews" by exhorting Catholics to "show reverence for the living religion of the Jews by acknowledging it as a valid and authentic supernatural reality." The exact relation between Israel and the Church, Father Sheerin confessed, "is a mystery." "But," he explains, "it would surely be wrong to say that Israel no longer has any function and that Christianity has replaced it as a permanent substitute."[30]

The desire to appreciate Judaism's persistent vitality and to understand how and in what ways *Judaism* can be an instrument for redemption is a major source of hope for the future. It promises an effort to make still further revisions in Church teaching. The fact that churchmen are now calling for dialogue and study with Jews in order to better understand the nature of Judaism, particularly in its post-biblical developments, is certainly one of the most welcome results of Vatican Council II.

THE SOCIOLOGICAL DIMENSION

There is a very practical, or sociological, dimension in the Catholic Church's teaching on Jews and Judaism. The fact is that anti-Semitism, whether motivated by a distorted notion of Christian belief or by diverse secular purposes, remains a scandal in the social order toward which the Christian Church ought to direct its full energies. As the Constitution on the Church in the Modern World explicitly affirms, "Every type of discrimination . . . is to be overcome and eradicated as contrary to God's intent." [31]

The Vatican Council was forthrightly unequivocal, particularly in its rejection of every form of anti-Semitism. In at least five different ways in the decree on non-Christian religions the Council Fathers asserted that the Church "reproves," "decries," "considers reprehensible," any act of discrimination directed against any man; and anti-Semitism, of course, was specifically named.

I am convinced, however, that the Church's attack on anti-Semitism will become more effective only when the Church will recognize its own past involvement in the making of anti-Semitism and the persistent power of religious factors in sustaining hatred of the Jews. Father Edward Flannery supports this idea by noting that Catholics have tended to repress any knowledge of the sufferings of Jews at the hands of the Church and warning that such pages of history "must be reinserted in our histories and publications if the Jewish-Catholic dialogue is to advance and succeed." Father Flannery contends that the Council declaration's "main defect was a failure to refer contritely to the role the Church played in the development of anti-Semitism throughout Christian history. . . . Anti-Semitism, despite all denials," he adds, "is still widespread among Catholics and much of it is still attributed to religious reasons. . . ." Speculating on the reason for the repression of this information about anti-Semitism, Father Flannery asks, "Was it guilt or was it a hidden form of anti-Semitism which simply considered Jews too unimportant to talk about in the great Christian era even when they were massacred in large numbers?"[32]

The Lutheran theologian, George A. Lindbeck, recalling the Council's confession of error against other Christians, says: "Surely all Christians need to ask forgiveness from the Jews even more urgently than Catholics do from Protestants or Orthodox."[33]

Can it be, then, that the Council's inability to face up to the Christian component in hatred is itself an indication of anti-Semitism still lurking within the Church? The Council's excellent statement decrying anti-Semitism needs to be translated into action. And certainly the first requirement must include a knowledge of past history. Not only will such knowledge provide the wisdom that may restrain Catholics from ever again taking the same course, but just as important, Catholics will learn to address the Jew sympathetically by knowing how history has influenced the Jewish people. Past injury has evoked a response of fear and suspicion. Experiences with Christians hardened Jewish resistance to the claim that a Redemption has visited earth. Certainly these factors must be understood for the dialogue to progress. As Father Flannery put it, "How can two persons confront one another on even ground when in the mind of one is the question never spoken—'Why are they so persecution-minded?'—while in the mind of the other is the question, again never spoken—'Why are they so indifferent to the oppression of my people?' "[34]

A proper appreciation of the declaration on the Jews will be based on awareness of the fact that the statement will not be nearly as important as the way it is used. Although the Conciliar document may fall short, it is clear that American Church officials intend to fill the breach. The statement makes no confession, expresses no contrition. Yet it is being interpreted and used by American officials with exactly such a spirit and purpose. Most Catholic commentaries on the decree are accompanied by profound expressions of remorse over the tragedies of past history and a clear call to cooperative labor against the anti-Semitism still prevalent in society. In America it is clear that the Conciliar statement will be used as an instrument of penitence and reconciliation. Representative of Catholic opinion is Father Benedict Ashley's moving declaration: ". . . this statement is essentially a confession by Catholics of their own guilt in the persecution of the Jews throughout two thousand years. If we Catholics are not absolving the Jews, we *are* seeking absolution of our own guilt through honest confession and a resolution to work against anti-Semitism and all forms of racial or religious discrimination."[35]

IMPLEMENTING THE DECLARATION

A proper appreciation of the sociological significance of the declaration on Judaism also requires that it be evaluated within the context of other schemata adopted and promulgated. The Council's decree must be seen as a moment in a dynamic process within the Church, rather than as a fixed and frozen expression of Catholic policy. The statement on Judaism is but the starting point in a general confrontation of Jews and Catholics. both of whom are eager to know each other better and to understand that which is most sacred in the other's perception of his divine election. The statement is a tool that can be used to fashion a more sophisticated theology of Jewish-Christian relations. The Church's fervent intention to implement the declaration and to move beyond it remains the most encouraging factor in the whole four-year episode. It is to this attitude that Jews must ultimately direct their energies and attention and not to the statement alone.

It must be confessed that if the four-year struggle demonstrated the existense of anti-Semitism and ignorance concerning Jews and Judaism within the Catholic Church, it disclosed, too, significant pockets of anti-Catholic bitterness inside the Jewish community. There are some Jews who will not—apparently cannot—ever forgive the Catholic Church. They pounced upon every news item concerning every equivocation at Rome as evidence justifying their lack of trust. They magnified the shortcomings of the statement out of all proportion, failing to recognize any progress in the Council's history. In their bitterness they assumed an attitude toward Catholicism not unlike the attitude some Catholics still take toward Jews and Judaism, namely, they held *all* Christians accountable for the crusades and inquisitions, the ritual murders, and the Nazi ovens. They insisted that anti-Semitism is inherent in Christianity itself and refused to recognize any reconciling tendency in the Church.

Catholics need to beware of the patronizing smugness that is sometimes the consequence of thinking oneself the sole possessor of the fullness of truth. Jews need to beware of the shrinking of spirit, the accusing pride, that accompanies a dwelling on hurt. Both Jews and Catholics need to understand the other's human failings. In the profound conviction that God has a purpose in our separate existence, we ought to seek Him better by serving humanity together.

THE SPIRITUAL STRUGGLE WITHIN THE CHURCH

By dwelling on the Jewish statement alone, Jews will fail to recognize that it emerged from the crucible of Council debate no more inadequate or compromised than many other schemata. From the very beginning it was clear that there was a deep rift inside the Church. On one side of the chasm were those who are ready to acknowledge that the Church in its earthly existence commits error and has sinned against God and man. When separated from other Christians and other men, the Church lacks wholeness. These churchmen were eager to place under scrutiny Church teachings and traditional ways of communicating the Word that seems to provoke human misunderstanding. They were eager to reach out in fraternity to other religions and to be in dialogue with them, to listen and to learn. They sought ways to bring the Church's power to bear upon the crucial social problems of the world, if only to know better God's will for the Church.

On the other side are those who feel assured that the Church, by virtue of its heavenly promise, is pure and without blemish and contains all truth. In their opinion ecumenicity will only weaken the hold of the faithful on that which is distinctive and different about Catholicism. They were anxious lest too rapid a change in the ways of doing things will be accompanied by impatience with the restraints required in any spiritual commitment. They wished to protect Catholics who may, in their innocence, sacrifice what is eternal and absolute for fleeting and temporary values.

A similar rift is experienced by all religions. Protestants have their fundamentalists and liberals, Jews their Orthodox and Reform. Pope John seemed willing to place the influence of his office on the side of ecumenicity against polemicism, charity against condemnation, human fraternity against dogmatic narrowness. Exactly such a commitment was required at that moment to unlock the windows and to expose the Church to the fresh winds of change. Pope Paul has tried to encompass both tendencies within an integrated movement toward change. He appeared to reason that conservatism provided a brake on the radical, even as the very stationing of the Church in the world required a new alertness and vitality from the Curia. For Pope Paul the key to a united Church that would contain such paradox was a strong centralized authority joined by a Conciliar instrumentality within which both conservatives and liberals could feel at home.

With Paul's ascendency to the papacy all Conciliar statements managed somehow, even if uneasily, to include assertions that acknowledged the viewpoints of both the conservatives and the liberals. Thus the Schema on Ecumenism reached out in love toward other Christians; but it also asserted that they suffered "defect." The Declaration on the Relation of the Church to Non-Christian Religions acknowledged that in their very distinctiveness these other religions often contained God's presence, yet it insisted that "the fullness" of religious life was to be found only in Christianity. The statement on Judaism acknowledged that Jews are not collectively culpable for the Crucifixion, but it hastened to remind Jews that they had been displaced collectively as "the people of God" by virtue of their enmity toward the

Gospel. The Decree on Religious Liberty proclaimed a stern assurance that the Church would never violate the conscience of adherents to other religions, and yet the schema also made room for special concordats betwen church and state. It urged men to consider that the Catholic Church is the custodian of the one true faith. The Council confirmed the collegial power of bishops, then left it up to the Pope alone to define how that collegial power would be exercised.

In my personal view, it will be impossible for the Church to maintain such a bipolarity of tendencies. As the Church moves inevitably toward a fuller ecumenicity, a more profound dialogue with non-Christians, and a more active involvement in the world, laggards will fall in the breach or change their direction. That is why I remain optimistic concerning the Catholic Church's attitude toward Judaism, despite reservations about the precise wording of a statement. I am confident, for example, that when Catholics come to know Judaism more deeply and have cooperated often enough with Jews in acting upon shared convictions in the social order, the Church will not only be able to acknowledge that Judaism remains a faith that can inspire men to seek God's truth and pursue justice, but will be "edified" in their own self-understanding and sense of a common mission.

The Process of the Council

It took four long years before the majority of the Council could assert its convictions with regard to Judaism. It took that long, too, for the Council to clear the way for statements on many other pressing questions. Before criticizing the Church for its lumbering process, therefore, we ought to appreciate how far this massive organization has already moved and recognize, now, how far it may go once it has been set on its course.

The point is that the Catholic Church has only recently returned to the world. It earlier looked upon freedom as dangerous, religious pluralism as a scandal, the secularization of society as a tragedy, and the development of interreligious experiences on the lay level as a threat to the orthodoxy of faith. When finally the world thrust itself upon the Church, the desire to revamp the structures of the Church could no longer be restrained. But change is never easy. It takes great courage to give up the security of old ways.

Jews certainly ought to appreciate, from their own experience, how considerable is the strength of the forces of reaction that would rather retreat from the world than face the need to relax old laws or adopt new ways in order to be part of the world. Let Jews imagine that authoritarian control over the policy-making procedures of the Jewish community were in the hands of exactly those officials with the most rigid mentality: how fast and unequivocally would change take place in the Jewish community? An experience for Jews comparable to the agonizing struggle in which Catholic leaders were engaged would be the suggestion that the Jews of Israel adopt an American-type pattern of separation of church and state. Jews are hesitant even to raise such a question for fear of creating a *Kulturkampf*. This is exactly the kind of agony the Catholic Church endured. In truth it is amazing that Catholic bishops were able to accomplish so much in such a short time.

It was very impressive to see how effectively the Church Fathers with the Pope created democratic instrumentalities enabling the Council to progress on its course. The regional conference of bishops, the skilled use of theologians and experts, the expansion of Council commissions to include a fair representation from every corner of the globe—all these served to break the grip of the Curia over the Church and insured the broadest type of participation in Council proceedings. It was a world-wide Council indeed. Furthermore, the right of each Church Father to have his say was zealously protected; radical as well as reactionary sentiments were spoken without fear. Every proposed amendment to a Council decree was given serious consideration, and in almost every case the minority on all issues received a hearing far beyond the minimal requirements of political democracy. The Council was not just a legislative body. It was an assemblage of religious leaders seeking by their actions to reveal the will of God and to serve Him. No wonder the Council moved slowly.

But by the time of its conclusion the Vatican Council had

spoken words more profound than most Catholics will be able to comprehend, interpret, and put into effect for years to come. It will take time for the Church faithful as well as the leaders of other religions to appreciate all that was intended by the actions of the Council. It will take a longer while for Church structures to be changed so as to give meaning to the Council's words.

The worldwide nature of this Council of course gave added dimension and greater significance to its deliberations. But one consequence was that the statement on Judaism was revealed to be not partcularly important to many of the Fathers of the Council. As important as it was for American and European prelates, generally speaking, the attitudes of the Middle Eastern clergy were antagonistic, and many of the Asian and African bishops were indifferent. It was of greater moment to the African and Asian prelates, for example, to have a statement that would enable them to approach, with tokens of respect, Hindus and Buddhists, followers of Islam, and primitive pagans. The Church was called upon to recognize truth, a reverence for life, and a seeking after values inherent in all sorts of spiritual expression— from that of superstitious tribesmen to that of sophisticated urbanized atheists of our technological civilization. If anti-Semitism and coercion of conscience were the issues that exercised the emotional energy of some Western churchmen, poverty, racial prejudice, and the anguish of overpopulation challenged the intellectual resources of the entire Church with a greater urgency. Some degree of vigilance must be maintained, therefore, by those who wish to eradicate anti-Semitism from our civilization, lest in man's concern for every other kind of social evil this particular disorder once again will be left to survive and fester.

The Council must be judged, finally, not alone by what it had to say about Judaism but also by the attitude it brought to the whole gamut of issues that confronted it. When we realize how much the Council set out to do, we will not so quickly make a negative critical judgment on what it accomplished. Many in the Church have already acknowledged the Church's need to learn and change and grow. More important than a final word on each issue, therefore, will be the Church's commitment to organize such structures of action as to keep it involved in the world. The Council's important achievement was the stimulation of a completely new atmosphere in Catholicism. The Catholic Church is ready now to expand the freedom and power of its world-wide clergy, make use of and consult with its laity, engage in conversation with other religions, and act in the world where required in order to be of greater service to humanity. This is a striking accomplishment.

14. Vatican Council II—Recapitulation and Projection

DURING THE FOUR-YEAR PERIOD of the Vatican Council, the question of Jewish-Christian relations received an attention quite unparalleled in emotional depth and spiritual intensity. Protestants, through their own international convocations, joined Catholics in reconsidering Christian teaching with regard to Jews and Judaism. And Jews, on their part, were also challenged to deliberate on their attitudes toward a past history of suffering and the nature of their kinship with Christianity. It was a period of profound reassessment and soul-searching.

Resolutions were adopted by the Protestant World Council of Churches[1] and by Lutherans who convened an international consultation on the Church and the Jews at Logumkloster, Denmark.[2] The statements by these and other Churches produced a powerful Christian repudiation of contempt for Jews and Judaism. However inadequate, theologically, the statements may have seemed from a Jewish perspective, there is no gainsaying their profound contribution to a more open atmosphere in the relations between Jews and Christians. The fact that each Church had to travel a labored course in order to achieve its statement reflects accurately on the actual depth of anti-Semitism in our culture. But the fact that such statements were eventually issued ought to be reassuring. A good will is at work attempting to undo a bitter past.

The Catholic Church's Ecumenical Council, more than any other Christian convocation, attracted world-wide attention. Its agenda items became headlines news. Its decisions, indeed, became better known even among Protestants than the resolutions adopted by international Protestant bodies. Thus, when at last the Catholic Church promulgated its repudiation of any form of discrimination, including anti-Semitism, it was an action of vast significance.

In this chapter I shall try to recapitulate the significant events in the Vatican Council's deliberation on the Jewish question, report on efforts to implement the Conciliar resolution, and assess future prospects for the Jewish-Christian dialogue.

As we have already seen, the Council had to deal with the following questions:

Should the Council consider a statement on Judaism? Why?

Under whose auspices should such a statement be introduced to the Council?

What ought to be the relationship of Jews and Jewish organizations toward the Council?

What should the Church say in a Conciliar statement on Jews?

How should it implement its decisions?

It is clear now that it was by decision of Pope John XXIII, personally, that Augustin Cardinal Bea was assigned responsibility for drawing up a statement on Judaism and maintaining cordial relations with Jewish officials. Undoubtedly, the horrendous sufferings of Jews under the Nazis, actually witnessed by Joseph Roncalli, were a decisive factor in this decision. Certainly, the scholarly writings of the French historian Jules Isaac and his audience with him in 1960 also contributed to the Pope's specific knowledge of the ways in which Christian teachers had inspired an attitude of contempt toward Judaism. As we have seen, Pope John felt free even before any Conciliar action to revise liturgical formulations that offended Jews. Furthermore, by virtue of Cardinal Bea's faithful devotion to the adoption of a Jewish statement and the vigorous battle of liberal prelates throughout the world, including the American bishops, there was a widespread Christian conviction that the Church could delay no longer in repairing the scandalous disorder which is anti-Semitism. Inevitably, a clarification of Christian teaching on Jews and Judaism became a major agenda item for the Vatican Council. It is plain now, however, that the Catholic leaders of the Council had no idea how difficult was the task they were undertaking.

THE OPPOSITION

Hostility toward any forthright statement on anti-Semitism or Judaism emerged almost immediately from at least four quarters:

There were a small number of hard-core Catholic anti-Semites in the Council itself, but mainly the bigots were to be found on the fringes. They revealed the typical anti-Semite's paranoic delusion that the Jews are the leaders of an international conspiracy. Not untypically, every liberal reform was considered by this claque to be part of a Jewish effort to weaken the Church.

Arab officials interpreted any positive, conciliatory action toward Jews as an act of political friendship for the State of Israel. In light of their grievances against Jews, they could not accept any statement on anti-Semitism unless it should also express a Christian sentiment of sympathy for the plight of Arab refugees or address a rebuke to Zionism. Arab governments brought severe pressure to bear on Arab Catholics, and it took a significant measure of courage for some of the Arab prelates to justify—even to explain—to their constituencies the reasons for the eventual Conciliar decision.

Eastern Orthodox Protestants, and some of the Eastern rite Catholics, are heir to a tradition of scriptural interpretation that views the Jews as a reprobate people and Judaism as a condemned faith. These Christians feared that a forthright repudiation of such interpretations would weaken the Christian faith of their adherents. It might lead them to question the truth of everything else they had been taught by their Church. The Eastern Christians were able to agree, nevertheless, that in light of their obligations to Christian charity they would have to judge as morally evil discrimination, hatred, and harassment directed against anyone, including Jews.

The most significant force in opposition to a Jewish statement was the conservative Catholic leadership who looked with suspicion and alarm upon *any* effort to revise traditional teaching. For this element, a proposal to change the approach to Jews and Judaism was as threatening as any other "innovation" recommended to the Council. It was no accident that this group adopted stiff resistance and delaying tactics toward the schemata on religious liberty, the church and the world, ecumenism, the chapter defining episcopal collegiality—as well as the statement on Judaism. Their fundamentalist approach was evident in their unswerving literalism in accepting and citing the harsh judgment of certain New Testament passages on Jews and Judaism. Not only did they ignore Scripture verses that balanced such testimony, they also remained insensitive to the difference between the first century and the post-Auschwitz era. For it makes a difference whether one writes as a member of a tiny struggling sect, disappointed and even angered by the resistance of an established Jewish officialdom, or as a representative of a powerful Christian structure in a world that has for centuries maligned and even destroyed a Jewish minority.

THE ROLE OF CHRISTIANITY IN ANTI-SEMITISM

The startling lack of agreement among Catholic officials regarding the importance of the religious component in anti-Semitism, particularly modern-day anti-Semitism, was a distressing feature of the Council. Illiteracy about the Church's record in past history and misinformation were to be found in every quarter of the Church. Catholic attitudes ranged from the suggestions of Vatican Radio during the swastika epidemic, that there was *no* religious component in contemporary anti-Semitism and that the Jews themselves had provoked prejudice, to the confession made by many prelates on the Council floor that Christians had harmed Jews and still do harm them. In no case, however, have Catholic scholars acknowledged as openly as have Protestant theologians that the New Testament can be a source of anti-Semitic sentiment. Nor do many Catholic historians admit that the Church, as church, had contributed its own particular ingredient to the anguish of Jews.

Obviously, the religious factor in hatred of the Jews remains a subject worthy of scholarly investigation, particularly in light of the University of California studies revealing that certain Christian beliefs contribute still to the anti-Semitism of American Christians.[3] Conservatively, these findings suggest that at least one-fourth of America's anti-Semites have a religious basis for their prejudice, while another fifth have this religious basis in considerable part. Indeed, only five per cent of Americans with anti-Semitic views lack all rudiments of a religious basis for their prejudice. In terms of absolute numbers rather than percentages, these data indicate that approximately 17.5 million Americans who hold fairly strong anti-Semitic beliefs would also be classified as religious bigots. Thirty-seven per cent of Protestants and 22 per cent of Catholics scored "high" in anti-Semitism. There remains prevalent in our civilization, therefore, a noxious heritage of religious attitudes that supports hatred of Jews. We shall need all the wisdom that can be derived from an understanding of the past in order to deal with this problem in the future.

Jews are justified in suspecting that the reluctance of Christians to confront the iniquitous past record stems, in part, from embarrassment. In view of that record, after all, how can Christians claim that the Redeemer has appeared on earth? Resistance to the testimony of history arises also from the severe challenge still posed by Judaism to the Christian claim that Jesus born of the Jews is the Christ. The "stiff-neckedness" of Jews regarding the Christian Messianic claim and the continued vitality of Judaism creates a problem for Christian theology of gigantic proportions. On the one hand, what does God intend by His continued fidelity to the Jewish people? And on the other hand, how can it be that a people who call Jesus "Lord and Saviour" should have lent themselves to the perpetration of such a bloody history of inhumanity and cruelty?[4]

Although the formal Conciliar statement was never permitted to express confession or contrition, the remorse of many individual Catholic prelates and their hopes that the statement would serve, nevertheless, as an instrument of reconciliation were clearly apparent. It is that attitude, in the end, more than the actual words of the statement, that will determine the future course of the Church in its relation to Jews.

RESPONSIBILITY FOR THE JEWISH STATEMENT

Once having decided that the Council ought to issue a statement on the Catholic attitude toward Jews and Judaism, Pope

John had to determine under what auspices such a statement should be written. His choice was made on the basis of his confidence in a *person* rather than in a rigid consistency of ideas. Thus, when he chose Cardinal Bea's Secretariat for the Promotion of Christian Unity as the proper commission to handle relations with Jews, he was obviously more concerned with Bea's liberalism and ecumenical outlook than with the question of Jewish inclusion in a "Christian unity" movement. In other words, Pope John paid greater attention to Cardinal Bea's willingness to acknowledge past Christian error, his respect for the truth nurtured in other faiths, and his commitment to the importance of biblical concepts than to a studious evaluation of the Church's theological stance with regard to Jews. Pope John made a wise choice.

Furthermore, there is wisdom in acknowledging somehow that the schism between the Synagogue and the Nazarenes was the original schism in the body of Israel and that later Christian divisions were no more scandalous a rupture in the unity of God's people.[5] If Christians share together the sacrament of baptism in Christ, so do Jews and Christians share together, according to the Gospel, the promises of Abraham, the claim to be God's Israel, and the prospect of a future harmony in God's end-time. The Church could hardly enact a constitution defining itself without taking into account its roots in the Synagogue and Temple and its relation to the Jewish people even at the very end of its pilgrimage on earth.

Many Jews, of course, objected to such a philosophy of Jewish-Christian interrelatedness. Their defensiveness was understandable in light of unhappy memories of a coercive Christian evangelism, frequently hidden behind the theologizing. Some Jews believed strongly also that the uniqueness of each faith permitted no "special ties" between them; Jews, they felt, had no place in a document of Christian self-definition. There were Church Fathers, too, who insisted that the Jews had lost all unique status by virtue of their rejection of Jesus, and thus the Church had no need to express a particular relationship to contemporary Jews. Paradoxically, therefore, both Orthodox Jews and conservative Catholics, each for their own different reasons, objected to Cardinal Bea's responsibility for a Jewish statement.

Ultimately, Cardinal Bea had to bend to such pressures. The Council from its very beginning decided to direct its major energies in ecumenical relationship toward Orthodox and Protestant Christians. Only later was it pressed into a consideration of Judaism, Islam, Hinduism and Buddhism, the pagan religions of Africa and Asia, and atheism. One cannot argue with this legitimate decision of the Catholics to place greatest emphasis on their relations with other Christians. But it should be clear by now that a doctrine of "the people of God" that is delimited to Christian components is an inadequate theological expression of God's profoundest dealings with other men and religions, and particularly it overlooks God's covenant with the Jews.

SHOULD THERE HAVE BEEN JEWISH OBSERVERS AT THE COUNCIL?

The Council's early decision to exclude official Jewish participation from the work of the Secretariat for the Promotion of Christian Unity was, in my opinion, an error. Provision should have been made for an official Jewish presence, in view of the Council's early announcement that a statement on Judaism would be on the agenda. Just as the Church needed and desired the help of other Christians in determining matters of church polity and policy, so did it need and desire consultation with Jews as it developed a Jewish declaration. In fact, the Church found the way to obtain such assistance. There were Jewish agencies, professionally concerned with the problems of anti-Semitism, who were ready to offer counsel. Council rules regarding secrecy and the later political machinations within the Church, however, lent an unfortunate air of stealth and subterfuge to what ought to have been an open relationship of trust and confidence. It did not help matters, of course, that Jewish and Catholic officials both played politics with "leaks" of documents.

The ugliness of such Jewish involvement in the Council was acerbated when Jews began to quarrel among themselves over who had the right to be in contact with the Church. Orthodox Jews paradoxically insisted that no Jews should intrude upon Christian deliberations, but then asserted that, if any Jews were to be consulted, they ought to be "Torah-true" Jews. American

Jewish community relations organizations, such as the American Jewish Committee and the Anti-Defamation League, countered: We are not intruding; the Church has asked for our help. The issues concern all Jews and therefore all Jews have a right to be involved.

Mistakes were made by both sides in this internal Jewish debate. Orthodox Jews frequently displayed a harsh anti-Church hostility coupled with a profound ignorance of Church politics. The community relations agencies often showed insensitivity to Jewish religious practices and attitudes.

In my own personal view, however, the contribution made by B'nai B'rith's Anti-Defamation League and by the American Jewish Committee remains of inestimable value. By their presence, the leaders of these organizations helped sympathetic Catholics ward off a powerful attack on the Jewish declaration. If the Orthodox Jewish attitude of disinterest in the Council and covert hostility had prevailed, these liberal Catholic prelates might have been overwhelmed. Instead, they were strengthened for their battle by the convictions of Dr. Joseph Lichten and Rabbi Marc Tanenbaum, and their European counterparts, B'nai B'rith's Dr. E. L. Ehrlich of Geneva and the American Jewish Committee's Paris-based European director Dr. Zachariah Shuster. These men helped the Council Fathers realize that Jews did care deeply about the Council's effort to improve Jewish-Christian relations, and that, furthermore, Jews and Christians do share enough of a heritage of faith so as to make possible and worthwhile interreligious dialogue and joint social action.

Obviously a historic situation as important as this Church Council encompasses complexities beyond the ken of any one author. I have hardly described all of the relationships between Jewish leaders in cooperation with Church officials, and I know even less about the manipulations of the opposition to the Jewish declaration. Other books by those directly involved will have to be written. I can report, however, that Jewish pressure, although necessary, was minuscule when compared to that exerted by the enemies of the declaration. Happily, despite the power of those who opposed Cardinal Bea's efforts, there was never any doubt that the majority of the Council Fathers were ready to denounce anti-Semitism and to repudiate any concept of the Jews as a people accursed of God.

THE SUBSTANCE OF THE JEWISH STATEMENT AND ITS LOCATION ON THE COUNCIL AGENDA

Exactly what the Church would say in a statement on Jews or Judaism depended, in part, on the context in which the statement would appear on the agenda. But theological considerations and evaluations of the public-relations posture of the Church were brought to bear upon the Conciliar officials charged with that responsibility.

The Secretariat for the Promotion of Christian Unity, primarily for practical reasons, decided at first to place the Jewish statement within the Schema on Ecumenism. That schema was to be written under their authority, it was certain to be considered early in the Council's agenda, and a case could be made for including a concern for Jews within the spirit of openness, respect, and acceptance already engendered by the ecumenical movement among Christians. But as we have noted, the proposal ran into stiff opposition. Some Catholics and Protestants, despite the friendliest of feelings for Jews, wanted to confine the ecumenical movement, officially, to Christianity. Other Catholics, out of disrespect for Judaism, opposed the inclusion of a statement on Judaism in the Schema on Ecumenism even as they opposed the schema itself. There were Jews, too, who preferred that the Council deal merely with anti-Semitism in the Schema on the Church in the Modern World as but another social problem. They hoped that the Church would eschew any effort to define the theological relationships between Judaism and Christianity.

Once it was agreed to separate the Jewish statement from the Schema on Ecumenism, the door was opened wide to many considerations. The following received some hearing:

It was proposed that the Vatican Council deal with anti-Semitism only as a problem in the social order and make no other statement with regard to Judaism. This proposal was rejected, ultimately, on the grounds that it would ignore exactly those distorted theological understandings of Christianity that had stimulated or justified, for some Christians, discrimination against Jews. Furthermore, the Church's statement would be more powerful were it placed within the context of the Church's own understanding of its indebtedness to Judaism and its theological affirmation of the role of the Jews in God's plan for the redemption of mankind.

It was proposed that the Council place the statement on Judaism within its Schema on the Church, and such a statement was in fact eventually written into that constitution. To define the Synagogue, however, only in terms of the Church's understanding of herself, would have meant failure to deal with the distortions of the Crucifixion account, the perverse theology of Jewish accursedness, or the social problem of anti-Semitism. Thus another, fuller statement was required.

It was proposed that the Council issue a separate statement on Judaism. This suggestion was rejected on the grounds that a world-wide Church could hardly justify a statement dealing with only one religion and offer no word regarding other religions. As one session after another took place, the conviction grew among the Church Fathers that the same open-mindedness required of them to recognize the presence of God in Judaism, the original non-Christian religion, could also be applied to other non-Christian faiths. In some ways, in fact, the problem of Judaism was even more complicated, since Jesus was Jewish and Jews rejected him as the Christ, whereas among other religions the awareness of the Christian claim to God's true nature was lacking completely. As we have seen, the Council Fathers ultimately pressed themselves to a re-assessment of that ray of truth and spiritual vitality that is to be found among many religions. By placing the Jewish statement in the context of the Catholic attitude toward all non-Christian religions, therefore, the Vatican Council opened a completely new and exciting chapter in Church history. Now, instead of emphasizing the blindness and the spiritual poverty of other faiths, instead of evoking a condescending spirit of pity or a compulsive manipulative effort to proselytize, the Church must approach other religions with respect. The Council statement on Judaism was changed, then, from a small chapter in the

Schema on Ecumenism to a full-scale decree on the Catholic attitude toward non-Christian religions.

The actual text of the Jewish statement also underwent numerous drafts and revisions and changes. But certain components remained constant throughout: The Church would denounce hatred; it would acknowledge its beginnings in biblical Judaism; it would emphasize the Pauline doctrine that the Jewish people remain dear to God and secure in their election. What remained uncertain was exactly how the Church would define the role or the guilt of some Jews in the Crucifixion, and ultimately how the Church would interpret the meaning of Jewish existence in light of the harsh scriptural judgments heaped upon Jews.

The Church's difficulty was not in its clear duty to renounce hatred or to express a sentiment of charity toward Jews; it was in the more complex problem of deciding exactly how to understand the words of its own Scripture. Not every opponent of the Jewish declaration was an enemy of Jews. Some persons were strongly motivated by a rigid, traditional, and literalistic approach to biblical exegesis. Hence the statement is a victory of no little proportion. The document offers a new understanding of the Bible.

At one point in the statement's history the Council would have acknowledged that only the Jews of today are free of a collective guilt for the Crucifixion, the implication being that the Jews of a former time were culpable. But then the statement clearly repudiated the concept of collective guilt, for the Jews both of the past and of this day. At one point the statement mentioned the crime of "deicide" by name; at another date it substituted for that word other less theologically perplexing formulations. The statement once contained what had been interpreted as a veiled invitation to Jewish conversion; that was later softened. The statement once condemned discrimination in general; now it repudiates and decries anti-Semitism specifically. In the course of this book I have tried to detail these various changes in the substance of the statement as they emerged in Council debate.

In all this, it is important to recognize that the actual wording of the statement is but the beginning in a new Jewish-Christian conversation. As good as the statement may be, it is not complete;

it is not fully adequate. What Jews will wish of the Church—and this becomes the agenda item for future dialogue—is not only a statement of Christianity's past relatedness to Judaism but a recognition also of the integrity and permanent preciousness of the contemporary Jewish faith. Jews want the Church to recognize that they are not a people unfulfilled or inferior in any way. No prayers for their conversion, no missionary enterprises are required. Rather, they welcome the opportunity for mutual study and inter-religious dialogue, mindful of God's promise that when men gather to speak of Him, His presence will be among them.

The renowned Catholic editor, Philip Sharper, after a visit to Israel gave intimation that Catholics are now aware of this Jewish concern. Writing in the January 1967 issue of *The Critic* he observed: "Even the most sophisticated Christians of good will seem, too often, to regard the theological relation of Christianity to Judaism to be exclusively to a Judaism locked in the past—the Old Testament, Hebraic thought-patterns, the creation of the Synagogue and the evolution of our liturgy from Jewish ritual forms. This is to assume that all the spiritual energy and religious force of Judaism became, after the advent of Christianity, a frozen waterfall. . . . It is with a living Judaism that the Christian is summoned to have dialogue today. . . ."

IMPLEMENTATION OF THE JEWISH STATEMENT

In the course of the four years of the Vatican Council's deliberation, a distinct pattern of political reaction emerged. As the Council Fathers became ever more resolute in their intention to move the Church toward change, Curial officials desperately devised one stratagem after another to delay that change. At each session of the Council, for example, the Jewish statement, when presented, was greeted with an affirmative response by the Fathers. In between sessions, however, when Curial officials were able to do their work outside the glare of public scrutiny, changes were frequently made in the Conciliar statement that restored traditional interpretations and weakened the text. When given the opportunity, the Council Fathers voiced with vigor a liberal approach in their relations with other faiths. But those who favored com-

promise were able to bide their time and behind closed doors
manipulate the machinery of the Church to inhibit ecumenism.
Fortunately, the Curia will not stop the Church from the progressive course set by the Council. A minority cannot block for long
the clearly expressed will of the majority. Life has a way of
moving far beyond the carefully planned compromises of the
moment. But in order to assure the permanence of the changes
in attitude expressed by the Council, the Church Fathers will have
to translate their new vision into structures of operation and
administration. Thus the powers, function, or personnel of the
Curia will have to be changed. The Synod of Bishops will need
to grow in power. Most importantly, the local hierarchy and the
regional associations will also have to implement the various
Council decrees. They will have to institute those structural patterns that will build the ecumenical spirit into every possible relation of the Church to other religions in the world.

As the debate in the Council seemed to linger on endlessly,
Jewish disappointment in the Catholic Church deepened and
signs of sullen anger appeared. Jews, too, will have to work out
their hurt in response to the good will that many churchmen
brought to the Council's declaration and have since constistently
demonstrated. It is unhealthy for Jews continually to nurture suspicion of the Christian world or to foster an attitude that suggests
"we stand alone without friends." As Rabbi Balfour Brickner, director of Reform Judaism's Department of Inter-Faith Activity, has
noted, "Hostilities are usually mutual and Jews too need to wrestle
with some of their own attitudinal difficulties!"[6] Jews ought to
accept, even encourage, continued discourse with Catholics. Urges
Rabbi Brickner, "we will need more, not less communication."
It is heartwarming to note, therefore, that a restructuring of the
institutional forms of the Church is now evident. A sincere effort
on the part of Catholic officials is being made to implement the
Conciliar statements and to stimulate continued Jewish-Christian
conversation. As Cardinal Bea has observed regarding the Council's decree on Judaism, "Its beneficial effects will depend on the
degree to which it will be understood, assimilated and put into
practice."[7]

In the United States the Catholic bishops established an official

Bishops' Commission for Ecumenical Affairs. Its first task was
to start dialogue and conversation with the major Church bodies
in this country, including the Jews. Theological conversations
have been initiated with Lutherans, Episcopalians, Presbyterians,
Methodists, and Orthodox Christians. In addition, a sub-com-
mission has been organized to inquire after and seek the ways of
maintaining contact with the Jewish community.[8]

Once again, unfortunately, that Bishops' Subcommission on
Catholic-Jewish Relations confronted the same confusing problem of organizational protocol that bedeviled the Vatican Council.
Should Jews be included officially within any ecumenical structure, considering that its major concern is for Christian unity?
If they are to be included, with whom in the Jewish community
should American Catholics converse? What is it that Jews and
Catholics can and should talk about? Will Jews be willing to
engage in theological conversation or must the agenda be limited
to those secular problems that men ought to confront together
in the social order?

To this point neither the Catholic Subcommission nor the
Jewish Community has resolved such questions; again Catholic officials are receiving conflicting opinion from within the Jewish
community. By early 1967, the Subcommission held one meeting
with officials of the Synagogue Council of America, an agency
coordinating the work of the three major religious denominational
groupings of American Jews. And it has promised to convene
individual meetings with the leaders of major Jewish community
relations organizations, such as the Anti-Defamation League, the
American Jewish Committee, the American Jewish Congress, and
the National Community Relations Advisory Council. At an Anti-
Defamation League Conference for Christian leaders on the problem of Christian beliefs and anti-Semitism, Msgr. George Higgins,
then Secretary to the Subcommittee, pleaded with Jewish officials
to create one coordinated leadership group with whom Catholics
could be in conversation. Unfortunately there is little likelihood
that they will do so in the near future. Instead, Catholic officials
will just have to find their way about the total Jewish community.
They will have to invite all Jewish agencies into conversation and
remain responsive to the wide variety of concerns and opportuni-

ties offered by each one. Certainly Catholics should not try to make a judgment on the variety of Jewish organizations and favor one above the other. They cannot restructure the Jewish community within categories that meet the definitions and need of the Christian Church.

Happily, relations with Jews do not have to remain as perplexing as they first appear. The National Council of Churches (Protestant), for example, has already worked out a satisfactory procedural arrangement for dealing with the Jewish community. For several years now the National Council of Churches has invited all Jewish religious, educational, welfare, and community relations organizations to meet regularly with the Protestant leadership for discussion of problems and issues of mutual concern. When placed in one room together, Jewish leaders tend to minimize their internal differences and to emphasize the programs on which they can stand together. Furthermore, when a problem is of major concern, such as the plight of the Jews in the Soviet Union or the safety of the State of Israel, the Jewish community manages to coordinate its reaction in a responsible way. In addition, the various departments and agencies of the National Council of Churches remain open to engaging in individual relationship with any and every Jewish organization on a project or concern worthy of attention. There is no reason why such a formalized pattern of consultations and dialogue of many types cannot now be built into the structure of the Bishops' Subcommission on Catholic-Jewish Relations.

What remains most constructive is the fact that on a national level the door has at last been opened officially for Jewish and Catholic leaders to meet with each other when the occasion warrants.

The Bishops' Commission for Ecumenical Affairs has also urged that a similar Diocesan Commission for Ecumenical Affairs be established in every local diocese, and has suggested that at least one member of the Commission be assigned specific responsibilities for maintaining cooperation with the local Jewish community. In a carefully planned listing of recommendations for diocesan commissions the bishops acknowledged that "the ecumenical movement in the strictest sense refers to the efforts to promote Christian unity and does not properly apply to the relations with non-Christian communities." Nevertheless, it exhorted each diocese "to seek a full measure of cooperation with these religious groups, notably the Jewish communities."[9]

The Bishops' Commission then went on to recommend activities that could be undertaken by every one of the major units within the Church; programs were suggested for the whole parish, for clergy, for theologians, for schools and colleges. The following were particularly underscored for action: a careful review of texts and recommended reading lists to eliminate anti-Jewish sentiment; the encouragement of Catholic seminarians to attend lectures and seminars in seminaries of other denominations; the preparation of sermon outlines in keeping with the diocesan program and policies and keyed to occasions of ecumenical importance; neighborhood ecumenical discussion groups for laymen across faith lines; the participation of priests in interreligious clergy dialogue.

The American bishops have also organized a Subcommission on Ecumenism and Catholic Education to consider specific changes that need to be made in the Catholic school system on all levels, from parish school to theological seminary, in light of the Conciliar decrees. This subcommission, too, has already met with national Protestant and Jewish leaders in order to ascertain feelings with regard to their effort.[10]

CATHOLIC BISHOPS ISSUE GUIDELINES

These actions by the American bishops culminated on March 16, 1967 when the Subcommission for Catholic-Jewish Affairs promulgated the text of official guidelines to govern relations with the Jewish community (see Appendix F). The guidelines reveal that American Catholics not only intend to fulfill the Council's mandate, but also in sensitivity to Jewish concerns they have moved far beyond it. Many of the objections raised by Jews toward the Conciliar statement are here met and overcome.

The Subcommission calls on Catholics to "take the initiative" in fostering Catholic-Jewish understanding. It makes it clear that the objectives of dialogue meetings should be mutually agreed upon in advance; the general purposes should be to eliminate

sources of tension, increase understanding, and promote cooperative social action. The guidelines explicitly caution, "it is understood that proselytizing is to be carefully avoided in the dialogue. . . ."

The guidelines again call for the examination of school texts,
prayer books, and other media. But they specify the changes
that will be brought into Catholic instruction:

Anti-Semitism must be confronted frankly and honestly in history books, courses, and curricula; and an explicit rejection must
be made of the "historically inaccurate notion that Judaism in
the first century, especially that of Pharisaism, was a decadent
formalism and hypocrisy." Finally the guidelines, recognizing the
inadequacy of Catholic theology in defining a relationship to contemporary Judaism, urge "an acknowledgment by Catholic scholars
of the living and complete reality of Judaism after Christ and
the permanent election of Israel," and the incorporation of the
results of such an attitude into Catholic teaching.

Given such a positive approach to Jewish-Christian understanding it is no surprise that many significant ventures in Jewish-
Christian cooperation have been initiated. At least fifty rabbis
have been invited to join the faculty of Catholic colleges. Lecture
programs on Judaism have been planned for seminarians. Educational in-service training programs on issues in Jewish-Christian
relations have been scheduled for teaching nuns. Textbooks or
units on Judaism are under preparation for use in Catholic
theology courses. So overburdened, in fact, was one Jewish scholar
who had been welcomed into parish meetings, invited to lecture
at Catholic school assemblies, and asked to participate in every
aspect of this ecumenical thrust that he quipped, "I am a victim
of ecumenical overkill." Obviously, it will be necessary to widen
the number of Jewish scholars and leaders who are equipped to
engage in such interreligious conversation.

Jewish religious leadership, responding to this outpouring of
good will, has begun to ignore those leaders in their own community who warn against theological dialogue. Both Reform and
Conservative religious leaders have created occasions officially to
indicate their support for and readiness to participate in religious
exchange with Catholic scholars. Both the Anti-Defamation League

and the American Jewish Committee have intensified their programming with Catholic institutions and have taken on additional staff to engage in the work.

The Union of American Hebrew Congregations (Reform) at its 48th Biennial General Assembly in San Francisco, November, 1965, issued the following resolution: "The new directions of American interreligious life, and, specifically, the call from our Christian brethren for a closer community and dialogue, offer fresh opportunities for the strengthening of these relations. We urge the expansion and deepening of the programs of our National Commission of Interfaith Activity and summon our congregations to enter more intensively into dialogue with our Christian compatriots *even into those areas which touch on matters of faith.*"[11]

At the Convention of the Rabbinical Assembly (Conservative) in Toronto, Canada, in June, 1966, Rabbi Abraham Heschel warned his co-religionists, "Parochialism has become untenable. Jews and Christians alike share the same perils and fears. It is no longer safe for Jews to cultivate aloneness and uniqueness, to refrain from sharing either perplexities or uncertainties with Christians."[12]

A debate on the subject of interfaith dialogue was featured at the Annual Meeting in April, 1966 of the National Community Relations Advisory Council, the coordinating agency of local and state Jewish community councils and national community relations organizations. The speaker in opposition was an executive of the Orthodox congregational body, the Union of Orthodox Jewish Congregations of America; the speaker in defense of dialogue was Morris Laub, lay chairman of social action for Conservative Jewry's congregational body, the United Synagogue. Mr. Laub argued that theological dialogue was legitimate "because it is already being done and it is right to permit it in the first instance." Reporting only on those dialogues in which laymen have been the participants, Mr. Laub revealed that the Anti-Defamation League had recorded over the past few years over sixty interfaith consultations; the American Jewish Committee reported six community dialogues in the three-month period ending January 15, 1966; and in April, 1966, the American Jewish Committee joined the National Council of Catholic Men in promoting a nationwide program of "grass roots ecumenism" intended "to place emphasis on participation by all Catholics in interreligious dialogue and community development." The Reform religious group announced that "dialogues on theological matters are being conducted currently in at least ten congregations." The University of Judaism in Los Angeles instituted a twenty-seven-session course to prepare laymen to participate in interreligious conversation. Mr. Laub summarized, "Dialogue causes the non-Jew to view the Jew with new eyes . . . his ignorance and prejudices about us begin to fall."[13]

The value of dialogue was seriously questioned in midsummer, 1967, however, when for most Jews the response of the official Christian churches to the crisis faced by Israel was so appallingly shallow. Charges and counter-charges were hurled through press headlines as Jews expressed their relief at Israel's stunning military victory and then articulated their disappointment at the failure of Christian bodies to have recognized the genocidal significance of the Arab threats. When all the facts were made known, however, it became clear there were many extenuating circumstances to account for the situation and its resolution required not Jewish self-righteous aloofness but more dialogue.[14]

In truth, the Church bodies were deficient in their response. Many had not realized that Israel was in such trouble; they had greater confidence in Israel's military ability than did the Jews themselves. They opposed unilateral action by the United States—given their unpopular opposition to American policy in Vietnam—and were hopeful of a United Nations solution. They were silenced, too, by their allegiance to Christians in Arab countries and their twenty-year commitment to relief programs in behalf of Arab refugees. But most significantly, Church leaders had no clear understanding of the relationship between American Jews and Israel. They looked upon Israel as but another secular state and failed to comprehend its religious meaning in Judaism. Jewish Leaders soon recognized that, in all their dialogues with Christians, the importance of Israel and the Zionist dimension in Jewish self-identification had rarely been placed on the agenda.

In truth, also, Jews quickly acknowledged that many individual Christians—those not bound by organizational and bureaucratic discipline—had spoken out openly in defense of Israel's integrity as a nation. Several of the hierarchy, Catholic newspapers, and many Catholic clergy not only supported Israel's cause but some criticized as well the papal statements calling for the peace of Jerusalem and its internationalization—a position that appeared to place property values above the human issues in that tense and complex part of the world.

Once the immediate crisis was over, most Jews and Christians recognized that the dialogue not only had to be intensified but redirected. Heretofore, much of the conversation had dealt with "defense" issues, i.e., the problem of the Crucifixion account and anti-Semitism, or religious problems, i.e., the role of religion in shaping public morality, the prayer life of Jews and Christians, the meaning of Old Testament passages, etc.; now the dialogue must acknowledge the corporate nature of Judaism and its peculiar combination of religious and secular elements. Christians will be called upon to confront the primary importance of Jewish peoplehood. In a word, Christians will be asked to make a greater effort to know the Jew as he is today, not as the Christian sees him through the spectrum of New Testament narration or medieval Christian theology.[15]

There is no doubt that the Vatican Council declaration and the changes it has inspired in Church structure will make possible a more intelligent Jewish-Christian encounter.

THE FUTURE OF JEWISH-CHRISTIAN RELATIONS

The enthusiasm and sincere warmth with which Catholics now cooperate in interreligious activities is most gratifying; some rather harsh realities on the horizon, however, ought properly to temper the general optimism.

To begin with, the very progressive spirit of the Church in the United States, particularly in relation to other religious groups, is not characteristic of the world-wide Church; nor, for that matter, has the Church moved at the same rapid pace everywhere in the United States.

The American Catholic Church, by virtue of a particular sociological position in this country, has been stimulated more than other national Churches to institute the changes promised in the

Decree on Ecumenism. In America, the Catholic Church is a minority religion, only recently given the freedom to burst forth from the confines of the ghetto. American Catholics thirst for the heady wine of the interreligious exchange, and their joy at its bouquet has warmed us all. In America, Jews properly expect Catholics to implement the Conciliar decrees calling for mutual study, intensive dialogue, and forthright cooperative social action ventures, and they have not been disappointed. In other countries, however, particularly where a conservative, majority Catholic culture-religion still prevails, Jews will be happy if Catholics only engage in the same type of interfaith brotherhood teas that characterized interreligious relations in this country more than thirty-five years ago; and they have not yet experienced even this minimal effort at interfaith fraternity. In other words, from a worldwide perspective, the Jew cannot yet feel completely secure and comfortable everywhere with the exercise of political power by Catholic-influenced officialdom. American Jews and Catholics, therefore, might consider developing such structures as will enable them together to bring the insights of their American experience to other countries, where the interreligious conversation has hardly begun and where social factors still resist civilized intercourse across faith lines.

But lest we think that all is perfect in the United States, it is well to remember the dioceses in this country where bishops still have been reluctant to allow their priests to enter interfaith dialogue groups or permit their Catholic seminarians to be exposed to Jewish scholars. Church-related organizations that may engage in the more radical type of social action still find it hard to operate. The Catholic Church in America has not yet everywhere, nor in a total sense, permitted freedom inside its own structures. Jews will watch with eager anticipation, therefore, as the Church struggles to remove herself from the shackles of a defensive immigrant status. We shall rejoice in Catholic achievement, for Jews, too, must yet win full freedom in Christian America. And we shall also have to learn how to forgo some of our defensiveness, fear, and suspicion.

In this respect, there is on the horizon another development in America that may give Jews pause: the possibility that intra-Christian *rapprochement* may be a threat to the Jew. Catholics and Protestants have suddenly rediscovered each other with such a zeal that their mutual delight in each other's Christianity has tended to make the Jew's belated reminder that he, too, is on the scene appear to some an annoying intrusion. Catholic priests are now ready to join ministerial associations and Catholic churches are seeking ways of relating themselves to the work of local (Protestant) church councils just at a time when Jewish participation in such communal religious organizations has resulted in a toning down of their manifest Christocentric character.

With a revival of sectarian Christian enthusiasm the Jews' insistence that public religious ceremonials and interfaith cooperative projects be couched exclusively in Old Testament language may wear thin the tolerance of some Christians. The Jew may find, when the behemoth Protestant and Catholic establishments join forces, that Judaism is really not the symbolic third in the religious constellation. Rather, Jews are a minuscule minority, less than 3 per cent of the population of this country. There is a way in which the achievement of a Christian consensus and its interpenetration into the culture of America may heighten the Jew's sense of alienation. It is possible, therefore, that many Jews will align themselves even more forcefully with a secularist tradition in America as a defense against the impositions of Christianity. Thus, we shall have to try, somehow, to find ways to strengthen religion's total involvement in the secular world without at the same time placing in jeopardy the right of each religious group to maintain its faith particularity.

Growth in Christian "churchiness," as a result of Catholic-Protestant ecumenicity, may also provide an internal problem for the Jewish community. We have long resisted organizing ourselves in terms of the Christian prototypes of ecclesiastical structure. But resistance to such a pattern is difficult to maintain. Even now, synagogue leaders, as part of an internal political power struggle, seek to win Church support for their claim that religious conversation and interreligious social action should be delimited to synagogue-church structures; thus they seek to exclude the Jewish community's non-synagogal-centered educational, philanthropic, and community relations organizations from some important interfaith activities. Some Christian leaders, in their innocence of the structures and sociology of American Jews, have found themselves trapped in this confusing maze of the Jewish minority's emotionally tinged fragmentation. Jewish-Christian relations will probably long be plagued with the fact that Jews do not maintain one united voice that can speak for the Jewish community with the same authority or inclusiveness as the Catholics' Bishops' Conference or the Protestants' National Council of Churches. Nor will Jews be as ready or as able to hold their own in the interfaith dialogue, in a period when the ability to define oneself theologically becomes more important. Jewish structures of education and patterns of group identity have been fashioned in ways far different from those of the Christian Church. The problem, therefore, of who speaks for the Jews to which Christians and what it is Jews are prepared to say at the time of confrontation remains to be resolved.

There are also hard-line political issues around which our religious communities still find themselves bitterly divided. While shared social-action ventures—rabbis walking together with nuns in Selma, Alabama; Catholic, Protestant, and Jewish officials testifying together in support of foreign aid programs, civil rights measures, increased educational spending and more effective campaigns against poverty—have increased the glow of the ecumenical spirit, nevertheless, dark antagonisms continue to threaten the mood of good will. The persistence of some Jewish and liberal civil liberties groups in attacking, through the courts, the many government-financed activities to aid church-related facilities for children remains a provocative source of tension. American Catholic bishops have remained also most passive on the issue of American military intervention in South Vietnam, at the very moment when this issue has strained the unity of many other religious groups. Thus, those who will choose to protest American policy the most vigorously, like those who are the most loyal supporters of the radical Negro rights movement, may find themselves more alienated from Catholic officialdom than from any other religious institutional leadership in this land. Jews and Catholics also still have their own quarrel with each other over the reluctance of the Vatican, in light of its far-flung commitments in the Arab world, to acknowledge in any official way the establishment of the State of Israel.

Finally, there is the possible prospect that the more we come to know about each other's faith commitment, the more hardened we shall become in insisting upon our differences and the more tense will be our relationship. Mutual study—unless it is initiated with the assumption of being limited to seeking understanding only, rather than scoring points or bringing about conversion—can lead to mutual antagonism, not growth in friendship. It is important, therefore, that every ecumenical relationship be undertaken with the rules and expectations as clearly defined as possible: We must respect each other in our differences; we must want to learn from the other and acknowledge some insufficiency in our understandings; we must cherish that which binds us together even as we affirm our sectarian convictions; we must agree to speak our minds in truth but remain alert to reformulate our conceptions when we have misunderstood or distorted the other's position; we must acknowledge our own human capacity to err and trust God to justify us in our virtue; we must never seek to violate conscience or manipulate, intimidate, or harass the other; we must be willing to join the other in the service of humanity and thus, by humility, sacrifice, pursuit of justice, and love, achieve at a depth beyond words that oneness which is often felt in a shared spiritual event.

Vatican Council II's promulgated decrees contain an appreciation of the attitudes that inform such rules of ecumenical behavior. Certainly, when such a spirit takes on the flesh of deed, then the Church will exercise a spiritual power that can transform intergroup suspicion into trust and refashion human alienation into a fraternal interdependence.

God's spirit certainly was present in the Council's deliberations. Protestants and Orthodox Christians and Jews and men of good will everywhere were touched by its achievement. They were moved to explore, each in their own way, their relation to God's purpose and their understanding of His will.

Now, God willing, by the quality of our associations with each other and the courage with which we shall seek to repair the world, we may increase the experience of godliness among men. To be a blessing unto people and a light unto nations is to be Israel. Toward that vocation both Christians and Jews feel themselves called. May we be worthy of our name.

Notes

INTRODUCTION

1. The full text of this Vatican Council declaration is to be found in Appendix D.
2. Delivered at a convocation on "Theological Issues of Vatican II," Notre Dame University, March 21, 1966. See John H. Miller, C.S.C., editor *Vatican II: An Interfaith Appraisal* (Notre Dame: University of Notre Dame Press, 1966), p. 373.
3. *Catholic Herald* (London), November 22, 1965.
4. *Ibid.*

CHAPTER 1. CONFRONTING THE PAST: THE CONSEQUENCES OF CONTEMPT

1. W. A. Visser 't Hooft, ed., *The First Assembly of the World Council of Churches: The Official Report* (New York: Harper & Brothers, 1949), p. 161.
2. *The New Delhi Report: Third Assembly of the World Council of Churches,* 1961 (New York: Association Press, 1962), p. 148.
3. Paul Démann, *Les Juifs dans la Catachèse Chrétienne* (Paris: Cahiers Sioniens, 1952). The results of a similar study in Germany in 1961 are contained in the book *Israel in Christian Religious Instruction,* Theodor Filthaut, ed. (Notre Dame: University of Notre Dame Press, 1965).
4. Quoted by James W. Arnold, "Religious Textbooks, Primer in Bigotry," *Ave Maria* (Notre Dame, Ind.), October 10 and 17, 1964.
5. *Evidences,* American Jewish Committee (Paris), January–February, 1961.
6. Quoted by John Slawson in *Realities of Jewish Integration,* American Jewish Committee (New York), November, 1961.
7. *Journal of Bible and Religion,* American Academy of Religion (Philadelphia), April, 1965, pp. 126–127.
8. Quoted in full in *The Church and the Jewish People,* an occasional publication of the World Council of Churches (Geneva), March, 1965.

9. Cited in the Relatio distributed by the Secretariat for the Promotion of Christian Unity to the Council Fathers at the fourth session, prior to their vote on the Declaration on Non-Christian Religions. They are also repeated and answered by Augustin Cardinal Bea, S.J., in his book *The Church and the Jewish People* (New York: Harper & Row, 1966), pp. 67 ff.

10. Gregory Baum, O.S.A., *The Jews and the Gospel* (Westminster, Md.: The Newman Press, 1961), p. 5.

11. John B. Sheerin's syndicated column in *Catholic News* (New York), January 14, 1965.

12. Dominick M. Crossan, O.S.M., "Anti-Semitism and the Gospel," *Theological Studies* (Woodstock, Md.: 1965), p. 214.

13. Edward Flannery, *The Anguish of the Jews* (New York: The Macmillan Company, 1965), p. 45.

14. Thomas Falls, *Justin Martyr* (New York: Christian Heritage, Inc., 1948), p. 172.

15. *Tertullian's Apologetic Works and Minucius Felix Octavius* (New York: Fathers of the Church, Inc., 1950), pp. 391–392.

16. *Ante-Nicene Christian Literature* (New York: Charles Scribner's Sons, 1912), Vol. 4, p. 506.

17. Heinrich Graetz, *History of the Jews* (Philadelphia: Jewish Publication Society, 1946), Vol. II, p. 625.

18. Cited by Baum, *op. cit.*, pp. 6–7. See also Flannery, *op. cit.*, pp. 48–49.

19. This quotation and others that follow, referring to Council decrees in past history, are taken from Heinrich Graetz, *History of the Jews, op. cit.* See especially Vol. II, pp. 563–64, 567, 617; Vol III, pp. 36–39. Other books on the life of the Jews include the following: Edward A. Synan, *The Popes and the Jews in the Middle Ages* (New York: The Macmillan Company, 1965).

Solomon Grayzel, *The Church and the Jews in the XIIIth Century* (Philadelphia: Dropsie College, 1933).

Jacob Marcus, *The Jew in the Medieval World* (Cincinnati: Sinai Press, 1938).

Salo Baron, *A Social and Religious History of the Jews* (New York: Columbia University Press, 1951).

Leon Poliakov, *The History of Anti-Semitism* (New York: Vanguard Press, 1965).

James Parkes, *The Conflict of the Church and Synagogue* (Cleveland and New York: The World Publishing Company, 1961).

20. Flannery, *op. cit.*, pp. 49–51.

21. Synan, *op. cit.*, pp. 95–96, 219–29.

22. Graetz, *op. cit.*, Vol. III, p. 510. See also Synan, *op. cit.*, pp. 234 ff.

23. Flannery, *op. cit.*, p. 174.

24. *Ibid.*, p. 113.

25. Martin Luther's statements are quoted by Aarne Siirala in his article "Luther and the Jews," *Lutheran World* (Switzerland), July, 1964.

26. Siirala *op. cit.*, is here quoting the Luther Scholars Armas A. Holmio: *The Lutheran Reformation and the Jew* and *The Birth of the Protestant Jewish Mission,* 1949; and Wilhelm Maurer, *Kirche and Synagogue,* 1951.

27. Cited by Sister Louis-Gabriel in "Kirche und Juden Zwischen den beiden Vatikan Konzilen," *Judenhass—Schuld der Christen?* (Essen: H. Driewer, 1965).

28. Flannery, *op cit.*, pp. 189–91. The story of the Jewish experience in Russia is told in detail in S. M. Dubnow, *History of the Jews in Russia and Poland* (Philadelphia: Jewish Publication Society, 1964), three volumes, and in Ismar Elbogen, *A Century of Jewish Life* (Philadelphia: Jewish Publication Society, 1946).

29. For short summary of the history of Anti-Semitism in the United States see Chapter 3, "Anti-Semitism in America," in my *A Jew in Christian America* (New York: Sheed and Ward, 1966). More detailed accounts are given in Rufus Learsi, *The Jews in America: A History* (Cleveland and New York: The World Publishing Company, 1954); Jacob Marcus, *Early American Jewry* (Philadelphia: Jewish Publication Society, 1951, 1953); Bertram Korn, *American Jewry and the Civil War* (Philadelphia: Jewish Publication Society, 1961); Lee Levinger, *Anti-Semitism in the United States* (New York: Bloch Publishing Co., 1925); G. Myers, *History of Bigotry in the United States* (New York: Capricorn Books, 1960); Carey McWilliams, *A Mask for Privilege: Anti-Semitism in America* (Boston: Little, Brown, 1948); Benjamin Epstein and Arnold Forster, *Some of My Best Friends* (New York: Farrar, Straus, 1962); N. C. Belth, ed., *Barriers, Patterns of Discrimination Against Jews* (New York: Anti-Defamation League, 1958).

30. George H. Tavard, *The Church, the Layman and the Modern World* (New York: The Macmillan Company, 1959), pp. 79–80.

31. *London Jewish Chronicle,* December 17, 1965.

CHAPTER 2. REDEEMING THE PAST: EFFORTS
  TOWARD RECONCILIATION

1. Mimeographed report issued by the Department of Racial and
   Cultural Relations, National Council of Churches (New York).
   The conference was held at McCormick Theological Seminary,
   Chicago, in July, 1956.
2. Adopted by the General Board, National Council of Churches,
   June 5, 1964. The full text appears in *The Church and the
   Jewish People,* an occasional publication of the World Council
   of Churches (Geneva), July, 1964.
3. Two of Jules Isaac's essays have been translated into English:
   Has Anti-Semitism Roots in Christianity? (New York: The
   National Conference of Christians and Jews, 1961) and *The
   Teaching of Contempt* (New York: Holt, Rinehart & Win-
   ston, 1964).
4. *The Seelisberg Conference* (New York: National Conference
   of Christians and Jews, 1947). In 1950 these ten points were
   changed slightly and adapted for use by German Catholic religious teachers. This version was granted an imprimatur by the
   archepiscopal office at Freiburg. The ten points were published
   with commentary by Karl Theime in *Judenfeindschaft* (Frank-
   furt Am Main: Fischer Buchner, 1963), pp. 74–79.
5. Paul Démann, *Les Juifs dans la Catachèse Chrétienne* (Paris:
   Cahiers Sioniens, 1952), p. 6.
6. Bernhard E. Olson, *Faith and Prejudice* (New Haven: Yale
   University Press, 1961). See *Religious Education* (New York),
   March–April, 1960, for a summary of Protestant, Catholic,
   and Jewish studies. For an earlier examination of Protestant
   school texts, see Mildred and Frank Eakin, *Sunday School
   Fights Prejudice* (New York: The Macmillan Company, 1953).
7. Sister M. Rose Albert Thering, O.P., "The Potential in Religious
   Textbooks for Developing a Realistic Self-Image," an unpublished dissertation submitted in partial fulfillment of doctoral
   degree requirements, Graduate School of Education, St. Louis
   University, 1961.
8. *Christian Century* (Chicago), June 10, 1964.
9. Personal letter, June 6, 1964, quoted by permission.
10. *London Jewish Chronicle,* July 26, 1963.
11. *Jubilee* (New York), January, 1965.

12. John M. Oesterreicher, ed., *The Bridge* (New York: Pantheon Books, 1955). Four volumes published to date.
13. *As the U.N. Probes Prejudice*, American Jewish Committee (New York), September, 1960.
14. *Ibid.*
15. *Ibid.*
16. Religious News Service, January 11, 1960.
17. *La Documentation Catholique* (Paris), 1960, Columns 299–300.
18. Religious News Service, January 6, 1960.
19. *America* (New York), March 24, 1961.
20. *The Lutheran* (Philadelphia), May 3, 1961.
21. Edward Flannery, *The Anguish of the Jews* (New York: The Macmillan Company, 1965), p. 206.
22. *Commonweal* (New York), May 12, 1961.
23. *Christianity Today* (Washington), November 10, 1961.
24. *Ungekundiste Bund* (Stuttgart: Kraig Verlag, 1962). For a brief report, see *Presbyterian Life* (Philadelphia), September 15, 1961.
25. *Interreligious Newsletter*, Anti-Defamation League (New York), May, 1962.
26. Religious News Service, April 15, 1961.
27. *Interreligious Newsletter* (New York), May, 1962.

CHAPTER 3. THE JEWISH ISSUE IN THE CONTEXT OF THE COUNCIL

1. Quoted by John Sheerin in *Catholic News* (New York), March 14, 1963.
2. *National Jewish Monthly* (Washington), January, 1965.
3. *Christianity and Crisis* (New York), October 1, 1962.
4. From the encyclical *Ad Petri Cathedrum*, quoted by Religious News Service, June 29, 1959.
5. *Information Directors Newsletter*, National Catholic Welfare Conference (Washington), July, 1965.
6. Msgr. Vincent A. Yzermans, ed., *American Participation in the Second Vatican Council* (New York: Sheed and Ward, 1967); see essay by Msgr. John M. Oesterreicher, pp. 596 ff.
7. Cardinal Bea has revealed that Pope John received him in audience September 18, 1960 and then formally "charged The Secretariat for Christian Unity with the task of preparing a Declaration dealing with the Jewish People." (*The Church and the Jewish People*, p. 22).
8. *America* (New York), March 4, 1961. Italics are Father Stransky's.

9. Quoted in a communication from the British Council of Christians and Jews, June, 1962.

10. Quoted in a survey on "The Jewish Attitude Toward Christian Unity," undertaken by Rev. Giles F. Spoonhour, S.A., published in *At-One-Ment* by the Franciscan Friars of the Atonement, Graymoor Friars, November, 1962.

11. *CCAR Journal* (New York), January, 1963, p. 50.

12. Translated and quoted in *Catholic Messenger* (Davenport, Iowa), May 4, 1961.

13. *Ibid.*

14. Bea, *op. cit.*, pp. 30 ff.

15. *National Jewish Post and Opinion* (Indianapolis), February 24, 1961.

16. Religious News Service, April 3, 1962.

17. Mimeographed copy, privately circulated February 27, 1962.

18. *Committee Reporter*, American Jewish Committee (New York), February, 1964; and private communication, "The Second Vatican Council's Declaration on the Jews, A Background Report," American Jewish Committee, November, 1965. See also "The Church and the Jews" by Judith Hershcopf in *American Jewish Year Book 1965*, (New York), pp. 109–10.

19. Hershcopf, *op. cit.*, p. 111.

20. Religious News Service, July 11, 1962.

21. *CCAR Journal* (New York), January, 1963.

22. Bea, *op. cit.*, p. 23.

23. Religious News Service, August 1, 1962.

24. *New York Times*, August 1, 1962.

25. Religious News Service, August 7, 1962.

26. *Ibid.*, December 24, 1962.

27. *London Jewish Chronicle*, August 10, 1962.

CHAPTER 4. THE LIBERALS EMERGE

1. *Council Day Book, Vatican II, Sessions One and Two*. Floyd Anderson, ed., (Washington, D.C.: National Catholic Welfare Conference, 1965), pp. 6–7.

2. *Catholic Messenger* (Davenport, Iowa), September 13, 1962.

3. *New York Times*, October 12, 1962.

4. Jewish Telegraphic Association, October 18, 1960.

5. Religious News Service, October 14, 1962. The full text may be found in the *Council Day Book, op. cit.*, pp. 36–37.

6. *Ibid.*, January 10, 1963.

7. *Ibid.*, October 10, 1962.

8. *Ibid.*, October 31, 1962.

9. *Ibid.*

10. *Catholic News* (New York), October 7, 1962.

11. *America* (New York), January 9, 1963.

12. *Ibid.*

13. Xavier Rynne, *Letters from Vatican City* (Garden City, N.Y.: Doubleday & Company, 1963), p. 144.

14. *Council Day Book, op. cit.*, pp. 108–109 for the full text.

15. Xavier Rynne, *op. cit.*, p. 212.

16. *Council Day Book, op. cit.*, p. 114.

17. Religious News Service, December 6, 1962.

18. *Christianity and Crisis* (New York), January 7, 1963.

19. Mimeographed release, Union of American Hebrew Congregations, New York, undated.

20. *London Jewish Chronicle*, December 7, 1962.

21. *Ibid.*

CHAPTER 5. DRAMA BETWEEN SESSIONS

1. Press release, National Catholic Welfare Conference, February 16, 1963.

2. *The Pilot* (Boston), December 7, 1963.

3. *The Dialogue*, National Conference of Christians and Jews (New York), February, 1964.

4. *Il Messagio Evangeli* (Milan: 1958).

5. Religious News Service, June 10, 1963.

6. *Ibid.*, July 2, 1963. See also *Report of the Plenary Session, June 27–30, 1963* (New York: National Community Relations Advisory Council, 1963), p. 59.

7. *Ibid.*

8. Private correspondence, July 12, 1963.

9. Private correspondence, July 12, 1963.

CHAPTER 6. CONFLICT AND MANEUVER IN SESSION TWO

1. Xavier Rynne, *The Second Session* (New York: Farrar, Straus and Co., 1964), p. 28.

2. Religious News Service, September 30, 1963. For the full text see Floyd Anderson, ed., *Council Day Book, Vatican II, Sessions One and Two* (Washington, D.C.: National Catholic Welfare Conference, 1965), p. 148.

3. Rynne, *op. cit.*, p. 130.

4. Cited by John M. Oesterreicher in *Herder Correspondence* (New York), February, 1964.

5. *Ibid.*
6. Religious News Service, October 28, 1965.
7. Rynne, *op. cit.,* pp. 182 ff.
8. Religious News Service, November 11, 1963. For the full text see *Council Day Book, op. cit.,* pp. 249–250.
9. *New York Times,* November 9, 1963.
10. Henri Fesquet, *The Drama of Vatican II* (New York: Random House, 1967), p. 219.
11. *Ibid.,* p. 229.
12. *The State of Our Union,* Union of American Hebrew Congregations (New York), November 16, 1963.
13. *New York Times,* November 19, 1963. The full text of Cardinal Bea's presentations to the Council may be found in *The Church and the Jewish People.*
14. *Jewish Life* (New York), November–December, 1963.
15. See Appendix A.
16. *New York Times,* November 19, 1963. For the full text see *Council Day Book,* pp. 277–282.
17. Msgr. Vincent A. Yzermans, *American Participation in the Second Vatican Council* (New York: Sheed and Ward, 1967), p. 306.
18. Rynne, *op. cit.,* pp. 235 ff.
19. Religious News Service, November 20, 1963.
20. *Council Day Book, op. cit.,* p. 271.
21. *Ibid.,* p. 272.
22. *Ibid.,* p. 285.
23. Yzermans, *op. cit.,* p. 307.
24. Robert McAfee Brown, *Observer in Rome* (Garden City, N.Y.: Doubleday & Company, 1964), p. 188.
25. *America* (New York), November 30, 1963.
26. *Council Day Book, op. cit.,* p. 272.
27. Yzermans, *op. cit.,* p. 570.
28. Brown, *op. cit.,* p. 222.
29. Rynne, *op. cit.,* p. 271.
30. For the full text, see *Council Day Book, op. cit.,* pp. 323–324.

CHAPTER 7.   PILGRIMAGE TO THE HOLY LAND

1. *New York Times,* December 4, 1963.
2. Alex Bein, *Theodore Herzl* (Philadelphia: Jewish Publication Society, 1945), p. 470. See also Pinchas Lapide, "Rome Comes to Jerusalem," *Congress Weekly* (New York), January 27, 1964.

3. John M. Oesterreicher, ed., *The Bridge* (New York: Pantheon Books, 1958), Vol. 3, p. 304.
4. *Ibid.,* p. 324.
5. *New York Times,* December 18, 1963.
6. *National Jewish Post and Opinion* (Indianapolis), December 13, 1963.
7. Reuben Slonim, *In the Steps of Pope Paul* (Baltimore: Helicon Press, 1964), p. 11.
8. Ralph Gorman, in *The Sign* (Union City, N.J.), April, 1957.
9. Slonim, *op. cit.,* p. 45.
10. *Ibid.,* p. 46.
11. *Christian News from Israel,* Chaim Wardi, ed. (Jerusalem), March, 1964, pp. 4–5.
12. *Ibid.,* p. 6.
13. Quoted in *Young Israel Viewpoint* (New York), January 17, 1964.
14. *London Jewish Chronicle,* January 10, 1964.
15. Quoted in *The Bulletin* (New York Board of Rabbis), January–February, 1964.
16. *Christian News from Israel,* March, 1964, p. 10.
17. *Ibid.,* p. 11.
18. *Commonweal* (New York), January 24, 1964.
19. Slonim, *op. cit.,* p. 99.
20. *Ibid.*

CHAPTER 8. CRISIS IN THE JEWISH COMMUNITY

1. *Jewish Life* (New York), November–December, 1963.
2. *Young Israel Viewpoint* (New York), May 31, 1964.
3. Rabbi Chaim Denburg (Orthodox), quoted in Religious News Service, March 18, 1964.
4. "A Statement of Principles," adopted by the (Orthodox) Rabbinical Council of America. Mimeographed release, February 5, 1964.
5. Rabbi Steven S. Schwarzchild (Reform), in *Judaism* (New York), March 4, 1964.
6. *The Ecumenist* (Glen Rock, N.J.), January–February, 1964.
7. "Statement of Principles," cited in Note 4.
8. *Jewish News* (Newark, N.J.), January 8, 1965.
9. Lubavitch News Service (Brooklyn, N.Y.), mimeographed release, March, 1965.
10. *Connecticut Jewish Ledger* (Hartford), April 16, 1965.
11. *Tradition* (New York), Fall, 1964.

12. *London Jewish Chronicle,* August 28, 1964.
13. Richard Cardinal Cushing, *Second Vatican Council, Its Meaning for Mankind* (New York: National Conference of Christians and Jews, March, 1961).

CHAPTER 9.   RUMORS BETWEEN SESSIONS
1. Religious News Service, April 17, 1964.
2. *Catholic News* (New York), May 7, 1964.
3. Dinner address before the American Jewish Committee, New York, April 30, 1964. Text distributed by A.J.C.
4. *America* (New York), May 2, 1964.
5. Xavier Rynne, *The Second Session* (New York: Farrar, Straus and Co., 1964), p. 334.
6. Religious News Service, May 23, 1964.
7. *Ibid.,* May 29, 1964.
8. *Ibid.*
9. *The Pilot* (Boston), June 6, 1964.
10. Religious News Service, June 8, 1964.
11. *Denver Catholic Register,* June 19, 1964. Italics are mine.
12. Private letter, June 16, 1964. See "Open Letter to American Catholic Bishops," *Commonweal* (New York), June 26, 1964.
13. *New York Times,* May 30, 1964. The American Jewish Committee delegation included: John Slawson, executive vice-president; Morris B. Abram, president; and Zachariah Shuster, director, European office.
14. Msgr. Vincent A. Yzermans, *American Participation in the Second Vatican Council* (New York: Sheed and Ward, 1967), p. 576.
15. Religious News Service, June 5, 1964.
16. *Orthodox Life* (New York), June, 1964.
17. *1964 Yearbook,* Central Conference of American Rabbis (New York), p. 14. See also critical reaction by Rabbi A. Klausner in *Jewish Spectator* (New York), December, 1964.
18. Mimeographed release, August 14, 1964.
19. *Christian Century* (Chicago), August 26, 1964.
20. Religious News Service, August 11, 1964.
21. *Catholic News* (New York), August 20, 1964.
22. *New York Times,* September 4, 1964.
23. *Ibid.*
24. *Catholic Reporter* (Kansas City, Mo.), September 25, 1964.
25. *Ibid.*
26. *America* (New York), September 19, 1964.

27. *Commonweal* (New York), October 2, 1964.

CHAPTER 10. A VOTE AT LAST

1. *New York Times,* September 15, 1964.
2. *The Pilot* (Boston), January 23, 1965.
3. Religious News Service, September 28, 1964.
4. *Herder Correspondence* (New York), January, 1965.
5. *A.D.L. Bulletin,* Anti-Defamation League (New York), January, 1965. These findings have been published in Charles Glock and Rodney Stark, *Christian Beliefs and Anti-Semitism* (New York: Harper & Row, 1966).
6. Cited in Msgr. Vincent A. Yzermans, *American Participation in the Second Vatican Council* (New York: Sheed and Ward, 1967), pp. 573–574.
7. *New York Times,* September 24, 1964.
8. *Ibid.*
9. *Ibid.* For full text of the speeches and interventions of American hierarchy at the Council see Yzermans, *op. cit.*
10. *Ibid.,* September 25, 1964.
11. Religious News Service, September 18, 1964.
12. *New York Times,* September 25, 1964.
13. *The Pilot* (Boston), October 3, 1964.
14. *New York Times,* September 25, 1964.
15. Religious News Service, September 28, 1964.
16. Graetz, *History of the Jews* (Philadelphia: Jewish Publication Society, 1946), Vol. III, pp. 575 ff., 602; Vol. IV, pp. 215, 251.
17. Religious News Service, September 25, 1964.
18. *London Jewish Chronicle,* October 2, 1964.
19. *Commonweal* (New York), November 6, 1964.
20. *The Pilot* (Boston), October 3, 1964. See also Yzermans, *op. cit.*
21. *Herder Correspondence* (New York), January, 1965.
22. Yzermans, *op. cit.,* pp. 587–589.
23. *Catholic Reporter* (Kansas City, Mo.), October 2, 1964. See also Yzermans, *op. cit.*
24. Floyd Anderson, ed., *Council Day Book, Vatican II, Session 3* (Washington, D.C.: National Catholic Welfare Conference, 1965), p. 64. See also Yzermans, *op. cit.*
25. *Ibid.,* p. 80. See also Yzermans, *op. cit.*
26. Yzermans, *op. cit.,* pp. 591–592.
27. *Council Day Book, op. cit.* See also Yzermans, *op. cit.*
28. Yzermans, *op. cit. pp.* 592–594.
29. Religious News Service, October 13, 1964.

30. *Ibid.,* October 27,1964.
31. Mimeographed release, October 12, 1964.
32. *National Catholic Reporter* (Kansas City, Mo.), October 12, 1964.
33. *New York Times,* October 14, 1964.
34. Xavier Rynne, *The Third Session* (New York: Farrar, Straus & Giroux, 1965), p. 117.
35. Fuller excerpts of the schema were published in *National Catholic Reporter* (Kansas City, Mo.), October 23, 1964.
36. Rynne, *op. cit.,* p. 262.
37. *Commonweal* (New York), December 25, 1964.
38. Cited in *Christian Century* (Chicago), December 2, 1964.
39. *London Jewish Chronicle,* November 27, 1964.
40. Religious News Service, November 23, 1964.
41. *Ibid.*
42. *National Catholic Reporter* (Kansas City, Mo.), November 25, 1964.
43. Religious News Service, November 23, 1964.
44. *Catholic News* (New York), December 6, 1964.
45. *Commonweal* (New York), December 11, 1964.
46. *Ibid.,* December 25, 1964.

CHAPTER 11.   ANXIOUS INTERLUDE

1. See *American Benedictine Review* (St. Paul, Minn.), March, 1964, and *Reconstructionist* (New York), April 16, 1965, for summaries of the colloquy from Catholic and Jewish perspectives.
2. The papers delivered at this colloquy have been published in Philip Scharper, ed., *Torah and Gospel* (New York: Sheed & Ward, 1966).
3. *New York Times,* March 31, 1965.
4. Religious News Service, February 9, 1965.
5. Quoted in full in *Here & There, #7,* Union of American Hebrew Congregations (New York), April 16, 1965.
6. *Intermountain Jewish News* (Denver, Colo.), April 16, 1965.
7. *Here & There, #7* (New York), April 16, 1965.
8. *London Jewish Chronicle,* April 9, 1965.
9. *National Catholic Reporter* (Kansas City, Mo.), April 14, 1965.
10. Religious News Service, April 6, 1965.
11. *Ibid.,* April 9, 1965.
12. *National Catholic Reporter* (Kansas City, Mo.), April 23, 1965.
13. *Catholic Reporter* (Kansas City, Mo.), May 7, 1965.
14. Religious News Service, April 28, 1965.
15. *Catholic Review* (Baltimore, Md.), April 12, 1965.

16. See critical response by Msgr. George Higgins in *Catholic Accent* (Greenburgh, Pa.), January 28, 1965, and editorial in *Christian Century* (Chicago), February 3, 1965.

17. Religious News Service, March 17, 1965.

18. *London Jewish Chronicle*, April 30, 1965.

19. Full text of the address is included in Arthur Gilbert, *A Jew In Christian America* (New York: Sheed & Ward, 1966).

20. *New York Times*, June 22, 1965.

21. *America* (New York), July 6, 1965.

22. Religious News Service, May 5, 1965. (Some evidence has been uncovered that leads some scholars to doubt the authenticity of this prayer.)

23. Alfred Klausler, "The Scandal of Particularity," a report on the conference, in *Christian Century* (Chicago), April 28, 1965. See J. Bruce Long, ed., *Judaism and the Christian Seminary Curriculum* (Chicago: Loyola University Press, 1966).

24. Religious News Service, June 16, 1965.

CHAPTER 12.   RECONSIDERATION AND PROMULGATION IN SESSION FOUR

1. *The Sign* (Union City, N.J.), September, 1965.

2. *New York Times*, September 10, 1965.

3. *Ibid.*, September 30, 1965.

4. *New York Post*, September 15, 1965.

5. *America* (New York), September 14, 1965.

6. Religious News Service, September 29, 1965.

7. *Ibid.*, October 1, 1965.

8. Jewish Telegraph Association, October 14, 1965.

9. Msgr. Vincent A. Yzermans, *American Participation in the Second Vatican Council* (New York: Sheed and Ward, 1967), p. 582.

10. *New York Herald Tribune*, October 1, 1965.

11. Religious News Service, October 5, 1965.

12. Address at a Theological Colloquium at Notre Dame, South Bend, Indiana, mimeographed release, March 21, 1966. The full text of Fr. Stransky's address, now somewhat revised, appears in John H. Miller, ed., *Vatican II: An Interfaith Appraisal*, (Notre Dame: University of Notre Dame Press, 1966).

13. It should be noted that while this Council hesitated to *condemn* anti-Semitism, there is on record a declaration of the Congregation of the Holy Office of March 25, 1928 which does include such a condemnation: ". . . In its charity the Apostolic See often protected the Jewish people against unjust molestation. And hence it condemns all forms of hostile rivalry between peoples

and consequently it very specially condemns hatred against a people, chosen of old by God, that hatred which is today commonly called anti-Semitism." See Bea, *op. cit.*, p. 12.

14. Floyd Anderson, ed., *Council Day Book, Vatican II, Session 4* (Washington, D.C.: National Catholic Welfare Conference, 1966), p. 133.

15. Henri Fesquet, *The Drama of Vatican II*, (New York: Random House, 1967), p. 706.

16. *Ibid.*, p. 712.

17. *Council Day Book, op. cit.*, pp. 133, 139.

18. Fesquet, *op. cit.*, p. 711.

19. Rabbi Jay Kaufman, Executive Secretary of B'nai B'rith, in a paper prepared for the Administrative Committee, Washington, D.C., August 28–29, 1965.

20. For several references to ritual murder charges throughout the centuries, see Joshua Trachtenburg, *The Devil and the Jews* (New Haven: Yale University Press, 1943).

21. *Reconstructionist* (New York), November 26, 1965.

22. Mimeographed press release, World Conference of Jewish Organizations, New York, October 15, 1965.

23. Jewish Telegraphic Association, October 29, 1965.

24. *Reconstructionist* (New York), October 29, 1965.

25. Jewish Telegraphic Association, October 18, 1965.

26. *The Criterion* (Indianapolis), October 22, 1965.

CHAPTER 13.   CATHOLIC TEACHINGS ON THE JEWS AND JUDAISM

1. This article appeared originally in *Civiltà Cattolica*, IV, No. 21 (November 6, 1965), pp. 209–229. A translation by Ann Rose Raia was published in *Thought*, New York, Spring 1966, pp. 9–32 under the title "The Jewish People in the Divine Plan of Salvation." See also Cardinal Bea's book, *The Church and the Jewish People* (New York: Harper & Row, 1966).

2. L. M. Carli, "La Questione Giudaica davanti al Concilio Vaticano II," in *La Palestra del Clero*, XLIV, 1965, pp. 185–203.

3. All the quotations from Council documents in this chapter are taken from *The Documents of Vatican II*, Walter M. Abbott, S.J., General Editor (New York: Guild Press—America Press—Association Press, 1966). See p. 15.

4. *Ibid.*, p. 25.

5. *Thought, op. cit.*, p. 12. Italics in original.

6. Privately circulated mimeographed translation of Cardinal Lercaro's address on the Council floor, September 28, 1964.

7. *The Documents of Vatican II, op. cit.,* p. 122.
8. *Thought, op. cit.,* p. 15.
9. Patriarch Maximos. See p. 172.
10. *Thought, op. cit.,* p. 22.
11. *Ibid.,* p. 31.
12. *Ibid.,* p. 23.
13. *Ibid.,* p. 20.
14. *Ibid.,* p. 31–32.
15. *The Documents of Vatican II, op. cit.,* p. 25. Italics supplied.
16. *Ibid.,* pp. 122–123.
17. See Appendix D.
18. See "The Jews," special issue of *Dialog,* A Journal of Theology (Minneapolis, Minn.), Summer, 1967, pp. 176–184; and Arthur Gilbert's article "The New Teachings of Protestant and Catholics with Regard to the Jews," in *Encounter* (Indianapolis), Vol. 28, No. 1, 1966.
19. *The Pilot,* (Boston), December 12, 1964.
20. *The Documents of Vatican II, op. cit.,* p. 346.
21. *Ibid.,* p. 345.
22. See pp. 88–89, and Chap. 6, note 2, p. 249.
23. *The Documents of Vatican II, op. cit.,* p. 347.
24. *Ibid.,* p. 353.
25. *Ibid.,* p. 349.
26. *Ibid..* p. 344.
27. *Ibid.,* p. 346, 348.
28. Gregory Baum, O.S.A., *Is the New Testament Anti-Semitic?* (Glen Rock, N. J.: Paulist Press, 1965), p. 9.
29. *Ibid.,* p. 348.
30. *Our Sunday Visitor* (Huntington, Ind.), May 22, 1966.
31. *The Documents of Vatican II, op. cit.,* p. 227.
32. Typewritten copy of address received from the author; it was delivered on May 12, 1966 at 56th Annual Convention of The Catholic Press Association, San Francisco, California.
33. *Christianity and Crisis* (New York), June 13, 1966, p. 134.
34. Father Flannery's Catholic Press Association address, *op. cit.,* See Note 32.
35. Quoted by Dr. Joseph A. Lichten in "The Vatican Decree and the Jews," a four-page article distributed by Anti-Defamation League, New York, undated.

CHAPTER 14. VATICAN COUNCIL II—RECAPITULATION AND PROJECTION

1. For a selection of the statements and resolutions adopted by the

World Council of Churches and other international and American church assemblies see *Christian Friends Bulletin,* "The Sin of Anti-Semitism," Anti-Defamation League, New York, December, 1965.

2. The papers delivered at this historic consultation in May, 1964, and the adopted resolutions are to be found in *Christians, Jews and the Mission of the Church,* Lutheran World Federation, Geneva, Switzerland, 1966. The Lutheran World Federation denounced anti-Semitism as "spiritual suicide" and as a "denial of the image of God in the Jew." It confessed "as Lutherans . . . our own peculiar guilt [for anti-Semitism]," adding "we lament with shame the responsibility which our church and her people bear for this sin. We can only ask God's pardon and that of the Jewish people." The consultation also urged the member churches of the Federation "to examine their publications and remove and oppose false generalizations about Jews." It said, "especially reprehensible are the notions that Jews rather than all mankind are responsible for the death of Jesus the Christ, and that God for this reason has rejected his covenant people."

3. Charles Y. Glock and Rodney Stark, *Christian Beliefs and Anti-Semitism* (New York: Harper & Row, 1966).

4. Commenting on the tendency of some Catholic theologians to deny that "authentic Christians" could lend themselves to anti-Semitism, Rev. John Reedy, editor of the Catholic weekly *Ave Maria* (Notre Dame, Indiana, June 11, 1966), observed: "The Church as the people of God is ourselves and that is the problem. . . . We must never forget that God, in becoming incarnate, came to men as they were; and they were and remained sinners. The temptation has always been present to deny the reality of the human church and it has expressed itself in the search for a Church which is not 'polluted and tainted by such human contact'—a totally Holy Church, a Church from which all sin could be excluded. To relegate what is polluted and tainted among Christians to 'folk religion' or 'inauthentic Christianity' is a throwback to pre-conciliar days when we had lost that understanding of the Church as the people of God on an earthly pilgrimage and fully human. . . . Christian theologians today (in view of the history of the last ten years) should be the least surprised at the Church's need at all stages in history for renewal."

5. The Protestant and Catholic editors of America's most distinguished theological journal, *The Journal of Ecumenical Studies* (Temple University, Philadelphia, Pennsylvania), announced the

addition to its Editorial Board in May, 1966 of a rabbi. In explaining this move, Rev. George Lindbeck wrote:

"For us . . . the first schism was the one which occurred in the New Testament times between Jew and Christian. It is inconsistent for us to seek to heal later divisions without wrestling also with the original rupture. There is, in Christian circles, a growing conviction that many of our ills stem from forgetfulness of our Jewishness. This is manifest not only in the appalling ills of Christian anti-Semitism, but also in the neglect of the eschatological and prophetic dimensions of our faith. . . . For us as Christians, therefore, the ecumenical dialogue is incomplete unless it includes the Jews."

6. Catholic-Jewish Cooperation, an address delivered at Merrimak College, October 22, 1967. Mimeographed, p. 3.

7. *The Church and the Jewish People* (New York: Harper and Row, 1966), page 8.

8. Moderator of the Subcommission for Catholic-Jewish Relations is Bishop Francis P. Leipzig of Baker, Oregon. Its membership reappointed in January, 1968, includes: Father Edward Flannery, Executive Secretary for the subcommission with headquarters at Seton Hall University in South Orange, New Jersey. Members of the Executive Committe of the Secretariat are: Bishop Aloysius J. Wycislo, Auxiliary Bishop of Chicago; Bishop Mark J. Hurley, Auxiliary Bishop of San Francisco; Rt. Rev. Msgr. George G. Higgins, Director of the Social Action Department, U.S. Catholic Conference; Rt. Rev. Msgr. John M. Oesterreicher, Director of the Institute of Judaeo-Christian Studies, Seton Hall University; Father John B. Sheerin, C.S.P., Editor of *The Catholic World;* Mother Katharine Hargrove, R.S.C.J., Professor of Theology, Manhattanville College, Purchase, New York; Mr. Philip Scharper, Editor, Sheed and Ward, New York; and Father Bernard Law, Executive Director of the Bishops' Committee for Ecumenical and Interreligious Affairs, ex officio.

A Board of Consultors, under the chairmanship of Rt. Rev. Msgr. George C. Higgins, has also been formed. It will include Rt. Rev. Msgr. John Doherty, Associate Superintendent of Schools, Archdiocese of New York; Rt. Rev. Msgr. Francis J. Lally, Editor of *The Boston Pilot;* Very Rev. Msgr. Philip J. Dowling, Executive Secretary, the Archbishop's Commission on Human Relations, Philadelphia; Father Dominic Crossan, O.S.M., Professor of Theology, St. Mary of the Lake Seminary, Mundelein, Illinois; Father Edward J. Duff, S.J., Catholic University of America; Father Thomas McFadden, Executive Secretary of the Diocesan Commission for Ecumenism, Brooklyn, New York; Brother C. Stephen Sullivan, F.S.C., Academic Vice-President, Manhattan College, New York; and Sister M. Rose Albert Thering, O.P., Catholic Adult Education Center, Chicago.

9. *Recommendations For Diocesan Commissions For Ecumenical Affairs,* Bishops Commission for Ecumenical Affairs (Washington, D.C.), March, 1966, p. 7.

10. A meeting between members of the subcommission on Ecumenism and Catholic Education and Protestant and Jewish educators was convened under the auspices of St. Meinrad Benedictine Seminary, St. Meinrad, Indiana, March 28–30, 1966. For a news report on this conference, see Religious News Service, Thursday, March 31, 1966. Some of the papers delivered at this conference have been published in the *American Benedictine Review,* Autumn 1966. They have been reprinted as a pamphlet, "Educating For Ecumenism," available through the Anti-Defamation League, New York.

11. Proceedings, Biennial General Assembly, Union of American Hebrew Congregations (New York), 1966. Mimeographed.

12. Religious News Service, June 20, 1966.

13. Report, Annual Meeting, National Community Relations Advisory Council (New York), 1966. For an opposing view see "Judaism in The Post-Christian Era," by Rabbi Eliezer Berkovitz, *Judaism* (New York), January, 1966, pp. 74–84. Rabbi Berkovitz asserts, "There is no reason on earth why Judaism should make itself available to 'fraternal dialogue' with a religion which, by its very premises, declares others to be in error and, thus, from the outset destroys the basis of a true dialogical situation." Pointing to the past history of Christian oppression of Jews, Rabbi Berkovitz adds, "We reject the idea of inter-religious understanding as immoral because it is an attempt to whitewash a criminal past." Finally, Rabbi Berkovitz claims, "Any close association with Christian thought is ultimately bound to cause confusion within Jewish thinking. It may cripple our ability to articulate the relevance of the specific Jewish position in our times."

A reply to Rabbi Berkowitz, written by Rabbi Seymour Seigel, a member of the Jewish Theological Seminary's faculty was published in *Congress-Bi-Weekly* (New York), May 23, 1966. Rabbi Seigel explained: "It is grossly unfair to hold that many good-hearted and pious Christians—both Protestant and Catholic—who sincerely wish to become friends—are responsible

for the unspeakable crimes of their co-religionists . . ." Furthermore, added Rabbi Seigel, "Large and important sections of
Christendom seem ready to modify those attitudes which have
caused us so much harm. Is it then a wise policy to close the
door in the face of such efforts?"

14. See the following summary articles and reports: Rabbi Marc
Tanenbaum's article "Israel and the Jewish-Christian Dialogue"
in *Conservative Judaism* (New York), Winter, 1967; Judith
Hershcopf Banki, *Christian Reactions to the Middle East Crisis*
(New York: American Jewish Committee, December, 1967);
American Reactions to the Six-Day War", a *Commentary* report
(New York), 1967; "The Middle East Conflicts," *Christian Cen-
tury* (Chicago), July 26, 1967.

15. See *A Statement of Conscience,* by Msgr. John M. Oesterreicher
and Rev. John H. Flannery, (Seton Hall University: The Institute
of Judeao-Christian Studies, December, 1967); Rabbi Balfour
Brickner, "Christian-Jewish Relations after the Arab-Israeli War,"
Christianity and Crisis, (New York), September 18, 1967; Rev.
Elwyn Smith, "Israel, the Jewish People and the World," *Reconstructionist* (New York), February 9, 1968.

Appendix A

ON THE ATTITUDE OF CATHOLICS TOWARD NON-CHRISTIANS AND ESPECIALLY TOWARD JEWS*

Latin text distributed to Council Fathers at Second Session, November 8, 1963.

Now that we have dealt with the principles of Catholic ecumenicism, we do not wish to pass over in silence the fact that the same principles should be applied, taking differences in condition duly into account, in the matter of speaking and cooperation with people who are not Christians, but who worship God, or at least in a spirit of good will conscientiously endeavor to observe the moral law innate in the nature of man.

This applies especially in the case of the Jews, as people who are connected with the Church of Christ in a special relationship.

The Church of Christ acknowledges with a grateful heart that the beginnings of the faith and of its election, along with the salutary mystery of God, can already be found among the Patriarchs and Prophets. For it is manifested that all the believers in Christ, the sons of Abraham according to the faith (cf. Gal. 3:7), come under the vocation of that Patriarch and that the salvation of the Church is mystically prefigured in the exodus of the chosen people from the land of bondage. The Church, a new creature in Christ (cf. Eph. 2:15), cannot forget that it is a continuation of that people with whom of old God, out of his ineffable mercy, was pleased to make his Old Covenant.

In addition the Church believes that Christ, our Peace, embraced both Jews and Gentiles in a single love and made them one (cf. Eph. 2:14) and by the union of both is one body (cf. Eph. 2:17) announced the reconciliation of all the world in Christ. Although a

*Translation made in Rome privately and mailed to author by Council observer October 15, 1963. This version never came to vote.

large part of the chosen people are still far from Christ, yet it is wrong to call them an accursed people, since it remains very dear to God because of the Fathers and the gifts given them (cf. Rom. 11:28), or a people that killed God, since the Lord, by his passion and death, washes away the sins of all men, which were the cause of the passion and death of Jesus Christ (cf. Luke 23:34; Acts 3:17; 1 Cor. 2:8). Yet the death of Christ was not brought about by the entire people then alive, and far less by the people of today. Therefore, let priests be careful not to say anything, in the instruction of the catechism or in preaching, that might give rise to hatred or contempt of the Jews in the hearts of their hearers. Nor does the Church forget that Christ Jesus was born of that people according to the flesh, that the Virgin Mary, the Mother of Christ, was thus born, that thus were born the Apostles, the foundation and pillars of the Church.

Wherefore, since the Church has so much of a common patrimony with the synagogue, this Holy Synod intends in every way to promote and further mutual knowledge and esteem obtained by theological studies and fraternal discussions; and, moreover, as it severely reproves injuries to men anywhere, even more so does it, with maternal heart, deplore and condemn hatred and persecution of Jews, whether committed of old or in our times.

Appendix B

ON THE JEWS AND NON-CHRISTIANS*

*Latin text debated by Council Fathers
early in Third Session, September 28–30, 1964.*

(On the inheritance common to Christians and Jews.) The Church
of Christ gladly acknowledges that the beginnings of its faith and
election, in accordance with God's mystery of salvation, are to be
found already among the Patriarchs and Prophets. Indeed, all Christians believe that, as sons of Abraham by faith (cf. Gal. 3, 7), they
are included in this Patriarch's vocation and that the salvation of the
Church is mystically prefigured in the exodus of the chosen people
from the land of bondage. Nor can the Church as a new creation
in Christ (cf. Eph. 2, 15) and as the people of the New Covenant
ever forget that it is a continuation of that people with whom God
in his ineffable mercy once designed to enter into the Old Covenant
and to whom he chose to entrust the revelation contained in the
Books of the Old Testament.

Moreover, the Church does not forget that from this Jewish
people were born Christ, the Virgin Mary, as well as the Apostles,
the foundation and the pillars of the Church.

Further, the Church was always mindful and will never overlook
Apostle Paul's words relating to the Jews, "whose is the adoption,
and the glory, and the covenants and the giving of the law, and the
service, and the promises" (Rom. 9, 4).

Since such is the inheritance accepted by Christians from the
Jews, this Holy Council is resolved expressly to further and to recommend reciprocal understanding and appreciation, to be obtained by
theological study and fraternal discussion and, beyond that, in as

*Translation appeared in the *New York Herald Tribune,* September
30, 1964. This version was presented as an appendix to the Schema on
Ecumenism. Cardinal Bea urged that it be strengthened.

much as it severely disapproves of any wrong inflicted upon men wheresoever, it equally deplores and condemns hatred and maltreatment of Jews.

It is also worth remembering that the union of the Jewish people with the Church is a part of the Christian hope. Accordingly, and following the teaching of Apostle Paul (cf. Rom. 11, 25), the Church expects in unshakable faith and with ardent desire the entrance of that people into the fullness of the people of God established by Christ.

Everyone should be careful, therefore, not to expose the Jewish people as a rejected nation, be it in Catechetical tuition, in preaching of God's Word or in worldly conversation, nor should anything else be said or done which may alienate the minds of men from the Jews. Equally, all should be on their guard not to impute to the Jews of our time that which was perpetrated in the Passion of Christ.

(All men have God as Father.) The Lord Jesus has clearly confirmed that God is the Father of all men, as this was already stated in the Writings of the Old Testament and is suggested by reason itself. But we surely cannot appeal or pray to God as the Father of all, if we deny brotherly behavior to some men who are all created in the image of God. The attitude of man toward God as Father and the attitude of man toward man as brother are so closely connected that any negation of human brotherhood carries with it or leads to the negation of God himself with whom there is no respect of persons (cf. 2 Par. 18, 7; Rom. 2, 11; Eph. 6, 9; Col. 3, 25; 1 Pet. 1, 17). The First Commandment is in fact so interwoven with the second that we cannot be acquitted from our debts unless we ourselves wholeheartedly acquit our debtors. Indeed, it was said already in the Old Law: "Have we not all one Father? Hath not one God created us? Why do we deal treacherously every man against his brother?" (Mal. 2, 10); the same is even more clearly reaffirmed in the New Law: "He that loveth not his brother whom he hath seen, how can he love God whom he hath not seen? And this commandment have we from him that he who loveth God love his brother also." (1 Jn. 4, 20–21.)

Impelled by such love for our brethren, let us consider with great diligence views and doctrines which, though in many points different from ours, in so many others, however, carry the ray of that truth which gives light to every man born into this world. Thus we embrace also, and first of all, the Moslems who worship one personal and recompensing God and who in religious feeling as well as through many channels of human culture came closer to us.

(Any kind of discrimination is to be condemned.) In consequence, any theory or practice which leads to discrimination between man and man or between nation and nation, insofar as human dignity and the rights flowing therefrom are concerned, is devoid of foundation.

It is imperative, therefore, that all men of good will and Christians in particular abstain from any discrimination or vexation of human beings on grounds of their race, color, social status or religion. As to the Christians, the Holy Council solemnly entreats them "to behave seemly among gentiles" (1 Pet. 2, 12) and if possible and insofar as it depends on them, to maintain peace with all men (cf. Rom. 12, 18); it enjoins them, moreover, to love not only the neighbor, but even the enemies, should they think to have them, that they should be in truth the sons of the Father who is in heaven and who makes his sun rise over all (cf. Mt. 5, 44–45).

Appendix C

[REVISED] DECLARATION ON THE CHURCH'S
RELATIONSHIP TOWARD NON-CHRISTIAN RELIGIONS*

*Latin text distributed to Council Fathers
near end of Third Session, November 18, 1964.
Approved by Council in preliminary vote, November 20, 1964.
1,651, yes; 242, yes with reservation; 99, no.*

In this age of ours when mankind is being drawn closer together, day by day, and the ties between peoples here and there are made stronger, the Church weighs earnestly her relationship toward non-Christian religions.

One is the community of all peoples, one their origin, for God made the entire human race live on all the face of the earth (cf. Acts 17, 26). One, too, is their ultimate end God: His providence, His goodness—of which creation is the witness—His saying design extend toward all men (cf. Wisd. 8, Acts 14, 17; Rom. 2, 6–7, 1 Tim. 2, 4). And in the end all the elect will be united in that Holy City whose light is the glory of God, that City where the nations will walk in His radiance (cf. Apoc. 21, 24f).

Men expect from the various religions answers to the unsolved riddles of the human condition, riddles that move the hearts of men today as they did in olden times: What is man? What is the meaning, what is the purpose of our lives? What is the moral good, what sin? Which is the road to true happiness? What are death, judgment, and retribution after death? What, finally, is that ultimate, inexpressible mystery which encompasses our existence, which is the fountain as well as the destiny of our beings?

Ever since primordial days, numerous peoples have had a certain perception of that hidden Power which hovers over the course of

*Translation appeared in *The Catholic Herald* (London), December 4, 1964.

267

things and over the events that make up the lives of men: some have even come to know of a Supreme Being and Father.

Religions, however, that are entwined with an advanced culture have been able to use, in their struggle for an answer to man's great questions, more refined concepts and a more developed language.

In Hinduism, for instance, men try to fathom the divine mystery, expressing it through an inexhaustible abundance of myths and through keen efforts of a philosophical kind; they seek freedom from the anguish of our human condition through ascetical methods, profound meditation, and a flight to God, full of love and trust.

Again, Buddhism realizes the radical inadequacy of this changeable world; it teaches a way by which men, with minds devout and confident, seek to liberate themselves, through a self-denial and inner cleansing, from the fleetingness of things, and to attain a state of lasting quiet. Other religions, everywhere on earth, counter the restlessness of the human heart, each in its own manner, by proposing ways, that is to say, doctrines, rules of life, and sacred rites.

The Catholic Church scorns nothing in these religions that is true and holy. For ceaselessly she proclaims Christ, "the Way, the Truth, and the Life" (Jn. 14, 6), in whom God reconciled all things to Himself (cf. 2 Cor. 15, 19). Having learned of various dispositions toward salvation (cf. Irenacus, Adv. Haer, IV, 28, 2; PG 7, 1062), she regards with sincere reverence those ways of action and of life, those precepts and teachings which, differ though they do from the ones she sets forth, reflect nonetheless a ray of that Truth which enlightens all men!

The Church, therefore, admonishes her sons that they converse and collaborate with the followers of other religions in order to preserve, indeed, advance those spiritual and moral goods as well as those socio-cultural values that have a home among men of other religious traditions.

The Church is filled with esteem for Moslems: they adore the one God who lives, exists in Himself, and wields all power; they adore the Creator of heaven and earth who has spoken to men; they strive to obey wholeheartedly even His incomprehensible decrees, just as Abraham did, to whose faith they like to link their own.

Though Moslems do not acknowledge Jesus as God, they revere Him as a Prophet. They also honor Mary, His Virgin-Mother; at times, they even call on her with devotion. Again, they await the day of judgment when God will reward all those who have risen.

Furthermore, as they worship God through prayer, almsgiving, and fasting, so they seek to make the moral life—be it that of the individual or that of the family and society—conform to His Will.

In the course of centuries, however, not a few quarrels and hostilities have arisen between Christians and Moslems. Hence this Sacred Synod urges all not only to forget the past but also to work honestly for mutual understanding and to further as well as guard together social justice, all moral goods, especially peace and freedom so that the whole of mankind may benefit from their endeavor.

As this Sacred Synod searches into the mystery of the Church, it remembers the bond that ties the people of the New Covenant to Abraham's stock.

With a grateful heart, the Church of Christ acknowledges that, according to God's saving design, the beginnings of her faith and her election were already among the patriarchs, Moses, and the prophets. She professes that all who believe in Christ—Abraham's sons according to faith—were included in the same patriarch's call, likewise that her salvation is typically foreshadowed by the chosen people's exodus from the land of bondage.

The Church, therefore, cannot forget that she received the revelation of the Old Testament from the people with whom God in His ineffable mercy concluded the former Covenant. Nor can she forget that she feeds upon the root of that cultivated olive tree into which the wild shoots of the Gentiles have been grafted (cf. Rom. 11, 17–24). Indeed, the Church believes that by His Cross Christ our Peace reconciled the Jews and Gentiles, making both one (cf. Eph. 2, 14, 16).

The Church keeps ever in mind the words of the Apostle about his kinsmen: "Theirs is the sonship, the glory, the covenants, the giving of the law, the worship, and the promises. Theirs are the patriarchs, and of them is the Christ according to the flesh," the Son of Mary the Virgin (Rom. 9, 4–5).

No less does she recall that the Apostles, the Church's mainstay and pillars, as well as most of the early disciples who proclaimed Christ's Gospel to the world, sprang from the Jewish people.

Even though a large part of the Jews did not accept the Gospel, they remain most dear to God for the sake of the patriarchs. This is the witness of the Apostle as is the utterance that God's gifts and call are irrevocable (cf. Rom. 11, 28 f.). In company with the prophets and the same Apostle, the Church awaits that day, known to God alone, on which all peoples will address the Lord in a single voice and "serve Him shoulder to shoulder" (Soph. 3, 9; cf. Is. 66, 23; Ps. 65, 4; Rom. 11, 11–32).

Since the spiritual patrimony common to Christians and Jews is of such magnitude, this Sacred Synod wants to support and recommend their mutual knowledge and respect, a knowledge and respect that are the fruit, above all, of biblical and theological studies as well as of fraternal dialogues.

Moreover, this Synod, in her rejection of injustices of whatever kind and wherever inflicted upon men, remains mindful of that common patrimony and so deplores, indeed, condemns hatred and persecutions of Jews, whether they arose in former or in our own days.

May all, then, see to it that in their catechetical work or in their preaching of the word of God they do not teach anything that could give rise to hatred or contempt of Jews in the hearts of Christians.

May they never present the Jewish people as one rejected, cursed, or guilty of deicide. All that happened to Christ in His passion cannot be attributed to the whole people then alive, much less to that of today.

Besides, the Church has always held and holds now that Christ underwent His passion and death freely, because of the sins of all men and out of infinite love. It is, therefore, the burden of Christians preaching to proclaim the Cross of Christ as the sign of God's all-embracing love and as the fountain from which every grace flows.

We cannot truly address God the Father of all, if we refuse to treat some men or other in a brotherly way, even though they are created in His image. Man's attitude toward God the Father and his attitude toward his human brethren are so intimately linked, one to the other, that Scripture is able to say: "He who does not love does not know God" (1 Jn. 4, 8; cf. 1 Jn. 2, 9–1; Lk. 10, 25–37).

Thus any theory or practice that, so far as their human dignity is concerned, discriminates between man and man or people and people, creating a different set of rights for each of them—any such theory or practice is shown to be without foundation.

All men, therefore, but especially Christians must refrain from discrimination against, or harassment of, others because of their race, color, creed or walk of life. But this is not enough. Treading the footsteps of the holy Apostles Peter and Paul, this Sacred Synod ardently implores the faithful that they rather "maintain good conduct among the Gentiles" (1 Pet. 2, 12) and live, if possible, that is, so far as it depends on them, in peace with all men (cf. Rom. 12, 18), so that they may really be sons of the Father who is in heaven (cf. Mt. 5, 44).

Appendix D

DECLARATION ON THE RELATION OF
THE CHURCH TO NON-CHRISTIAN RELIGIONS*

APPROVED TEXT
November 20, 1964
(3rd version)

1. *(Prooemium)* In this age of ours, when day by day mankind is being drawn closer together, and the ties between various peoples are becoming stronger, the Church considers attentively her relationship to non-christian religions.

One is the community of all peoples, one their origin, for God made the whole human race to

EMENDED TEXT
October, 1965
(4th and final version)

1. *(Prooemium)* In this age of ours, when day by day mankind is being drawn closer together, and the ties between various peoples are becoming stronger, the Church considers *more* attentively her relationship to non-christian religions. *In her task of promoting unity and love among men, indeed among nations, she above all considers in this declaration what men have in common and what leads to mutual fellowship.*

One is the community of all peoples, one their origin, for God made the whole human race to

*This appendix sets side by side the Declaration adopted by the Council Fathers at their third session, November 20, 1964, with the final emended version of the statement circulated to the Council Fathers October 1, 1965. Approved by the Council, this last version was promulgated by the Pope. The italicized text are the words that were added or changed between Sessions Three and Four. The translation was made by Professor Ralph Lazzaro (Harvard Divinity School).

live on the entire face of the earth. One, too, is their ultimate end, God. His providence, His manifestations of goodness, His saving design extend to all men, until that time when the elect will be united in the Holy City, which the radiant glory of God will illumine, where the nations will walk in His light.

Men expect from the various religions answers to the unsolved riddles of the human condition, which today, even as in olden times, deeply stir the hearts of men: What is man? What is the meaning, the aim of our life? What is the moral good, what sin? What are death, judgment and retribution after death? What, finally, is that ultimate inexpressible mystery which encompasses our existence: whence do we come, and where are we going?

2. *(The Variety of Non-Christian Religions)* Already from ancient times, there is found among various peoples a certain perception of that hidden power which hovers over the course of things and over human events; at times some indeed have come to a recognition of a Supreme Being and a Father.

live on the entire face of the earth (cf. Acts 17:26). One, too, is their ultimate end, God. His providence, His manifestations of goodness, His saving design extend to all men (cf. Wis. 8:1; Acts 14:17; Rom. 2:6–7; 1 Tim. 2:4), until that time when the elect will be united in the Holy City, which the radiant glory of God will illumine, where the nations will walk in His light (cf. Apoc. 21:23 f.).

Men expect from the various religions answers to the unsolved riddles of the human condition, which today, even as in olden times, deeply stir the hearts of men: What is man? What is the meaning, the aim of our life? What is the moral good, what sin? *Whence suffering and what purpose does it serve?* What are death, judgment and retribution after death? What, finally, is that ultimate inexpressible mystery which encompasses our existence: whence do we come, and where are we going?

2. *(The Variety of Non-Christian Religions)* From ancient times *continuing to the present,* there is found among various peoples a certain perception of that hidden power which hovers over the course of things and over human events; at times some indeed have come to the recognition of a Supreme Being, *or even of* a Father. *This perception and recognition pene-*

Religions, however, that are entwined with an advanced culture have struggled to answer the same question by means of more refined concepts and a more developed language. Thus in Hinduism, men contemplate the divine mystery and express it through an inexhaustible abundance of myths and through searching essays into philosophy; they seek freedom from the anguish of our human condition through ascetical practices, through profound meditation, and a flight to God with love and trust. Again, Buddhism realizes the radical inadequacy of this changeable world; it teaches a way by which men, in a devout and confident spirit, may be able to liberate themselves, through self-denial and inner cleansing, from the fleetingness of things, and to attain a state of lasting quietude. Likewise, other religions found everywhere counter the restlessness of the human heart, each in its own manner, by proposing ways, that is to say, teachings, rules of life, and sacred rites.

The Catholic Church rejects nothing that is true and holy in these religions. Indeed, she ever proclaims Christ, "the way, the truth and the life" (Jn. 14:6), in whom God has reconciled all things to Himself (cf. 2 Cor.

trates their lives with a profound religious sense.

Religions, however, that are entwined with an advanced culture have struggled to answer the same question by means of more refined concepts and a more developed language. Thus in Hinduism, men contemplate the divine mystery and express it through an inexhaustible abundance of myths and through searching essays into philosophy; they seek freedom from the anguish of our human condition either through ascetical practices or profound meditation or a flight to God with love and trust. Again, Buddhism, *in its various forms,* realizes the radical inadequacy of this changeable world; it teaches a way by which men, in a devout and confident spirit, *may be able either to acquire the state of perfect liberation, or attain, by their own efforts or through higher help, the supreme illumination.* Likewise, other religions found everywhere *try to* counter the restlessness of the human heart each in its own manner, by proposing ways, that is to say, teachings, rules of life, and sacred rites.

The Catholic Church rejects nothing that is true and holy in these religions. She regards with sincere reverence *those* ways of action and of life, *those* precepts and teachings which, though differing in many aspects from

5:19). Having been instructed about various dispositions toward salvation (cf. Irenaeus, Adv. *Haer.* IV, 28, 2), she regards with sincere reverence ways of action and of life, precepts and teachings, which, though differing in many aspects from the ones she sets forth, nonetheless reflect a ray of that Truth which enlightens all men.

The Church, therefore, exhorts her sons, that without violating the integrity of the Catholic faith, through dialogue and collaboration with the followers of other religions, they preserve and promote those spiritual and moral goods as well as those socio-cultural values found among these men.

3. *(The Mussulmans)* The Church looks with esteem also upon the Mussulmans. They adore the one God who is living, subsisting in Himself, and all-powerful, the Creator of heaven and earth who has spoken to men; they strive to submit wholeheartedly even to His incomprehensible decrees, just as Abraham submitted to God, to whom the moslem faith takes pleasure in linking itself. Though they do not acknowledge Jesus as God, they revere Him as a Prophet. They also honor Mary, his virgin mother; at times they even call on her with devotion. In addition, they await the day of judgment when God will

the ones she *holds and* sets forth, nonetheless *often* reflect a ray of that Truth which enlightens all men. *Indeed,* she proclaims, *and* ever *must proclaim,* Christ, "the way, the truth, and the life" (Jn. 14:6), *in whom men may find the fulness of religious life,* in whom God has reconciled all things to Himself (2 Cor. 5:19).

The Church, therefore, exhorts her sons, that through dialogue and collaboration with the followers of other religions, carried out *with prudence and love and in witness to the Christian faith and life,* they *recognize,* preserve and promote those spiritual and moral goods as well as those socio-cultural values found among these men.

3. *(The Religion of Islam)* The Church looks with esteem also upon the *Moslems.* They adore the one God, living and subsisting in Himself, *merciful* and all-powerful, the Creator of heaven and earth who has spoken to men; they strive to submit wholeheartedly even to His incomprehensible decrees, just as Abraham submitted to God, to whom the faith *of Islam* takes pleasure in linking itself. Though they do not acknowledge Jesus as God, they nevertheless revere Him as a Prophet. They also honor Mary, his virgin mother; at times they even call on her with devotion. In addition, they await the day

reward all those who have been raised up. Finally, as they worship God especially through prayer, almsgiving and fasting, so they endeavor to lead the moral life—be it that of the individual or that of the family and society —in obedience to Him.

Since in the course of centuries not a few quarrels and hostilities have arisen between Christians and Mussulmans, this Sacred Synod urges all to forget the past, and to work sincerely for mutual understanding and to preserve as well as to promote together social justice, all moral goods, as well as peace and freedom for the benefit of all mankind.

4. *(The Jews)* As this Sacred Synod searches into the mystery of the Church, it remembers the bond that ties the people of the New Covenant to Abraham's stock.

In truth, *with a grateful heart* the Church of Christ acknowledges that, according to God's saving design, the beginnings of her faith and her election are already found among the Patriarchs, Moses and the prophets. She professes that all who believe in Christ—Abraham's sons according to faith (cf. Gal. 3:7) —are included in the same Patriarch's call, likewise that the salvation of the Church is mysteriously foreshadowed by the chosen people's exodus from the

of judgment when God will reward all those who have been raised up. Finally, *they value* the moral life and worship God especially through prayer, almsgiving and fasting.

Since in the course of centuries not a few quarrels and hostilities have arisen between Christians and *Moslems,* this Sacred Synod urges all to forget the past, and to work sincerely for mutual understanding and to preserve as well as to promote together social justice, all moral goods, as well as peace and freedom, for the benefit of all mankind.

4. *(The Jewish Religion)* As this Sacred Synod searches into the mystery of the Church, it remembers the bond that *spiritually* ties the people of the New Covenant to Abraham's stock.

In truth, the Church of Christ acknowledges that, according to God's saving design, the beginnings of her faith and her election are already found among the Patriarchs, Moses and the prophets. She professes that all who believe in Christ—Abraham's sons according to faith (cf. Gal. 3:7)—are included in the same Patriarch's call, likewise that the salvation of the Church is mysteriously foreshadowed by the chosen people's exodus from the land of bondage. The Church, land of bondage. The Church, therefore, cannot forget that she received the revelation of the Old Testament from the people with whom God in His ineffable mercy concluded the Ancient Covenant. Nor can she forget that she feeds upon the root of that cultivated olive tree into which the wild shoots of the Gentiles have been grafted (cf. Rom. 11:17–24). Indeed, the Church believes that by His cross Christ Our Peace reconciled Jews and Gentiles, making both one (cf. Eph. 2:14–16).

The Church keeps ever in mind the words of the Apostle about his kinsmen: "theirs is the sonship and the glory and the covenants and the legislation and the worship and the promises; theirs are the fathers and from them is the Christ according to the flesh" (Rom. 9:4–5), the Son of the Virgin Mary. She also recalls that the Apostles, the Church's mainstay and pillars, as well as most of the early disciples who proclaimed Christ's Gospel to the world, sprang from the Jewish people.

Even though a large part of the Jews did not accept the Gospel, nevertheless, as the Apostle testifies, God holds them most dear for the sake of the Fathers; His gift and call are irrevocable (cf. Rom. 11:28–29). In company with the Prophets and the same Apostle, the Church awaits the day, known to God alone,

therefore, cannot forget that she received the revelation of the Old Testament *through* the people with whom God in His ineffable mercy concluded the Ancient Covenant. Nor can she forget that she feeds upon the root of that cultivated olive tree into which the wild shoots of the Gentiles have been grafted (cf. Rom. 11:17–24). Indeed, the Church believes that by His cross Christ Our Peace reconciled Jews and Gentiles, making both one *in Himself* (cf. Eph. 2:14–16).

The Church keeps ever in mind the words of the Apostle about his kinsmen: "theirs is the sonship and the glory and the covenants and the legislation and the worship and the promises; theirs are the fathers and from them is the Christ according to the flesh" (Rom. 9:4–5), the Son of the Virgin Mary. She also recalls that the Apostles, the Church's mainstay and pillars, as well as most of the early disciples who proclaimed Christ's Gospel to the world, sprang from the Jewish people.

As Holy Scripture testifies, Jerusalem did not recognize the time of her visitation (cf. Lk. 19:44), *nor did the Jews, for the most part, accept the Gospel; indeed many opposed its spreading* (cf. Rom. 11:28). *Nevertheless*, according to the Apostle, God holds *the Jews* most dear for the sake of the Fathers: His on which all peoples will address the Lord in a single voice and "serve him shoulder to shoulder (Soph. 3:9).

Since the spiritual patrimony common to Christians and Jews is thus of such magnitude, this Sacred Synod wants to foster and recommend a mutual knowledge and respect which is the fruit, above all, of biblical and theological studies as well as of fraternal dialogues.

Moreover, this Synod, in her rejection of injustice of whatever kind and wherever inflicted upon men, remains mindful of that common patrimony and so deplores, *indeed condemns* hatred and persecution of Jews, whether they arose in former or in our own days.

May all, then, see to it that in catechetical work or in preaching they do not teach anything that could give rise to hatred or contempt of Jews in the hearts of Christians. May they never present the Jewish people as one rejected, cursed, *or guilty of deicide*. All that happened to Christ in His passion can in no way be attributed to the whole people then alive, much less to the people of today.

gift and call are irrevocable (cf. Rom. 11:28–29; cf. *Constitution on the Church*, n. 16). In company with the Prophets and the same Apostle, the Church awaits the day, known to God alone, on which all peoples will address the Lord in a single voice and "serve him shoulder to shoulder" (Soph. 3:9).

Since the spiritual patrimony common to Christians and Jews is thus of such magnitude, this Sacred Synod wants to foster and recommend a mutual knowledge and respect which is the fruit, above all, of biblical and theological studies as well as of fraternal dialogues.

Although the Jewish authorities and those who followed their lead pressed for the death of Christ (cf. Jn. 19:6), *nevertheless* what happened to Christ in His passion cannot be attributed *to all Jews, without distinction*, then alive, *nor to the Jews of today. Although the Church is the new people of God, the Jews* should *not* be presented as rejected *by God or* accursed, *as if this follows from the Holy Scriptures.* May all see to it, then, that in catechetical work or in preaching the word of God they do not teach anything *that is inconsistent with the truth of the Gospel and with the spirit of Christ.*

Moreover, the Church, which rejects every persecution against any man, mindful of the common patrimony with the Jews and moved not by political reasons but by the Gospel's spiritual love, deplores hatred, persecutions, displays of anti-Semitism, directed against Jews at any time and by anyone.

Besides, the Church has always held, and holds now, that Christ underwent His passion and death freely—out of infinite love— because of the sins of men. It is, therefore, the burden of the Church's preaching to proclaim the cross of Christ as the sign of God's all-embracing love and as the fountain from which every grace flows.

Besides, *as* the Church has always held and holds now, Christ underwent His passion and death freely, because of the sins of men and out of infinite love, *in order that all may reach salvation.* It is, therefore, the burden of the Church's preaching to proclaim the cross of Christ as the sign of God's all-embracing love and as the fountain from which every grace flows.

5. *(Universal Brotherhood, excluding Every Discrimination)* We cannot truly call on God, the Father of all, if we refuse to treat in a brotherly way any man, created as he is in the image of God. Man's relation to God the Father and his relation to men his brothers are so linked together that he who does not love does not know God.

5. *(Universal Brotherhood, excluding Every Discrimination)* We cannot truly call on God, the Father of all, if we refuse to treat in a brotherly way any man, created as he is in the image of God. Man's relation to God the Father and his relation to men his brothers are so linked together that *Scripture says:* "He who does not love does not know God" (1 Jn. 4:8).

The foundation is therefore removed for any theory or prac-

The foundation is therefore removed for any theory or practice that leads to discrimination between man and man or people and people, in so far as their human dignity and the rights flowing from it are concerned.

All men, therefore, especially Christians, must refrain from any discrimination against men or harassment of them because of their race, color, condition in life, or religion. On the contrary, following in the footsteps of the holy Apostles Peter and Paul, this Sacred Synod ardently implores the Christian faithful to "maintain good fellowship among the nations" (1 Pet. 2:12), and, if possible, to live for their part in peace with all men (cf. Rom. 12:18), so that they may truly be sons of the Father who is in heaven (cf. Mt. 5:44).

tice that leads to discrimination between man and man or people and people, in so far as their human dignity and the rights flowing from it are concerned.

The Church thus reproves, as foreign to the mind of Christ, any discrimination against men or harassment of them because of their race, color, condition in life, or religion. On the contrary following in the footsteps of the holy Apostles Peter and Paul, this Sacred Synod ardently implores the Christian faithful to "maintain good fellowship among the nations" (1 Pet, 2:12), and, if possible, to live for their part in peace with all men (cf. Rom. 12:18), so that they may truly be sons of the Father who is in heaven (cf. Mt. 5:44).

Appendix E

EXCERPTS FROM THE "EXPLANATIONS" OF THE CHANGES MADE IN THE DECLARATION ON THE RELATION OF THE CHURCH TO NON-CHRISTIAN RELIGIONS*

Venerable Fathers

May it be permitted me only very briefly to point to some things before voting on the suggestions which have been proposed relative to the Schema of the Declaration "On the Relation of the Church to non-Christian Religions." The Secretariat for the Promotion of Christian Unity with grateful heart has received and has both diligently and soundly examined all the proposals, but, as is almost always the case, has decided to accept some and others no. Now, the criterion in bringing this examination to its completion has been none other than that the Schema might, as far as it could, come out clearer and more accurate, so long as there was *faithful adherence*, however, *to the content of the text* approved by you a year ago with a majority vote.

First of all, *in three Sections* the sense of the Declaration seems to us more clearly expressed. For the purpose of the Declaration does not aim to set forth a complete exposition of religions and their divergences amongst themselves and with the Catholic religion. Rather, the Sacred Synod wants through this Declaration to point to the bond among men and religions as a basis for dialogue and collaboration. Therefore, more attention is paid to what things bind men together and lead to mutual fellowship. One must proceed with prudence, to be sure, but indeed with trust and love. Your

*Translation made by Professor Ralph Lazzaro (Harvard Divinity School). These explanations made by Cardinal Bea in behalf of the Secretariat for the Promotion of Christian Unity justify the changes made in the Declaration and account for amendments accepted or rejected. Abridgement by the author.

proposed suggestions and observations were a great help to us, so that the Declaration, through which the Catholic Church is now for the first time proposing a dialogue of the brethren with the great non-Christian religions, is in greater accord with this purpose.

The fourth Section demanded greater attention both for the weight of the question dealt with therein and for the many and various observations proposed thereto. Therefore the Synod proposed to itself this method of dealing with this matter: besides applying careful scrutiny in daily discussions to the suggestions proposed, we deemed it important also that a number of trips be undertaken to contact members of the Sacred Hierarchy, both Catholic and non-Catholic, in those various regions where the greatest difficulties arose a year ago concerning this Schema. All these attempts were aimed at this end, especially: (1) to obviate, as far as possible, incorrect interpretations of the theological doctrine proposed in the Schema; (2) to express clearly the exclusively religious [spiritual] nature of the Schema, so that the road was by all means closed to any political interpretation.

1. As for this last point, the Secretariat has decided that in the rejection of persecution of the Jews, the reasons for such rejection should be clearly expressed by the insertion of these following words: "The Church, moved not by political reasons but by the Gospel's spiritual love . . . deplores," and by the additional rejection also of *every* persecution directed against any man. Therefore the text now goes thus: "Moreover, the Church, which rejects every persecution against any man, mindful of the common patrimony with the Jews and moved not by political reasons but by the Gospel's spiritual love, deplores hatred, persecutions, displays of anti-Semitism, directed against Jews at any time and by anyone." May we hope that thus, finally, along with the repeated declarations, any political interpretation of the decree that will arise from any quarter at all is definitely excluded or that its falsity, at least, is clearly shown.

2. Moreover, as to theological clarity, may we explicitly bring this to mind—namely, that most difficult point of the Schema relative to the question of the responsibility of the Jews for the things that happened in the Lord's Passion. That my explanation may turn out clear, first I cite the new text, as it is now proposed by the Secretariat: "Although the Jewish authorities and those who followed their lead pressed for the death of Christ (cf. John 19:6), nevertheless what happened in His Passion cannot be attributed to all Jews, without distinction, then alive, nor to the Jews of today.

Although the Church is the new people of God, the Jews should not be presented as rejected by God or accursed, as if this follows from the Holy Scriptures." From this text it clearly appears: (1) The Schema entirely preserves and sets forth the truth of the Gospel; (2) At the same time it excludes the unjust assertions and accusations brought against all the Jews, without distinction, living at that time as well as against the Jews of our day, namely, that they are all guilty of the condemnation of the Lord and therefore rejected by God and acursed; (3) The Council urges all that in this matter their catechetical work and preaching be consistent with the truth of the Gospel and the Spirit of Christ.

From a comparison of this text with the text you approved a year ago it also appears that the Secretariat is recommending the deletion from the text of the expression "guilty of deicide." It is known that difficulties and controversies have *in fact* arisen from the use of this word, as though, to be sure, the Schema were contradicting the Gospel. On the other hand, it is clear to whoever reads the text just cited and explained that the *matter* we were trying to express by this word in the former text is expressed carefully and completely. I know indeed that a great so-called psychological weight is attributed by some to this word. I reply, however: if that same word is erroneously understood in so many regions and if, moreover, the same thing can be expressed more clearly in other more suitable words, do not pastoral prudence and Christian love forbid us to use this word, and require us to explain the matter in other words? I maintain that this is required by that same "spiritual love of the Gospel" under whose impulse John XXIII ordered this Declaration to be prepared and inspired by which you yourselves approved the Declaration a year ago. Our Secretariat deems this emendation to be of great importance for the correct understanding of the Declaration itself and for its acceptance on all sides, in spite of difficulties of every sort. Accordingly I earnestly ask that you would give consideration to this emendation in the light of pastoral prudence and Gospel love.

In general. It is asked that the whole section (No. 4) be deleted. *Reason:* As being unnecessary and ambiguous.
Decision: The text was approved by the Council. The section on the Jews is necessary in the Declaration on the Attitude of the Church toward non-Christian Religions for the sake of the completeness of the Declaration, which ought to deal with all religions, in accordance with the intent of the Constitution on the Church, No. 16.

It is asked that the true meaning of the words of St. Paul in 1 Thess. be explained ("for the wrath [of God] is come upon them to the uttermost," 2:16), as well as of other loci in Holy Scripture where the Jews are censured.

Reason: The text is to be harmonized with the teaching of St. Paul in Rom. 11.

Decision: The function of this ancient people in the history of salvation is a doctrinal theme which runs throughout all Scripture. Therefore it is impossible to explicate the significance of a single text apart from the total biblical doctrine on Israel. In general, however, for an understanding of those severe judgments on the Jews, the following principles are to be applied:

1. Many of the harsh words were intended not as specific judgments but as prophetic admonitions (threats) calling the people to repentance, and they therefore remain as admonitions to us Christians whensoever we are forgetful of our calling (for example, Matthew 3:7–10; Acts 7:51–53; Matthew 8:11–22).

2. Many of the harsh judgments relate to the leaders (rulers) of the Jews and to that section of the inhabitants of Jerusalem who followed the leaders in the rejection of Jesus. For this "wicked generation" Christ foretold chastisement and punishment, which reached their height in the destruction of the temple and city. But we cannot apply whatever is contained in these judgments to all the generations of the Jewish people (Matthew 23:29–39, 27:25; 1 Thess. 2:15; Luke 19:42–46).

3. Some of the harsh judgments declare that the Synagogue had shut itself out from the messianic blessings imparted by Christ, inasmuch as it did not receive Him (John 1:11, 8:21–24; Acts 28:23–29; Gal. 4:25–26; Rom. 9:30–31). It is true therefore that Israel is now not a sacrament of salvation for the world. This fact, however, is not suitably expressed through such words as "rejected" and "accursed." Holy Scripture teaches us that God's love ever pursues any people. This is best expressed in chapter 11 to the Romans, where in verse 28 it is said that the promises of God made to the fathers have not been withdrawn.

Instead of the title "The Jews" one should say "The Jewish Religion."

Reason: That it appear clear that here the religion and not the people is being dealt with.

Decision: The suggestion is accepted that one say *"The Jewish Religion."*

The words "with a grateful heart" should be deleted.
Reason: The meaning is not clear. It could be understood as if we had to give thanks to the Jews of today (2 Fathers).
Decision: The suggestion is accepted.

The word "feeds upon" should be deleted or replaced by "springs from" (2 Fathers).
Reason: The Church does not feed upon earthly and human food but is fed by God through Christ.
Decision: The suggestion is not accepted. The Revelation of the Old Testament remains a source of spiritual life in the Church; for example, the Psalms in the liturgy.

After "did not accept" should be added "and not a single time did Christ Jesus charge them that they had not recognized the time of their visitation."
Reason: The rejection of the Gospel was a guilt the punishment for which was the destruction of the Holy City and of the Jewish nation.
Decision: It ought clearly, and in the spirit of this Declaration, be expressed:
(a) according to the Catholic faith, that the Jewish people, after the rejection of Jesus on the part of Jerusalem and the Synagogue, was no longer the Church [Assembly] of God as it had previously been, and
(b) according to Scripture, that many Jews at the time of the Apostles had been inimical to the Gospel and to its spreading. Therefore, the [new] text reads thus: *"As Holy Scripture testifies, Jerusalem did not recognize the time of her visitation* [cf. Luke 19:44], nor did the Jews, *for the most* [*magna,* "large"] *part,* accept the Gospel; *indeed, many opposed its spreading* (cf. Rom. 11:28). *Nevertheless,* according to the Apostle, God holds the Jews most dear for the sake of the Fathers: His gift and call are irrevocable" (cf. Rom. 11:28–29; cf. Const. dogm. *Lumen Gentium,* A.A.S.57 [1965], n. 1, p. 20). The reason that verse Rom. 11:28 is twice cited is found in the following paragraph.

It should read thus: "Nevertheless, a large part of the Jews did not accept the Gospel. Their leaders put Jesus to death, and the responsibility of this crime somehow affects not the individuals altogether and one by one, but the Hebrew people taken collectively. Moreover, inasmuch as the entire calling of the Hebrew people was headed toward Christ and inasmuch as Christ 'came unto his own, and his own received him not' (John 1:11), the Hebrew people is no longer God's people; the Church has become the true Israel, the new Israel, God's Israel, Israel according to faith (cf. Gal. 3:29, 6:16; Rom. 9:6–8; 1 Cor. 10:18). Nevertheless, as the Apostle testifies, God, whose gift and call are irrevocable, holds them most dear for the sake of the Fathers, although, at times, as concerning the Gospel, [they are] enemies for the sake of the faithful." (cf. Rom. 11:28).

Reason: To affirm that the responsibility for the Crucifixion somehow affects the Jewish people taken collectively. Furthermore, the content of the entire verse (Rom. 11:28) should be given, where the Jews are said to be "most dear for the sake of the Fathers" and also "enemies for your sakes."

Decision: The proposal is accepted in part to the extent that in the new redaction, in accordance with the requirements of the Declaration, the Jewish people is said not now to be the Church of God, and that it was the leaders of the people who required the death of Christ. However, the notion of the collective responsibility for the Crucifixion is not accepted. It is also to be noted that the verse Rom. 11:28, wherein the Jews are called "most dear" and "enemies" has not been cited literally; nevertheless, the entire teaching of the verse is given. Therefore reference to Rom. 11:28 is twice made in the notes. In the new redaction, there is mention of the Jews who at the time of the Apostles were inimical to the Gospel. The whole verse is not cited because the part where the Jews are called "enemies" refers to the time of the Apostles, when many Jews were opposed to the spreading of the Gospel, but can in no wise apply to later generations; the part, however, wherein they are called "most dear" for the sake of the fathers obtains for all ages and even our times: for the gift and call of God are irrevocable. Cf. Dogmatic Constitution *Lumen Gentium,* No. 16: "a people most dear, as touching election, for the fathers' sakes."

The word "such" [*adeo*] should be deleted.

Reason: The expression is too strong.

Decision: The suggestion is not accepted. The common inheritance [patrimony] of the Church and the Synagogue is very great.

"Condemns" should be removed.

Reasons:

1. That discrimination against the Jews be not more strongly repudiated than discriminations against others (2 Fathers).

2. In a Conciliar document it seems better to reserve words of

condemnation for matters which pertain to formal heresy (1 Father).
Decision: The suggestion is accepted.

The words "May they never present the Jewish people . . ."
should be deleted (8 Fathers).
Reasons: The doctrine is uncertain, dangerous, contradicted in the
Gospel. The argument of many Fathers is as follows: *In regard to
deicide:*

1. That the Jewish people, as a people, through their leaders, has
become guilty of *material* deicide, is clear: for Christ, the Son of
God, was killed by them, as St. Paul himself asserts, "[the Jews], who
killed both the Lord Jesus . . ." (1 Thess. 2:15).

2. That some of the leaders at least were guilty even of *formal*
deicide is beyond doubt, and cannot prudently be denied, because
of the Lord's words: "If I had not done among them the works
which none other man did, they had not had sin; but now have they
both seen and hated both me and my Father" (John 15:24).

In regard to reprobation [rejection]:

That the Jewish people, as a people, was rejected is clear from the
parable of the vineyard (Matthew 21:34–36 [33–44]), whose conclusion the Lord himself formulates thusly: "Therefore I say unto
you, the kingdom of God shall be taken from you, and given to a
nation bringing forth the fruits thereof." [verse 43].

There ought also to be deleted the remaining words, which, although
true in every respect, could nevertheless in this context lead to a certain
justification of the crime of the priests and chieftains of the Jews; and
then someone could equally argue for the justification of even Judas,
the traitor, whom the Lord called "the son of perdition" (John
17:12).

Decision: The text approved by the Council in regard to substance
cannot be changed.

Moreover, the arguments by which attempts are made to prove the
guilt deicide and rejection are invalid. It is true that the Synagogue
shut itself out from the messianic blessings conferred by Christ, but
this did not eventuate directly because the leaders of the Jews gave
Jesus over to death, but because they would not believe in Jesus
preached by the Apostles.

As an illustration, in 1 Thess. 2:15 St. Paul is not speaking of
the Jewish people as such, but of their leaders in Jerusalem and
Judaea who persecuted Jesus and the faithful and in whom he sees
the heirs of those who long ago killed the prophets (cf. Mt. 23:30–
32; Acts 7:51–52). The words of Christ in John 15:24 refer to the

sin of those of the leaders and of the crowd who had put it in their mind to kill Him. These men St. John often terms "the Jews." But neither in the Fourth Gospel nor in any other passage in the New Testament is the sin of those who put Christ to death represented as the sin of formal deicide. According to the sacred authors, the enemies of Christ, whatever their guilt may have been, were unaware that they were killing the Holy One of Israel (cf. Acts 3:17, 13:27; 1 Cor. 2:8), although this could be attributed to their blindness and hardness of heart. Furthermore, in the parable of the vineyard (Mt. 21:33–45) the Lord threatened the leaders of the people and not the people itself, and thus was it understood by the hearers: "When the chief priests and Pharisees had heard his parables, they perceived that he spake of them" (Mt. 21:45).

The following emendations have been proposed:

(a) to add: "for, according to the Gospels, the leaders of the Jews and a part of the inhabitants of the Jerusalem of that day, by pressing for the death of Christ, called the responsibility of His blood upon themselves and upon their children . . ."
Reason: This is more faithful to the Gospel.

(b) to omit: "or guilty of deicide." Then it should read: "For all that happened . . . can in no way be attributed to every individual Jew then alive, much less to those of today, with individual guilt."
Reason: Thus is avoided the question of collective guilt.

(c) to add: "It is true that the Jewish people, as is clear from the Gospels, had in its rejection of Christ a certain social responsibility which, indeed, had its consequence in the historic fact of the destruction of the Holy City of Jerusalem and the dispersion of the Jewish people, as predicted by Christ himself."
Reason: This social responsibility shines clearly from Christ's words (cf. Mt. 23:37 ff., 21:33–41).

(d) to correct thus: "Nevertheless, all that happened . . . in His passion cannot be attributed indiscriminately to all the Jews then alive, much less to the Jews of today. Moreover, although the Church is the new people of God, [to] the Jews, nevertheless, neither as being reject of God . . ."
Reason: Thus it is clearly stated that the Church is the true Israel, and speculative expression is entirely avoided.
Decision: In order to satisfy the requests of the Fathers, the text, although substantially preserved, has been emended to respond to five difficulties:
The Gospel truth must be taken into account.

The crime committed by the leaders of the Jews in pressing for the death of Christ must be acknowledged.

Care must be taken lest the condition of the Jewish people in the scheme of salvation seem the same after the death of Christ as before, though the collective guilt of that people in the death of Christ cannot be allowed. Therefore the new text says: "Although the Church is the new people of God, the Jews should not . . ." There is no more reference to the Jewish people, but to the Jews, who did not all indiscriminately play a part in Christ's death. However, in accepting those suggestions, the Secretariat for the Promotion of Christian Unity in no way intends to lay down a decision in regard to the sense in which the Jewish people remains, in accordance with the words of the dogmatic Constitution On the *Church*, No. 16, "a people most dear as touching election for the Fathers' sakes."

Several Fathers have requested that the words "or guilty of deicide" be deleted or at least be explained more carefully, for such an expression seemed ambiguous to them. Furthermore, certain Fathers have been caused to wonder at these words, as if the Catholic Church no longer seemed to teach that He who was slain for us is in fact the Son of God.

Decision: Weighing all these things carefully in the balance . . . the words "or guilty of deicide" have been deleted for the following reasons:

1. The word "deicide," in any context, has an odious ring. Therefore, such terms as "deicide" (*"Gottesmorder,"* "Christkiller," *"peuple déicide,"* and such other expressions) should be proscribed entirely from the Christian vocabulary.

2. Moreover, the word "deicide" could lead to false theological interpretations. Such false interpretation have already arisen and have provided an opportunity to difficulties both in pastoral activity in general and in the ecumenical dialogue with some Churches.

Therefore, all things having been taken under consideration, the new text reads thus:

"Although the Jewish authorities and those who followed their lead pressed for the death of Christ (cf. John 19:6), *nevertheless what happened in His passion cannot be attributed to all Jews, without distinction, then alive, nor to the Jews of today. Although the Church is the new people of God, the Jews should not be presented as rejected by God, or accursed, as if this follows from the Holy Scriptures."*

must also be given a high priority. Since many of the problems in this area of Catholic-Jewish relations are intellectual in nature, research in history, psychology, sociology, and the Bible by individual Catholic and Jewish scholars as well as collaborative scholarly enterprises are to be highly commended.

10. The following themes which, among others, are viewed by Christian and Jewish dialogists as important issues affecting Christian-Jewish relations merit the attention and study of Catholic educators and scholars:

(a) Scholarly studies and educational efforts to show the common historical, biblical, doctrinal, and liturgical heritage shared by Catholics and Jews, as well as their differences.

(b) As the Statement requires, the presentation of the Crucifixion story in such a way as not to implicate all Jews of Jesus' time or of today in a collective guilt for the crime.

(c) In keeping with the Statement's strong repudiation of anti-Semitism, a frank and honest treatment of the history of Christian anti-Semitism in our history books, courses, and curricula.

(d) A study of the life of Jesus and of the primitive Church in the setting of the religious, social, and cultural features of Jewish life in the first century.

(e) An explicit rejection of the historically inaccurate notion that Judaism of that time, especially that of Pharisaism, was a decadent formalism and hypocrisy well exemplified by Jesus' enemies.

(f) An acknowledgment by Catholic scholars of the living and complex reality of Judaism after Christ and the permanent election of Israel, alluded to by St. Paul (Rom. 9:29), and the incorporation of the results into Catholic teaching.

(g) A full and precise explanation of the use of the expression "the Jews" by St. John and other New Testament references which appear to place all Jews in a negative light. (These expressions and references should be fully and precisely clarified in accordance with the intent of the Statement that Jews are not to be "presented as rejected or accursed by God as if this followed from Holy Scripture.")

Appendix G

CHRONOLOGY OF THE COUNCIL'S JEWISH STATEMENT AND AMERICAN JEWISH REACTION

October 1958	Angelo Cardinal Roncalli elevated, he becomes Pope John XXIII.
January 20, 1959	Pope John reveals to his Secretary of State his intention to call a Council.
June 18, 1959	Domenico Cardinal Tardini circulates the members of his hierarchy requesting their suggestions regarding the Council agenda.
December 24, 1959	Cologne Synagogue is desecrated. Swastika epidemic erupts throughout Europe and the United States.
January 18, 1960	B'nai B'rith delegation visits Pope John to discuss Swastika outbreak.
June 5, 1960	Pope John creates preparatory commissions to organize material supplied by bishops worldwide. Augustin Cardinal Bea is requested to preside over a Secretariat for the Promotion of Christian Unity.
July 1960	Pope John receives in audience the noted Jewish historian Jules Isaac.
September 18, 1960	Pope John receives Cardinal Bea in private audience and charges him to prepare a declaration dealing with the Jewish people.
October 1960	Pope John meets with officials of United Jewish Appeal.
October 24, 1960	Secretariat for the Promotion of Christian Unity opens an office in Rome.
November 1960	Cardinal Bea informally invites American Jewish organizations, Anti-Defamation League, and American Jewish Committee to submit memoranda on Jewish question.

June 27, 1961
American Jewish Committee submits first of its three memoranda to Cardinal Bea's Secretariat. It deals with the image of the Jew in Catholic school books.

November 1961
World Jewish Congress and International B'nai B'rith together submit to Cardinal Bea's Secretariat a memorandum on anti-Semitism.

West European Orthodox rabbis resolve that Jews ought not participate in Vatican Council even if invited.

American Jewish Committee submits its second memorandum dealing with anti-Jewish material in Catholic liturgy.

Secretariat for the Promotion of Christian Unity approves first draft of its statement on the Jews.

May 1962
Secretariat for the Promotion of Christian Unity reaffirms the general outline of its statement on Jews, entitled *De Judaeis*. The existence of a statement is still a secret to most Jewish leaders.

June 12, 1962
World Jewish Congress announces the appointment of Dr. Chaim Wardi as its "unofficial observer and representative." There is a massive protest from Arab nations.

June 19, 1962
Vatican Secretary of State withdraws Jewish statement from agenda of crucial meeting of Central Preparatory Commission.

August 1, 1962
Nine Arab states ask Vatican for Moslem representation at Council with status similar to Israel's—a reference to Wardi.

October 1962
Secretariat for the Promotion of Christian Unity decides not to press for consideration of Jewish statement during first session of Council.

October 11, 1962
First session of Council opens. Elio Toaff, Chief Rabbi of Rome, sends greetings. He urges Council to eliminate all derogatory expressions in church ritual and education.

October 19, 1962
Secretariat for the Promotion of Christian Unity made a Council Commission.

American bishops organize a study comittee on Christian unity.

December 2, 1962	Just before first session concludes, anti-Semitic literature distributed to Council Fathers.
December 7, 1962	First session ends. No action is taken on the Jewish statement. Pope John, in a move to strengthen the liberal forces, orders that all schemata be reworked by a new Central Coordinating Commission.
December 13, 1962	Pope John associates himself with the decision not to have placed the statement on the Jews on the agenda of the first session of the Council—an alleged consequence of the Wardi incident.
February 20, 1963	Rolf Hochhuth's play, *The Deputy,* premiers in Berlin.
March 1963	Cardinal Bea visits United States and, under auspices of American Jewish Committee, addresses Jewish leaders of all religious persuasions.
June 3, 1963	Pope John dies.
June 21, 1963	Giovanni Battista Cardinal Montini becomes Pope Paul VI.
June 27, 1963	Fr. Gustave Weigel, S.J., informs American Jewish leaders at meeting of National Community Relations Advisory Council that Council Fathers would rather "avoid" Jewish question.
July 12, 1963	Official of the Secretariat for the Promotion of Christian Unity assures Jewish leaders in a private communication that Secretariat will in fact submit a statement on the Jews at the next session of the Council.
Summer 1963	Behind the scenes, the Secretariat prepares a new statement. It is to be attached to a Schema on Ecumenism. Delegations of American Jews from the American Jewish Committee and the Anti-Defamation League visit the Pope. He is cordial but noncommittal.
September 29, 1963	Second Session of Council begins. Pope Paul asks Protestant and Orthodox Christian observers for their pardon and forgiveness, if

	any feel themselves to have been injured by the Catholic Church.
October 1963	The Council proceeds at a snail's pace. The printing of Chapter IV and Chapter V— chapters dealing with the Jews and Religious Liberty, as part of the Schema on Ecumenism is mysteriously delayed.
	Two anti-Semitic pamphlets, supporting from Scripture the concept of the Jews as an accursed people, are distributed to Council Fathers.
October 16, 1963	Milton Bracker, *New York Times* reporter, leaks the outline of the contents of the official but secret statement on the Jews, entitled *De Catholicorum Habitudine ad Christianos et Maxime ad Judaeos*—"On the Catholic Attitude Toward Non-Christians and Especially Toward Jews."
November 8, 1963	Official text of the statement is now distributed to Council Fathers. Cardinal Bea issues communiqué to press. Jewish leaders express gratitude. Rabbi Israel Miller, Orthodox, Vice-President of the Rabbinical Council of America, hails proposal "if adopted." However, Jewish officials have not yet seen the actual text of Chapter IV.
November 16, 1963	Rabbi Maurice Eisendrath calls on Reform Jews to reappraise attitudes toward Jesus.
November 19, 1963	Cardinal Bea officially introduces Chapter IV and addresses Council session. Some Jewish leaders are distressed by his introduction.
November 20, 1963	Text of Chapter IV at last released to the public.
	Opposition grows from many sides against including a Jewish statement within a schema dealing with Christian ecumenism.
November 21, 1963	Council Fathers approve first three chapters of Schema on Ecumenism: 1,966, yes; 86, no.
November 29, 1963	Bishop Charles Helmsing of Kansas City asks for vote on Chapters IV and V. He receives no answer.

December 2, 1963	Cardinal Bea announces that no vote will be taken on Chapters IV and V due to "insufficient time."
December 5, 1963	Pope Paul announces his trip to "the holy places."
January 5, 1964	Pope Paul spends day in Israel. He never once refers by name to the Jewish State.
February 5, 1964	Rabbinical Council of America (Orthodox) issues a Statement of Principles warning against interreligious exchange.
February 27–March 7, 1964	Secretariat for the Promotion of Christian Unity in secret sessions approves a strengthened statement on the Jews as an appendix to the Schema on Ecumenism. It will deal also with Islam.
April 30, 1964	Cardinal Spellman of New York, addressing a dinner of the American Jewish Committee, lashes out against anti-Semitism.
May 2, 1964	Arab League Council Meeting in Cairo decides that all its thirteen member nations will seek accredited diplomatic status with the Vatican.
May 20, 1964	Pope Paul appoints Cardinal Marella to head a new Secretariat for Non-Christians. Jewish leaders are confused by this move. They are not certain now whether the Jewish statement will be handled by Cardinal Bea or Cardinal Marella.
May 29, 1964	Dr. Joseph Lichten, Anti-Defamation League official, and Rabbi Marc Tanenbaum of the American Jewish Committee attend Catholic Press Association Convention. They give voice to rumors that the Jewish statement may be abandoned or weakened by removing explicit condemnation of deicide charge.
May 30, 1964	American Jewish Committee leaders visit Pope Paul in Rome. He does not allay their fears.
June 11, 1964	Robert C. Doty, *New York Times* reporter, reveals that Jewish statement has been weakened. A.D.L. and A.J.C. intensify lobbying efforts. Some Jewish leaders, in contrast, insist that a Jewish appeal for a statement can only be

"revolting to the Jewish spirit."

Cardinal Spellman, in private intervention to papal Secretary of State, protests any weakening of the statement.

Fall 1964 — Rabbi Joseph Soloveitchik attacks those Jewish leaders who are involved in negotiations with Catholic Church. He explains why no Jewish-Christian conversation is possible.

Rabbi Marc Tanenbaum defends Jewish organizations involved with Cardinal Bea's Secretariat and criticizes attitude of Orthodox Jewish officials.

September 3, 1964 — *Herald Tribune* publishes text of the secret statement on the Jews. It has been watered down. It now includes a hope for the conversion of Jews. Jewish leaders unanimously repudiate it.

September 14, 1964 — Third Session of Council Opens.

Rabbi Abraham Heschel visits Rome and has audience with Pope Paul.

September 16, 1964 — American Bishops caucus and agree to fight for a strengthened statement. Six bishops are designated to prepare speeches to be delivered on the Council floor at the appropriate time.

September 17, 1964 — An A.D.L.-sponsored survey on the beliefs of American Catholics regarding Jewish culpability for the Crucifixion is distributed to Council Fathers by Dutch Documentation Center.

September 21, 1964 — The text of the weakened Jewish statement is distributed to the Council Fathers.

September 26, 1964 — Cardinal Bea formally introduces the seventy-line Jewish statement now entitled "On the Jews and Non-Christians." It is no longer attached to the Schema on Ecumenism. He urges the Council Fathers to amend it and strengthen it.

September 29, 1964 — Two anti-Semitic pamphlets circulated among Council Fathers.

September 28–
30, 1964 — American Bishops argue strongly in behalf of an improved statement. They call for restoration of the word "deicide," and urge elimina-

tion of any call for Jewish conversion.

October 8–9, 1964   Cardinal Bea receives instructions from Cardinal Cicognani, allegedly speaking in the name
of the Pope, to resubmit his now strengthened
Jewish statement to Cardinal Ottaviani's theological commission, where it will undoubtedly
again be weakened. Cardinals Cushing and
Spellman intervene with the Pope protesting
any such move.

October 12, 1964   In obvious pique, Jewish organizations unanimously warn their officials against any further
effort "to offer suggestions regarding religious
doctrine to the Vatican."

October 14, 1964   Gaston Cruzat, director of Latin American
Information Center, breaks Vatican secrecy
and reveals that Pope Paul has still not decided
where Jewish statement should be located
among Council documents.

October 27, 1964   Arab League instructs its ambassadors to seek
contacts with cardinals and bishops and to
report back the result of the conversations.

November 18, 1964   Newly revised and much strengthened state-
ment, now entitled "Declaration on the
Church's Relationship Toward Non-Christian
Religions," is distributed to Council Fathers.

November 20, 1964   Council Fathers vote on the Jewish statement:
1,651, yes; 242, yes with reservations; 99, no.

A very strong statement, it both deplores and
condemns discrimination against Jews and
warns against considering Jews a *deicide
people.* Any reference to conversion of Jews
is eliminated. While Jewish reactions are favorable, they are more restrained than past con-
gratulatory messages. Anything can yet occur
between Council sessions.

November 21, 1964   Third Session Concludes. Pope Paul announces
that the next session will be the last.

November 23, 1964   Pope arranges to meet with the President and
Premier of Lebanon. In a front page editorial
in *L'Osservatore Romano,* Cardinal Bea seeks
to assuage anger of Arabs over the adoption

of a positive statement on the Jews.

December 1964	American Christian observers at Council, while hailing statement on Jews, voice apprehension over the power of the Curia, behind the scenes, to scuttle Council actions.
January 1965	Jewish Catholic Theological Colloquy convened at St. Vincent Archabbey in Latrobe, Pa.
March 17, 1965	Msgr. Luigi Carli of Italy writes an article for a Rome priests' magazine accusing Jews "as a whole for the crime of deicide."
March 31, 1965	Pope Paul orders revision of Good Friday prayers to omit references offensive to Jews.
April 5, 1965	In a Lenten homily, Pope Paul speaks of Jews killing Christ. Jewish leaders are critical. Vatican radio dismisses incident as misunderstanding. Orthodox Christian leaders hail the sermon.
April 30, 1964	Rabbi Heschel reacts angrily to the rumor that Pope Paul has deleted the reference to "deicide" in the approved Jewish statement.
Late Spring and Summer 1964	Msgr. Jan Willebrand journeys to the Middle East and visits with Orthodox Christian and Arab Catholic officials in a last effort to win their support for a Jewish statement.
March and May 1965	Secretariat for the Promotion of Christian Unity deletes word "deicide" from Jewish statement and adds a series of conditional phrases and qualifications.
September 11, 1965	Secretariat publically reveals that it had changed the statement "in order to clear up any eventual misunderstandings." Full text of revised statement, however, has not yet been distributed to Council Fathers.
September 14, 1965	Last session of Vatican Council II begins. Pope Paul announces his intention to visit United Nations in New York on October 4.
September 23, 1965	It is announced that a Declaration on Non-Christian Religions will be distributed to the Council Fathers during the week of October 4.
	Pope Paul grants an audience to a four member delegation from the Palestine-Arab

	liberation organization.
October 1, 1965	Text of the Declaration with its paragraphs dealing with the Jewish religion is circulated to the Council Fathers. Bishop Leven of San Antonio, Texas, angered by the changes made between sessions of the Council, mounts a campaign to reject this revised version.
October 4, 1965	Pope Paul visits United Nations. New York rabbis boycott Catholic Mass at Yankee Stadium. Pope reads lesson of the day from Scripture. It speaks of the disciples' "fear of the Jews." American Jewish officials are disappointed.
October 11, 1965	In violation of Council's rules, some conservative Church Fathers distribute letter calling upon the Council to reject the Jewish statement.
October 12, 1965	Four-page tract signed by Catholic organizations throughout the world, charges that only an "anti-Pope or a secret conspiracy could approve" the Declaration. It is circulated among Council Fathers.
October 14–15, 1965	Council approves Declaration:

On rejecting the collective guilt of Jewish people for the death of Christ: Yes, 1,875; No, 188; Null, 9.

On declaring that Jews must not be represented as accursed or rejected by God: Yes, 1,821; No, 245; Null, 14.

On rejecting anti-Semitism and persecutions against the Jewish people: Yes, 1,905; No, 199; Null, 14.

A Summary on universal brotherhood: Yes, 2,064; No, 58; Null, 6.

On the Declaration as a whole: Yes, 1,763; No, 250; Null, 10.

| October 28, 1965 | Prior to its promulgation by the Pope, the Council renders its final vote on the Declaration: Yes, 2,221; No, 88; Null, 3. |
| October 29, 1965 | Congregation of Rites forbids any further veneration of relics or saying of masses in |

name of two-year-old Simon of Trent, allegedly murdered by Jews five centuries ago for ritual purposes.

October 28–
30, 1965

Jewish leaders in New York meet for two days in an effort to issue one unified statement on Council declaration. Division is so severe that separate statements are released to the press, some critical and others most favorable.

Appendix H

GLOSSARY OF JEWISH ORGANIZATIONS

The *American Jewish Committee* was organized in 1906 in the United States by a group of distinguished Jewish citizens in order to assist the Jewish victims of persecution in Czarist Russia. At first only a small organization of outstanding national Jewish leaders, it has intensified its efforts to develop a broader local membership and now comprises 100 chapters or units with a total membership of 33,000. It maintains a European office in Paris, two offices in South America, and one in Tel Aviv. Its main purpose remains "to combat anti-Semitism and other forms of bigotry." Rabbi Marc Tanenbaum, A.J.C.'s Director of Inter-religious Affairs, and Dr. Zachariah Shuster, its European Director in Paris, were in regular contact with Vatican Council officials.

The *B'nai B'rith* is the oldest and largest Jewish fraternal organization in the United States. Organized by German Jewish immigrants in New York in 1843 as a mutual aid society, it rapidly expanded its program to include philanthropy, youth and adult education, service to college-age students through its Hillel Foundations, and many other forms of political and social service. It has a membership of 400,000 members with national headquarters in Washington, D. C. It has lodges in forty-four countries and offices in Toronto, London, Geneva, Basle, Tel Aviv, and Santiago, Chile. Dr. E. L. Ehrlich in Geneva maintained contact with Vatican officials in behalf of International B'nai B'rith.

The community relations arm of B'nai B'rith is the *Anti-Defamation League,* which was organized in 1913 specifically to expose anti-Semitic calumnies and combat discrimination. The largest of such agencies, it grew enormously in size and scope of operation particularly during the Nazi period and now maintains a national office in

302

New York and twenty-five regional offices across the United States. Approximately 4,000 lay volunteers participate in its regional programs. Dr. Joseph Lichten, director of A.D.L.'s Department of Intercultural Affairs, was the one American Jewish official to be present in Rome throughout the entire period when the Vatican Council considered the Jewish statement.

The *American Jewish Congress* was convened between 1916 and 1918 as an association representing national Jewish organizations and elected representatives of local Jewish communities. Its founding purpose was to represent American Jews in negotiations at the peace tables following World War I. It remained in existence as a membership organization, growing in size and importance as the Jewish community rallied to fight against anti-Semitism during the Nazi period, and in recent years, it has been most vigorous in the struggle for civil rights, for maintaining the American pattern of Church-State separation, and for the strengthening of Jewish identity. It supports eighteen regional offices throughout the United States. It was represented in Rome through its association with the *World Jewish Congress,* a group that had been convened in 1936, with American Jewish Congress groups playing a leading role. Today there are sixty-five Jewish communities in affiliation, most of these the central representation body of Jews in their respective countries. Mr. Fritz Becker, Rome representative of the World Jewish Congress, was on the scene throughout the Council. From time to time also, the secretary general of the World Jewish Congress, Dr. Gerhard Reigner of Geneva, met with Catholic officials.

In 1944 the leaders of Jewish organizations involved in community relations work organized a coordinating agency, the *National Community Relations Advisory Council (NCRAC).* Participation was limited at first to national organizations: the American Jewish Committee, B'nai B'rith, the American Jewish Congress, Jewish Labor Committee, Jewish War Veterans, and the lay organizations of the three religious groupings: The Union of American Hebrew Congregations (Reform), The United Synagogue of America (Conservative), and the Union of Orthodox Jewish Congregations. Its program was restricted to advisory and consultative functions only. Later it brought into its deliberations representatives of local Jewish community-relations councils.

In 1952, an effort was made to strengthen the NCRAC's power to allocate functions and responsibilties among the Jewish organizations. B'nai B'rith and the American Jewish Committee thereupon withdrew. In 1963, B'nai B'rith's Anti-Defamation League returned to the NCRAC, and in 1966 negotiations were initiated for the return of the American Jewish Committee. The NCRAC today includes in its membership representatives of 69 local and regional community relations councils.

Reform Judaism in America grew chiefly through the immigration to this country of German Jews in the mid-1800s. It initiated patterns of institutional organization that have subsequently been followed by Conservative and Orthodox Jews, whose membership was increased by the immigration to this country of the more religiously traditional eastern European Jews in the early 1900s. Reform Jews established first a federation of congregations, the Union of American Hebrew Congregations (U.A.H.C.) in 1873. In 1875, they founded a rabbinical school, the Hebrew Union College (H.U.C.) in Cincinnati; in 1950, H.U.C. merged with the Jewish Institute of Religion (J.I.R.), a theological school established by Rabbi Stephen S. Wise in New York in 1922. The combined Hebrew Union College–Jewish Institute of Religion now has centers in New York, Cincinnati, Los Angeles, and Jerusalem. In 1889, Reform rabbis established a clerical association, the Central Conference of American Rabbis (CCAR). As of 1963, there were more than 650 Reform synagogues belonging to the U.A.H.C.

In 1926 there was organized a *World Union for Progressive Judaism*. Today it coordinates the work of Reform–Liberal synagogues in twenty-six countries, the largest constituencies next to the United States being found in England, Canada, and South Africa.

Conservative Judaism began in America with the founding of the Jewish Theological Seminary (J.T.S.) in New York City in 1887. A Rabbinical Assembly (R.A.) was established in 1900, and in 1912, Conservative congregations came together as the United Synagogue, which now has more than 800 member congregations. A World Council of Synagogues was formed in 1957, coordinating the work of Conservative congregations in twenty-two countries; the largest number of affiliates is in Latin America.

Orthodox Judaism is divided into several groups distinguished from one another chiefly by the patterns of worship and theology that have their sources in European Jewry. In 1902, a union of Orthodox rabbis (Agudas Harabbanim) was founded; it supported the Rabbi Isaac Elchanan Theological Seminary, which was the first unit in the developing Yeshiva College, an institution that achieved university status in 1945. In 1930, a group of Orthodox rabbis, trained at Yeshiva Seminary, broke with their European-trained elder colleagues of the Agudas Harabbanim to form the Rabbinical Council of America (R.C.A.). This association of rabbis sponsors a congregational affiliate, the Union of Orthodox Jewish Congregations of America (U.O.J.C.A.) which receives support from approximately 650 member synagogues.

Orthodox Jewry in America supports a number of theological seminaries: In addition to the Isaac Elchanan Seminary at Yeshiva University in New York, there are Yeshiva Torah V'Daath in Brooklyn, the New Israel Yeshiva in Baltimore, and the Hebrew Theological Seminary in Chicago. In addition there are several other Orthodox congregational bodies. Next to the U.O.J.C.A. in size and strength is the National Council of Young Israel, organized in 1912 in New York, which now has over 100 affiliate synagogues.

A *Synagogue Council of America* was organized in 1926 to coordinate the major rabbinical and synagogue associations. It speaks with a united voice on issues of political and social importance on which there is consensus among these religious groups. On the issue of interreligious dialogue, the Synagogue Council has been prevented by the Orthodox exercise of veto power from sponsoring theological conversation. Its budget is also severely limited and it maintains a minimal national staff in New York City. During the period of the four sessions of the Council, the executive director of the Synagogue Council of America was Rabbi Philip Hiat. He maintained unofficial contact with officers of the Secretariat for the Promotion of Christian Unity.

Reconstructionist Judaism is the youngest of the Jewish religious denominations in the United States today. Its formation was in large measure a response to the publication in 1934 of Rabbi Mordecai Kaplan's epoch-making book, *Judaism As a Civilization*. With headquarters in New York, the Jewish Reconstructionist Foundation publishes a biweekly magazine, *Reconstructionist,* maintains a press, and coordinates the activities of twenty-four synagogues and fellowships located throughout the United States, Canada, and Mexico.

Reconstructionist thought has effectively influenced Reform and Conservative Judaism, Zionist and secular Jewish groups. Emphasizing that Judaism is an evolving religious civilization, it has urged Jews to act as one people in order to strengthen the contributions that each group can make to the wholeness of Jewish life. Thus the Reconstructionist movement has served as a bridge between secular and religious forces in American Jewish life. It also maintains a significant contact with university students through its Reconstructionist University Fellowship. In the Fall of 1968, it will open the first new rabbinical school in the United States in forty-five years. This school will be housed adjacent to Temple University in Philadelphia. Students will pursue Ph.D. studies at Temple's Department of Religion and concurrently engage in rabbinical studies at the Reconstructionist school. After five or six years, a graduate of the program will earn both a Ph.D. degree and rabbinical ordination.

The first *Zionist* group to be established in the United States in 1896 called itself the Knights of Zion. In 1913 it became part of a federation of local and national Zionist societies that had sprung up everywhere across the country. In 1917 the federation was replaced by a membership organization, the Zionist Organization of America (Z.O.A.). *Hadassah,* the woman's Zionist organization, had its beginnings in 1913. Soon other Zionist groups sprang up that reflected the stance of political parties in Palestine.

The membership and activity of Zionist organizations grew swiftly during the period of the establishment of the State of Israel; membership has now leveled off to about 700,000 persons, since much work in support of Israel is also carried on by other Jewish organizations. In 1939, the Zionist groups in the United States formed a coordinating agency, The Emergency Committee for Zionist Affairs. Its name was changed in 1950 to The American Zionist Council; thirteen major national American Zionist groups are currently in association with the A.Z.C. Each of these groups also participates in a World Zionist Organization whose administrative arm is called the Jewish Agency for Israel, with executive offices in Jerusalem, Geneva, London, Paris, and New York.

In 1952 the presidents of twenty-one major American Jewish organizations, including religious, Zionist, and community-relations agencies, formed a *President's Council* to strengthen action by Jews on issues that were considered to have central political and international significance, such as the plight of Jews in the Soviet Union, negotiations with the German government, and the security of Israel.

For essays that interpret each of the religious groupings in American Judaism, as well as the philosophy and structures of organization for non-synagogue affiliates see Belden Menkus, ed., *Meet The American Jew* (Nashville: Broadman Press, 1963); Nathan Glazer, *American Judaism* (Chicago: University of Chicago Press, 1957); and Joseph L. Blau, *Modern Varieties of Judaism* (New York: Columbia University Press, 1966).

Index